ESSENTIALS

OF

SPEECH

BY

JOHN R. PELSMA

*Department of Public Speaking, Kansas State
Teachers' College of Pittsburg*

NEW YORK

THOMAS Y. CROWELL COMPANY

PUBLISHERS

PREFACE

THIS book is a fundamental treatise covering the whole field of oral expression except dramatics. It is intended as a text-book for high schools, academies, normal schools, and also for elementary college courses. Most of it has stood the class-room test for many years. Part I deals with oral reading and the technique of expression, and Part II treats of the various forms of public speaking.

There is a growing conviction on the part of educators that in most of the preparatory schools our methods of teaching English need revision, and that in all schools the class-work in English needs vitalizing; that since we speak hundreds of times where we write once, relatively more attention should be given to oral English than has been the case in the past.

A few years ago the Illinois Teachers' Association carried on an experiment which proved that classes in English devoting an hour a week to oral expression were, at the end of the year, not only more proficient in *writing* English than the parallel classes devoting all their time to written composition, but at the same time acquired the ability to speak effectively before an audience.

To meet this need the present volume has been prepared. It is intended not alone for teachers who are conducting separate classes in public speaking, but for all teachers of English. When used as a text in connection with the regular class-work in English, all parts of the book would not necessarily be used by a single teacher with a particular class; but since the text is a complete treatise, teachers may use it for all the work in oral English that should be incorporated in the regular high school course in English. The best results are secured when the technique in Part I is assigned simultaneously with the practical speaking as outlined in Part II. When students make extempore speeches they more readily appreciate the value of the drill in technique. When the book is used with separate classes in oral expression, the whole text would naturally be covered in one semester or in a whole year's course.

The author feels very grateful to the many publishers and authors who have so generously given permission to use selections and quotations from their productions.

The author also wishes to express his indebtedness to the many excellent books on public speaking now on the market; to Professor E. D. Shurter for his valuable criticism; to his worthy instructors, including Professors H. B. Gough of DePauw, S. S. Curry, School of Expression, S. H. Clark and F. M. Blanchard of Chicago, I. L. Winter of Harvard, and Miss G. E. Johnson of Wisconsin; and to his many interesting students for valuable suggestions.

J. R. P.

PITTSBURG, KANSAS,
February 1, 1924.

CONTENTS

PART I—ORAL READING

ESSENTIALS OF SPEECH

PART ONE

ORAL READING

I

INTRODUCTION

Definitions.—The greatest discovery of mankind next to that of making fire was the discovery of a means of oral communication. It is now the greatest art of all arts. This book attempts to formulate the essential fundamental laws and principles underlying the science and art of expressing vocally our thoughts and emotions. It may be possible to express the thoughts of others, but quite impossible to express emotions not our own. The printed page, at best, can record only the ideas and thoughts of the writer. What the author *felt* is purely conjectural on our part. Sympathetic experience is our best teacher.

Speech includes all forms of the spoken word. It may be divided into two main divisions:

(1) *Oral Reading* and (2) *Public Speaking.*

Oral Reading relates to the verbal reproduction and sympathetic expression of the ideas and emotions of another. The ideas and thoughts of an author can be made our own, and these can be reproduced in the exact language of the writer or speaker, but the emotions of another can be only suggested. A reader can interpret the meaning of the printed page and express this meaning to his auditors; and may to a limited extent feel emotions *similar* to those of the writer or speaker, and be able to arouse concordant emotions in his audience through proper voice modulations and appropriate physical expression.

Public Speaking presupposes an audience, and refers to the expression of our own thoughts and emotions. Private conversation and public speaking differ only in the number of auditors. Effective speaking, whether private or public, must be governed in manner and character by the size and nature of the audience.

Value of Oral English.—Ruskin says, "If I could have a son or daughter possessed of but one accomplishment in life, it should be that of good reading."

The human race always has had some method of communication. At first only inarticulate sounds and simple signs were used. Man's expression became more varied as his thoughts and emotions became more complex. Mankind has profited from many inventions, but from none other so much as from the invention of articulate language. There is a striking analogy between the development of speech and of the general intelligence in the human race and in the individual. Vocal expression preceded by many aeons a written language. The child learns to talk many years before he learns to write, and after he has learned to do both, he speaks a thousand words to writing one. In actual practice, the communication of thought and feeling is, for the most part, by word of mouth.

Literary Value.—Poetry and song spring spontaneously from the heart. The poem and the lyric, to be appreciated, must be recited and sung. "Literature is not in the book. She has to do with the living speech of men. Her language is that of the lips. Her life is in the song and ballad, the story and the oration, the epic and the drama, as they sound and are heard of men. We, too, no less than the scientist, must get behind the book to that of which the book is but the record and notation, the mere tablet of memory—to enchanted speech. Where there is no enchantment there is no literature," says Percival Chubb. Literature is life. It must not merely be read but lived. It is sensuous, and to be appreciated must be heard. Like a bar of music, it must be played and sung before its beauty and melody can thrill the heart.

The great literary masterpieces can never be appreciated fully without being heard. Manifestly this is true of oratorical literature, which is addressed to a hearer and not to a reader; and it is quite as true of the idealized language of poetry. To Shakespeare, as Professor Corson points out in his little book, *The Voice and Spiritual Education,* "language was for the ear, not the eye. The written word was to him what it was to Socrates, 'the mere image or phantom of the living and animated word.' Reading must supply all the deficiencies of written or printed language. How comparatively little is addressed to the eye, in print or manuscript, of what has to be addressed to the ear of a reader! There are no indications of tone, quality of voice, inflection, pitch, time, or any other of the vocal functions demanded for a full intellectual and spiritual interpretation. A poem is not truly a poem until it is voiced by an accomplished reader who adequately has assimilated it—in whom it has to some

extent, been born again, according to his individual spiritual constitution and experience."

The art of printing has caused language to be overmuch
transferred from its true domain, the sense of hearing,
to the sense of sight.   Then, too, the multiplication of
books, magazines, and newspapers in modern times, has
encouraged silent reading.   The practice of the olden
time, when the family gathered together to hear a book
read by some one of their number, gave the family a
unit now largely lost.   The picture of Longfellow is realized rarely to-day when a member of the household
is asked to

> . . . read from the treasured volume
>   The poem of thy choice,
> And lend to the rhyme of the poet
>   The beauty of thy voice.
>
> And the night shall be filled with music,
>   And the cares that infest the day
> Shall fold their tents like the Arabs,
>   And as silently steal away.

Emotional Value.—From the first year in the primary
to the last year in the college, the student daily has opportunities for *impression,* but few opportunities for
expression.   The child longs to express his ideas, emotions, his images; the adult is "cold and moveless as a
stone."   It is thought that a practical man should not express, but suppress his emotions.   The result is that he
soon learns that he is wholly incapacitated to enjoy a
beautiful painting, good music, fine literature, or a summer sunset.   Nature's laws cannot be violated with
impunity.

Proper emotions should be developed, cultivated.   The

man who is merely a "thinking machine" is only half a man. As we learn to sing by singing, we learn to smile by smiling. We learn to be happy by making others happy; we learn to love by loving. We must *express* what is within us. Who has not been thrilled through and through by a beautiful song, by a selection well read? Actors are frequently moved to tears by the sound of their own voices. We must *express* our ideas, our thoughts, our ideals, or they will suffocate within. Says Professor S. H. Clark, "I believe there is no better way to inculcate the love of literature than by having the pupil read it aloud. We talk glibly of the sonorous rhythm of Milton's verse, but cannot quote a line. We talk of the fertile imagination and sublime passion of Shakespeare, but how many of us ever pick him up for an hour's reading? We talk of the tenderness, of the homeliness of the lyrics of Burns, but never read them."

Cultural Value.—Jane Addams says, "The person of the highest culture is the one who is able to put himself in the place of the greatest number of other persons." Self identification with the characters in a drama, or the personification of the monologue develops the highest instincts and the noblest motives in a child. The boy and girl must be permitted to live their ideals found in literature. The ability to see, feel, and will as our associates; to appreciate the beauties in life through the eyes and ears of the masters, is the acme of culture. Beauty and pleasure must be shared. No life can develop without expression.

Professor Edward Dowden, in his *New Studies in Literature,* says, "Few persons now-a-days seem to realize how powerful an instrument of culture may be found in modern, intelligent, and sympathetic reading aloud. The reciter and the elocutionist of late have done much to rob us of this which is one of the finest of the fine arts. A mongrel something which, at least with the inferior adepts, is neither good reading nor yet veritable acting, but which sets agape the half-educated with the wonder of its airs and attitudinizing, its pseudo-heroics and pseudo-pathos, has usurped the place of the art of true reading aloud, and has made the word 'recitation' a terror to quiet folk who are content with intelligence and refinement."

Social Value.—"Education is social efficiency." "No man liveth unto himself alone." Our joys magnify many fold, when told, our sorrows decrease when poured into a sympathetic ear. The ability to converse fluently, agreeably, accurately, with a well modulated voice is the outward sign of a cultured mind. The voice is the thermometer of the soul. Again, could not a long lonely hour be shortened by reading a poem, a story to a sick friend? Why is not this done more frequently? We are ashamed of letting others know how poorly we read!

Educational Value.—Not long ago one of the world's greatest athletes died at the age of thirty. Large external muscles do not insure longevity. Strong internal muscles are of greater importance—muscles of respiration and assimilation—muscles of life. A knowledge of their development is of vital interest to every boy and girl.

Our memory is quickened by using the sense of hearing and the kinesthetic sense as well as that of sight. Selections read aloud are retained in memory longer than those read silently.

Confidence in your ability to express yourself in good, pure, forceful English will encourage you to undertake tasks that you would otherwise hesitate in attempting.

The student who can express well what is within him usually stands at the head in every branch in school.

Says Orison Swett Marden, "The attempt to become a good public speaker is a great awakener of the mental faculties. The sense of power that comes from holding attention, stirring the emotions or convincing the reason of an audience, gives self-confidence, assurance, self-reliance, arouses ambition and tends to make one more effective in every particular. One's manhood, character, learning, judgment of his opinion—all things that go to make him what he is—are being unrolled into a panorama. Every mental faculty is quickened, every power of thought and expression spurred. Thoughts rush for utterance, words press for choice. The speaker summons all his reserves of education, of experience, of natural or acquired ability, and masses all his forces in the endeavor to capture the approval and applause of the audience."

Vocational Value.—Recently a Wall Street business man said to a group of college students: "Unless you acquire in your college course the ability to write and speak effectively, it will not be worth the time and money spent upon it." Every applicant for a business position must stand a satisfactory test in the use of correct oral English. Who wants a teacher with a rasping, throaty, shrill, irritating voice; a stammering, hesitating, mumbling clerk; bashful, forceless, lisping salesman; or a weak-voiced, ineffective, "throaty" preacher or lawyer?

Thousands of men and women have put themselves on record as saying, "Oh, if I could only make a good speech to-day! the occasion is the opportunity of my life."

The ability to express effectively one's own thoughts and to interpret vocally the thoughts of others is an inestimable asset in the struggle for supremacy in the economic world. To be able to speak to a purpose, clearly, distinctly, gracefully and forcefully is an open sesame to leadership.

Who Needs Oral English?—Only those who expect to live a Robinson Crusoe life can afford to omit a knowledge of the theory and practice of the art of reading and speaking. If you expect to communicate with your associates, you need a pleasing conversation; if you intend to convince them, you need a logical and forceful address; if you desire to persuade them, you need an effective delivery; briefly, if you wish to be a man among men, take the advice of Martin Luther, *"He who speaks well is a man."*

How May the Ability to Read and Speak Well be Acquired?—By following the laws and principles of vocal expression patiently and intelligently; by persistently practicing under competent criticism. Practice alone does not make perfect; but *practice under criticism.* Be your own critic to a large degree. Heed well the suggestions made by your instructor. Remember that what is worth doing at all is worth doing well. One of the Swobodian principles of muscular development demands that when you exercise or lift a weight you must lift all you can if you desire to grow strong physically. Exercise with light weights may be sufficient to retain your health, but it will not *develop* your muscle. So it is with reading and speaking. Every time you speak or read do your *very best;* otherwise you may hold your own, but you will not become more efficient.

Who Can Become a Good Reader and Speaker?— Every person with an ordinary intelligence and a normal physique. Perhaps, you should possess a few other qualities. A desire—a will—strong enough to overcome your vocal defects if you have any; confidence in yourself and faith in your purpose in life, and enough perseverance to conquer as others have, who have gone this way before you.

A friend who lived on a farm adjoining that of Byron King relates an incident connected with the latter's early life. One day Mr. King came over to borrow a wheelbarrow. It took him one-half hour to make known his errand. Mr. King inherited about all the vocal defects in the catalogue. Through the wise teaching of a friend and by persistent and heroic effort, he overcame them all. Dr. Byron King is now president of the King School of Oratory and a reader and speaker of unusual power and eloquence. The old story of Demosthenes has had many modern parallels.

Certainly the masters of the art of speech, both ancient and modern, did not become masters without laborious and long-continued training. Such training was the life-long work of the Greek and Roman orators. Curran, the celebrated Irish orator, was so handicapped in his youth that he was called "stuttering Jack Curran." He said of himself, "My friends despaired of my ever making a speaker, but I would not give it up." Says one of his friends, "He turned his shrill and stumbling brogue into a flexible, sustained, and finely modulated voice; his action became free and forcible; and he acquired perfect readiness in thinking on his legs." With reference both to matter and manner, Webster said of himself: "When I was a young man, and for several years after I had acquired a respectable degree of eminence in my profession, my style was bombastic in the extreme. Some kind friend was good enough to point out that fact to me, and I determined to correct it, if labor could do it. Whether it has been corrected or not, no small part of my life has been spent in the attempt."

II

PHONOLOGY

Definitions.—*Phonology* is the science of vocal sound. It treats of the physical laws involved in the production of sound, and the physiological laws governing all the organs of speech.

Sound is the auditory sensation produced by the vibrations of air or some other media. These vibrations in the media are the result of the vibration of some object. For example, a violin string is touched. The string moves to and fro causing condensations and rarefactions in the air; these waves set in motion the ear-drum, and it, in turn, communicates these vibrations to the inner ear where very small delicate cords are set in sympathetic vibration. This is communicated to the brain by the auditory nerve.

Each string of a violin is said to have a certain *pitch*. Pitch depends on the number of vibrations per second. The number of vibrations depends on the length, thickness, and tension of the string. The *volume*, or loudness, of the sound depends on the amplitude or distance the string vibrates, which in turn is caused by the force of the blow given the string. The *quality*, or character of the sound is dependent on the overtones, the texture of the string, and the resonance of the frame work of the violin.

However, the violin is too simple in construction to

serve as a basis of explanation of the human voice. There is no instrument made in exact imitation of the human speech apparatus. The single reed-pipe of a church organ is a near approach in principle, and serves well as an illustration of its general structure. Again, the cornet serves very well when the lips are made to represent the vocal cords.

Before making this comparison, however, it will be necessary to explain briefly the technique of the voice.

Technique of the Voice.—In order to understand how the voice is produced it will be important to sketch briefly the anatomy of the vocal apparatus.

The *larynx,* the most important organ in voice production, consists of cartilages, muscles, vocal bands, true and false mucous membrane, ligaments, etc. It is situated between the hyoid bone above and the trachea below. For a complete description see any standard text on physiology.

With reference to the voice, the most important part of the larynx is the vocal bands. They are the chief sound producers. The false vocal cords lie above the true cords. They fold over the latter in coughing, swallowing, etc. The vocal cords are attached to the arytenoid cartilages which move freely on their base, swivel-like, and the movements and tension of the vocal cords are produced by adjustments of these cartilages. The hyoid bone is at the top of the larynx. It has no definite function in sound production except as it affords attachment for the muscles of the tongue.

The *glottis* is the chink or opening between the true vocal cords.

The *tongue* is a very important organ in phonation and articulation. Its wonderful ability of adjustments in shape and position in the mouth cavity determines the greater number of modifications of tone resonance.

The *uvula* is the small curtain which closes the back of the mouth. It and the soft palate determine the direction the breath takes when it comes from the pharynx. If

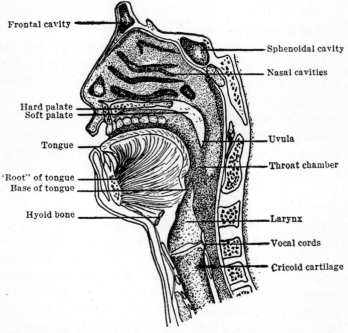

Frontal cavity

Sphenoidal cavity

Nasal cavities

Hard palate
Soft palate

Tongue

Uvula

Throat chamber

'Root" of tongue
Base of tongue

Hyoid bone

Larynx

Vocal cords

Cricoid cartilage

Median section of the head and neck, giving general side view of the organs of speech and the resonators above the larynx.

dropped, the air goes partly through the nose, as in sounding the letter "m." If raised, very little passes through the nose. Snoring is caused by the vibration of this curtain.

The *teeth, hard* and *soft palates,* and the *lips* modify the resonance and aid materially in phonation.

In comparing the voice to a single reed-pipe of a church organ, three general analogies are noted: 1. A box or wind-chest into which the air is forced by the bellows; 2. A reed or vibrator which is the source of the sound; and 3. A resonator, or resonance chamber, aiding in modifying the volume and quality of the sound.

The air is pumped into the wind-chest of the organ and as it meets resistance, it is under considerable pressure. The only outlet is through the narrow slit between the edges of the vibrator or "reed." The air, in passing between the free edges of the vibrator, causes these edges to oscillate in such a manner that they open and close this narrow slit at regular intervals; thus transmitting to the surrounding air a series of sound waves of the same frequency. The air chamber or resonator above the "reed," by virtue of its resonating property, favors those vibrations that are adaptable to the size of the hollow interior. Those vibrations that are favored are reënforced; those that are not, are suppressed. Each pipe of the organ is so constructed as to favor, or harmonize the vibrations of its own "reed."

In the human body the lungs act as the wind-chest. Air is drawn into them and placed under pressure. It can escape only through the narrow slit between two elastic tissue membranes—the vocal cords—which form the "reed" of our vocal machinery. The free elastic edges of these cords vibrate and communicate these waves to the air chamber above them in the same manner as the "reed" of the organ transmits the sound to the resonator. The resonator of the voice is the throat, mouth, and nose.

So far there is a great similarity between the single reed-pipe of the organ and the human voice mechanism. Some of the differences must now be noted: 1. The vibrator in the organ always produces the same vibrations; the vocal cords can be regulated at will to perform the function of many organ "reeds." 2. The resonator of the organ is as unchangeable as its vibrator. The resonating chamber in the human voice is adjustable and with proper care may be made to reënforce, modify and harmonize the sound waves of all the minute shades of tones produced by the vocal cords, normally ranging through two octaves.

The human voice may be compared, in effect, to the entire church organ. Though the range of pitch is not so great, the voice is capable of an infinitely greater variety of vibrations and character of tone within its limited range. It was claimed that Madame Mara, within her range of three octaves, could produce 2100 changes of pitch, which would represent a successive change in the length of the vocal bands of approximately 1/17000 of an inch.

Control of the Voice.—The production and control of vocal sound is a very complex process. The ability to coördinate this complicated apparatus, more delicate than any instrument ever manufactured, capable of producing incalculable modulations; so attuned that it responds automatically and unconsciously to our mental perception—demands our utmost care and attention.

First of all, it must be observed that this complex machinery is coördinated by the nervous system. Parts are under direct control of the will and parts are involuntary. This complex machinery must be made to respond to our mental percepts, that is, to the ideas we have to be expressed. Without a definite, conscious effort this complex mechanism must respond to our wishes. Hence, (1) definite mental images and proper sound-perceptions develop; (2) the capacity and conscious control of the breath; and (3) control of the vocal cords, resonance mechanism and other organs of articulation; and (4) the harmonious involuntary adjustment of all these processes.

Breathing.—Voice is vocalized breath. In ordinary breathing we inhale and exhale the breath with approximate regularity. In reading or speaking, however, we inhale quickly and exhale slowly, converting the exhalations into vocal sounds. Now, as a fundamental prerequisite in the use of the voice, we must learn to perform properly this inhaling and exhaling process. How often do we hear people who gasp for breath while talking, or who "get out of breath" before finishing a clause or sentence. There is lacking either sufficient breath-quantity, or breath-control, or both. The proper management of the vocal organs requires that the voice have due support and control. This involves the necessity of deep breathing.

There are three ways of breathing whereby the chest capacity is enlarged and the lungs filled with air: Clavicular, or collar-bone breathing; costal, or rib breathing; and diaphragmatic, or abdominal breathing.

In *clavicular* breathing, the upper ribs are raised, the breastbone is thrust forward, and the shoulders and collar-bones are elevated. By this method, only the upper part of the lungs is inflated; but the exclusive use of this method (which may sometimes be required temporarily by disease and permanently by tight lacing), is as bad for the voice as it is for the health. In the first place, proper vocal support is lacking. The lungs in this kind of breathing can be filled only partially, and hence there is not sufficient reserve supply of air to produce a sustained tone. Secondly, it prevents vocal control. As the shoulders and collar-bones are forced upward, they press against the vocal organs, causing a constriction of the throat; this necessitates an attempt to control the breath in the throat, which was never intended for such purpose; and this, in turn, causes the breath to come in spurts, making the voice trembly, jerky, wheezy, or "throaty." It rasps the vocal cords, and often results in a huskiness known as "clergyman's sore throat."

In *costal,* or rib breathing the lower or floating ribs are distended sideways, employing the middle portion of the lungs in breathing. This method provides a larger cavity than does clavicular breathing, and thus makes it possible to produce a fuller, rounded, and more sustained tone. It should be employed in connection with the lower portion of the lungs, or deep breathing.

In *diaphragmatic* or abdominal breathing, the diaphragm contracts, moves downward, while at the same time the abdominal muscles expand the lower chest laterally, thus creating a large cavity for the air to enter. This is the method of breathing that the singer or speaker must adopt. Deep breathing is absolutely essential for a strong, pure, resonant, sustained tone. It furnishes a reserve supply of air for a sustained tone. It allows the throat freedom for proper relaxation and control. It permits one to control the voice from the diaphragm, and this is frequently necessary, as in ringing, dynamic utterance.

Physicians and writers on hygiene have shown, from statistics carefully compiled, that comparatively few persons breathe correctly; that is, so manipulate the diaphragm that the breathing apparatus is used in the way best suited to physical development.

Do you use the lower part of your lungs in breathing?

If not, you should learn to do so, for the muscles controlling respiration are both involuntary and voluntary, that is, we can by conscious attention acquire the habit of deep breathing. In forming this habit, give primary attention to the diaphragm, and the rib breathing will take care of itself; think of filling the lower part of the lungs. Place the hands above the hips, press firmly as you inhale, and you can soon discover whether or not you are using the diaphragm in breathing.

Respiratory Coördination.—The delicate adjustment of mental-perception, breath-control, and the voice mechanism, must not be overlooked in cultivating a good speaking or singing voice. Mental attitude has much to do with this adjustment.

The amount of air which can be forced into the lungs is estimated ordinarily as 330 cubic inches. The quantity used in quiet respiration is about 30 cubic inches. This is called *tidal* air. The quantity that can be added to this by taking a deep breath is about 100 cubic inches. This is called *complemental* air. The quantity that can be expelled by a forceful expiration is about 100 cubic inches. This is called *reserved* air. The quantity that cannot be expelled at all is about 100 cubic inches, and is called *residual* air.

One very important fact that should always be borne in mind is that all reading and speaking should be done with at least 200 cubic inches of air in the lungs. This demands frequent inhalations while speaking. When shall you take breath? Whenever you can do so; each time there is a rhythmic pause in the thought expressed. Again, the chest should always remain expanded. The upper part of your chest should never be permitted to sink. As you use the lower part of the chest and diaphragm in respiration, there is no necessity of any movement in the upper chest region. This upper chest should be moved in pantomime only and not for the purpose of respiration. It *must* be used for the purpose of resonance. It acts like a drum. This chest resonance is essential to the production of pure, clear, forceful, resonant tones. The early collapse of the chest leads generally to dropping the sound at the end of phrases and gasping for breath at the pauses, two very common defects in reading and speaking.

Get into the habit of breathing through the nose with mouth closed when not using the vocal cords. When you speak or sing, breathe through your mouth.

The lungs must perform two functions: breathing (1) to support life, and (2) to produce pure tone. Some have great difficulty in harmonizing these. Life breathing goes on continually; it is paramount in importance and the speaker must adjust his voice breathing to this.

The following are some simple exercises for practice. Two cautions in connection with practicing these and other exercises that follow farther on should be carefully noted. First, *do not overdo the exercises*. Never strain the lungs or the vocal organs to the point of weariness or exhaustion. Learn proper relaxation as well as effort; the proper use of the throat, for example, requires relaxation of the muscles, quite as much as contraction. And secondly, *systematic and persistent practice* is the thing that counts. Take ten minutes, say, twice a day, and practice the breathing and vocal exercises, and *keep at it* until faults are overcome and new habits formed. It is the moderate and continued practice that counts. You cannot practice in an hour what should be distributed through regularly recurring periods during a week.

Without overstraining, then, or without too prolonged effort at any time, practice the following breathing exercises:

EXERCISES IN BREATHING AND VOICE CULTURE

I. Lie on your back on a couch and breathe normally, quietly. This may be done in the morning before you get up. Your body will then be free from all tight fitting clothing. You will discover that you breathe in the middle of the body, not near your collar bone.

II. Now take in just a little more air than is needed. Hold it a few seconds and then let go completely.

III. Take in more air; hold it a little longer, and again relax completely—let go all at once.

IV. Repeat I, II and III breathing through your mouth.

V. Sit erect in a chair and make yourself breathe in just the same way you did while lying down, repeating II, III, and IV.

VI. Now stand erect and perform II and III.

This may be difficult at first, especially is it difficult for many girls. But intercostal, combined with diaphragmatic breathing must be secured, or you may as well give up all hopes of ever becoming a reader, a speaker, or a singer.

VII. Now open your mouth about an inch; keep tongue lying flat and with no feeling of weight, between the lower teeth, the tip touching the lower front teeth. Now open your mouth in the back as well as in the front; open your throat as wide as possible; and while you are doing all this take in a good, deep breath, and be sure your waist-band seems to tighten. By placing your hands on your hips you may be able to detect this lateral expansion. Now let the breath escape slowly, and control the escape by the diaphragm and not by closing the epiglottis.

VIII. Repeat VII, but as you let the breath escape say, "ah," as lightly as you can, and then relax completely. Be sure this sound is cut off short—just a little, little tap —not a prolonged *ah—ah—ah*. When you relax let go completely, and your breath will escape normally. It requires an effort to inhale, not to exhale.

IX. Repeat VIII twenty times. You may get dizzy at first, but if this exercise is practiced a short time daily you will soon become accustomed to the excess of oxygen.

There are four points that should be carefully observed: 1. Be sure that your tongue lies perfectly flat, especially in the back. 2. Be sure that your mouth opens in the back as well as in front. Let your jaw drop. This can be detected by observing that the lower lip covers the lower front teeth. Again, if you will place your finger against the side of your face just in front of the ear you will notice a depression forming as you open your mouth. 3. When you give the sound of "ah" you must know that the breath is checked by the diaphragm and not by closing the epiglottis. The breath must never be held by any stoppage in the throat. 4. The open throat is essential. In the initial stage of the yawn the throat opens properly, and the jaw drops down in the correct way. This feeling of relaxation should be felt in performing the above exercises.

X. Pant like a dog, only be sure your tongue stays at its proper place—flat on the floor of the mouth.

XI. Repeat with one breath, the following line from Browning: "Boot, saddle, to horse, and away." Have four distinct diaphragmatic impulses.

XII. Laugh: Ha, ha, ha; ha, ha, ha. Note that you breathe naturally with the diaphragm when you laugh, and that the quick spurts of air causing the laughing sound are controlled by the diaphragm.

XIII. Practice for pure tone:

1. "Yo ho, lads! Yo, ho, yo, ho!"
    The captain calls to all below,
    "Joy, joy to all, for we must go,
    Yo ho, lads! Yo, ho! yo, ho!"

2. O hark, O hear! how thin and clear,
    And thinner, clearer, farther going!
    O sweet and far from cliff and scar
    The horns of Elfland faintly blowing!
    Blow, let us hear the purple glens replying:
    Blow, bugle; answer, echoes, dying, dying, dying.

3. Since to all earthly work an end must come, our words of farewell to a fellow-workman should not alone be those of grief that man's common lot has come to him; but of pride and joy that his task has been done worthily. Powerful men so weave themselves into their hour that, for the moment, it all but seems the world will stop when they depart. Yet, it does not stop or even pause.

III

VOICE CULTURE

Definitions.—Broadly speaking, there are **two** kinds of tone—I. Pure, and II. Impure.

I. A Pure tone is one that contains only harmonious overtones, and in which all the breath is vocalized.

II. An Impure tone is one that contains discordant secondary vibrations. These secondary vibrations usually come from meeting obstructions in the resonating cavities in their passage from the vocal cords. "Eighty-five per cent. of all impure tones," says Dr. Muckey, "are caused by false cord interference."

The *Pure* tone may be said to be *Normal, Oral, Falsetto, Orotund,* or *Pectoral.*

1. The *Normal* tone is one used in ordinary conversation. It has a pure, clear resonance.

2. The *Oral* is thin, feeble—with the center of resonance in the forward part of the mouth.

3. The *Falsetto* is shrill and clear; it is known as "the false voice." It is heard where the voice is said to "break." The vocal cords are tightly pressed together at one end, permitting only part of their length to vibrate. In a cultivated voice there is no break in passing from the lower to the upper register.

4. The *Orotund* is clear, smooth, and voluminous, with the resonance in the upper chest.

5. The *Pectoral* is a deep, hollow, sepulchral tone, with the resonance in the lower part of the chest.

The *Impure* tones are: *Aspirate, Guttural,* and *Nasal.*

1. The *Aspirate* is a breathy, hissing, whispered tone.

2. The *Guttural* is harsh, raspy, grating, and often throaty.

3. The *Nasal* is a twanging, head tone with the center of resonance in the nasal cavities.

Cultivation of the Voice. — Talking is perhaps such a common thing that little attention is paid to the control and cultivation of the voice for conversational and public speaking purposes.

There are many beautiful women with dazzling complexions and graceful carriage who, when they open their mouths to speak, destroy the first flattering impression they have made by a vulgar quality of voice. Again, there are those who, in personal appearance, might be called plain, but who have such pleasant and melodious voices that hosts of admirers are always in waiting to be thrilled to admiration by the sound of their pure, distinct, cultured, and agreeable accents.

As an attraction for charming, a sweet, melodious voice is invaluable and often outweighs many physical shortcomings.

The voice is a wonderful instrument, but it must be properly used to render its greatest service. By nature, nearly all our voices are clear and pure. When we were children we breathed naturally, and barring natural impediments, spoke with clear, pure, pleasing accent. Modern social customs and the stress and strain incident to getting ahead of the other fellow is daily occasioning many defective voices. *Back to nature* is the cry of the voice specialist as truly as that of the social reformer.

To control the breath properly, and to coördinate mental images, breath and resonance are the two fundamental principles in vocal culture. The muscles of the vocal cords are so completely involuntary that we never pay any direct attention to them. They will deport properly if we establish the necessary coördination. Remember that the active center of breath control is the diaphragm. You should practice the exercises suggested until the mental percepts or emotions coördinate and regulate the amount of breath; open the jaw and throat, and the proper movements of the tongue, lips, and soft palate are made to express these percepts or emotions; and you should learn to do this unconscious of these vocal adjustments. Correct habits must be formed. The earlier the better. You see some object on the ground in the distance; you think of picking it up. Immediately you take the proper steps, stop when you reach it and stoop to pick it up. You are not conscious of these movements. You have learned to coördinate your mental percepts with your muscular organization. In the same way you must unconsciously control your speaking apparatus; so that when you have an idea, the diaphragm, vocal cords, jaw, tongue, etc., will express your idea without thought as to just what part each one performs. The best speaker and reader is he who performs his work properly with the least expenditure of energy.

While performing an exercise to correct any defect, center your mind upon that part. If you do not speak clearly because your teeth are too close together, center your thoughts on this opening. In practicing any exercise, do not be afraid of overdoing it just a little. A tree that has been bent the wrong way for a number of years needs to be bent, not straight, but far over in the opposite direction for a short time, so that if let entirely alone it will assume a natural and erect position.

Think while you perform the exercise. Doing it listlessly and in a half-hearted manner will represent just that much loss of time. Constantly watch your speech whenever and wherever you speak. To repeat these exercises for a few days will not correct a defect that has been growing on you for years; but faithful and patient practice will be rewarded.

The conscientious and competent teacher will tell you of your most prominent defect and suggest what exercises should be followed in your particular case. The same remedy cannot be prescribed in each case, for the defects are not all alike. However, proper breath control, the open throat, relaxed condition of the muscles of the throat and neck, a loose jaw and a flexible tongue will remedy about all the vocal defects that are not due to actual malformations.

Some of the exercises are mere devices, which, when properly used, will aid; but do not confound them in importance with the fundamental law of coördination. Learn to breathe properly and to relax the muscles of the throat as suggested in Chapter II. Unless this is observed, no amount of facial contortions will ever improve your tone. A good singing teacher may be able to aid you greatly in teaching you how to breathe properly.

VOCAL EXERCISES

I. *Lips.*—Some people never use the lips in articulation. Flexibility and control may be cultivated by practicing the following exercises:

1. Open the mouth and bring the lips together quickly and firmly; then compress the breath against lips and cheeks, resisting with these muscles finally forcing the lips open.

2. Pronounce *oo* with the lips rounded, and projected as far as possible.

3. Pronounce *ee,* drawing the lips sideways as far as possible.

4. Repeat rapidly: e-ah-oo; oo-ah-e; e-oo-ah.

II. *Jaw.*—A most common fault is that of talking, as we say, with the mouth shut. If one does not drop the lower jaw enough to let the tone pass freely, the voice is either muffled or swallowed. Cultivate the mouth-opening habit.

1. Relax the lower jaw. Move from side to side and forward and back. Repeat while singing *ah* in a single key.

2. Drop the back part of the jaw as far as possible and repeat, very slowly at first, and gradually faster at each repetition, *we-wick-wack-walk.*

III. *Tongue.*—In cases where one is really "tongue-tied," a surgeon may be needed to clip the small cord attached to the lower part of the tongue. But many faults of speech arise from the improper use, or lack of use, of the organ. A blurred articulation, for example, may come from using the middle part of the tongue, instead of the very tip; and failure to let the tongue lie low in the mouth makes one "mouth" his words, or obstructs the vocal passage so as to produce a nasal tone.

1. Open the mouth, keeping the tongue flat; then thrust the tongue out straight and draw it back as far as possible several times.

2. With the very tip of the tongue touch, in turn, the lower teeth, upper teeth, and the roof of the mouth.

3. Pass the tip of the tongue forward between the teeth, and then draw the whole tongue vigorously backward, as if trying to swallow it.

IV. *Correcting a Nasal Tone.*—When the tongue is raised behind and the soft palate lowered so as to nearly or quite meet it, the breath is directed upward and passes chiefly through the nose, producing the nasal tone or twang which is a deplorably common fault in America. To correct this, attention must be given to two things: (1) Lowering the tongue and raising the soft palate, so that there may be a free passageway from the pharynx to the front part of the mouth; and (2) projecting the tone forward in the mouth—a matter that is referred to under another topic.

1. With the aid of a mirror look at the back part of the mouth. Inhale through the nostrils, with the mouth wide open and the tongue still and flat: this will cause the soft palate to fall. Now exhale *through the mouth,* and note the rise of the soft palate.

2. Look in a mirror and with the mouth wide open go through the movement of gaping. Practice this until you can raise and lower the soft palate at will.

3. With soft palate raised sing *ah* and *oh* in pure, projected tone.

4. With the thumb and forefinger close the nostrils and repeat *"O precious hours,"* first in normal (nasal) tone, then in a pure tone, that is, sending the vocalization wholly through the mouth. Repeat with the nostrils open.

V. *The Guttural or Throaty Voice.*—This arises from a constriction of the throat muscles, and the process of correction lies in coaxing the muscles gradually in and about the throat into a state of relaxation. Take a deep breath, open the mouth widely in every way, open the throat by a relaxation of all the muscles, and vocalize, in turn, in a single breath, each of the open vowel sounds, such as *ah, aw, oh, oo.* Let the sounds *float* out, without effort at first. *Think* of the voice as coming from the lungs, and not from the throat. Note the quality of the tone, as you give these vowel sounds, and gradually acquire the habit of opening the voice channels so that the sound is free and unobstructed—pure.

VI. *The Aspirate, Breathy Voice.*—When all the air is not vocalized, the voice is said to be "breathy." It is often due to taking into the lungs too much air before speaking, so that it cannot be controlled properly. The remedy lies in applying to the vocal cords just enough air to produce the given sound.

1. Inhale deeply. Exhale in saying *ah*. Apply the air very gently to the vocal cords and use as little air as possible.

2. Count from one to ten in a whisper; then in a pure vocal tone.

3. To make sure that you are vocalizing all your breath, use this test: Take a deep breath and at your ordinary rate read as many lines as you can of the following:

> Collecting, projecting,
> Receding and speeding,
> And shocking and rocking,
> And darting and parting,
> And threading and spreading,
> And whizzing and hissing,
> And dripping and skipping,
> And hitting and splitting,
> And shining and twining,
> And rattling and battling,
> And shaking and quaking,
> And pouring and roaring,
> And waving and raving,
> And tossing and crossing,
> And flowing and going,
> And running and stunning,
> And foaming and roaming,
> And dinning and spinning,

And dropping and hopping,
And working and jerking,
And guggling and struggling,
And heaving and cleaving,
And moaning and groaning,
And glittering and frittering,
And gathering and feathering,
And whitening and brightening,
And quivering and shivering,
And hurrying and skurrying,
And thundering and floundering.

Placing the Voice.—Among other classifications, vocal sounds are distinguished as being *head* tones or *chest* tones. The head tone, whereby the head is the center of resonance, is the ordinary conversational tone, and is expressive of unemotional matter which is addressed to the intellect: hence it is sometimes called the *intellective voice*. In the chest tone, the center of resonance is deeper. This type of voice is properly employed in the expression of ideas of breadth, bigness, grandeur, sublimity, or solemnity. But both the head and the chest tones require that the voice be projected properly from the resonance chamber; that it be given due carrying power; that it neither be swallowed, (the squeezed-back voice), nor forced by the position of the tongue and mouth cavity to bang against the roof of the mouth (the hard, or quacky tone), nor made to rebound because of the mouth's being partially closed.

A successful plan to place the voice properly is to imagine it coming from your diaphragm and hitting gently the hard palate just back of the front teeth.

Tone Projection.—To make a tone carry well it must come from the mouth unobstructed by secondary vibrations of the false cords, soft palate, tongue, teeth, etc. It must have good support from the diaphragm which sends it out on its journey. Imagine it hitting the hard palate just back of the front teeth and going right through and coming out between your eyes. This will insure the proper face resonance so essential to the reënforcement of the tone.

I. Give the short sound of *a* (as in flat), first with the chest tone, then with the metallic hard tone, then with a pure, clear resonant head tone, deflecting the center of resonance to the hard palate just behind the front teeth.

II. Count from one to twenty, prolonging the "n's," and feel the vibration of the face, especially at the base of the nose.

III. Repeat ten times with strong projecting force in a pure clear ringing tone, observing proper breath control: ah, mo, po; to, po, ee.

IV. Repeat in the same way: ring, sing, thing, wing; bend, end, lend, mend, rend, send, tend, wend.

V. Prolong with a musical quality and clear resonance the repetition of "bells" in the following lines from Poe:

Hear the mellow wedding bells—
Golden bells!
What a world of happiness their harmony foretells!
Through the balmy air of night
How they ring out their delight
From the molten-golden notes,
And all in tune!—
Oh, from out the sounding cells,
What a gush of euphony voluminously wells!
How it swells!
How it dwells
On the future! how it tells
Of the rapture that impels
To the swinging and the ringing
Of the bells, bells, bells, bells,
Bells, bells, bells—
To the rhyming and the chiming of the bells!

Lisping.—This is merely the confirmed habit of advancing the tip of the tongue too far in articulating the sibilant consonants. Care should be exercised with small children who exhibit a tendency to lisp. The proper position of the tongue required to make the sound *s* and *z* should be shown them.

Stammering.—This defect is due to lack of control over the muscles of articulation, and seldom to any anatomical defect. Just as it is necessary to learn to walk, so everybody must learn to speak. It is not a natural gift. Some people have never succeeded in coördinating the movements of the organs of speech. Especially is this lack of control obvious when attempting words beginning with *b, p, t,* or *d,* and generally when the next sound is a consonant, as, *bl, br, pr,* etc.

Some children have a tendency to repeat the initial letter in their efforts to pronounce the word—this is called *stuttering.* This defect usually begins at five years of age or earlier, and seldom lasts later than twenty. Sickness, fear, embarrassment may be assigned as causes. The principal active causes are:

I. Pressing lips tightly together.

II. Pressing the lips too tightly against the teeth.

III. Not opening the glottis so that the air may pass through.

IV. Tension in the lower jaw.

V. Pressing the tongue too tightly against the teeth or palate.

A young child who begins to stammer should be told to speak slowly and thoughtfully, assuring him that he has nothing to fear; for embarrassment frequently makes many stammer who under normal conditions never show this defect. A strong determination to be cured; the exercise of more self-control and self-reliance, and a patient, persistent effort to speak slowly and to articulate distinctly, will go far to remove this defect. When proper articulation is impossible, stop. Take a deep breath, and then slowly force out the word. Speak in a slow, rhythmic measure; stammerers seldom have any difficulty in singing. To accompany each word with some physical movement is often a great aid. It is said that Demosthenes overcame this defect by reciting poems while running up hill.

Care of the Voice.—Breathing through the nose should be enforced upon children at a very early age. It is of great value to the nose itself and protects the vocal cords. Some tribes of the American Indians enforce this rule by tying up the babies' mouths while they are not being fed. The child should be taught deep breathing and correct phonological coördination.

When girls and boys have reached the age when their voices undergo a very rapid change, no strain should be placed on them by vigorous training, either speaking or singing. At the age of seventeen, girls and boys may begin rigorous vocal training.

The bright glare of the sun is fatal to the eyesight. The noise of cannon and deafening machinery is not good for the delicate ear. Likewise, those who have any regard for the voice should not indulge in shouting or screaming themselves hoarse, whatever the excitement may be.

Vocal malformations can often be modified by the surgeon, and the sooner this is done the better; especially such as clipping the small membrane under the tongue to correct a lack of flexibility of the tongue; clipping of the uvula to correct a nasal tone; and the removal of adenoids to increase the purity of resonance. Catarrh and other nasal affections usually can be remedied through nasal vibration, proper diet, and the application of salt water to the mucous lining of the nose.

Do not speak in a room where the atmosphere is over-heated or vitiated with dust, smoke, and disease germs. A cold will destroy a good voice more quickly, per-haps, than anything else except smoking and alcoholic drinks.

Use a medium tone when you are obliged to speak for a long time. Trying to make yourself heard above the noise of the street or train has a tendency to coarsen the delicate tones of the speaking voice. A speaker should exercise great care not to expose himself to damp or cold air immediately after exercising his voice. The neck should never be muffled.

If the sympathetic nervous system suppresses the free flow of saliva when you first begin to speak, and your tongue clings to the roof of your mouth, just a sip of water may effect temporary relief; but do not get into the habit of drinking when on the platform. Unless you are very much excited the saliva may be made to flow by chewing a bit of paper before you being to speak.

It is never too late to cultivate a good speaking voice. If your voice be of a shrill, rasping, thick, nasal, high-pitched, or of indistinct quality, you can accomplish a wonderful change if you set about the task with the characteristic determination which a desire to be attract-ive incites. The voices of the American girl and boy are noted for being unpleasant in quality. The nervous temperament that is characteristically American has a great deal to do with the tense, strident tones that are heard so frequently. Climate is sometimes indirectly the cause of an unpleasant voice. But, on the whole, we must confess that we alone are at fault for our vocal shortcomings, and should immediately set about developing a good voice and refrain from doing those things destructive to its highest possible development.

IV

ENUNCIATION AND PRONUNCIATION

Definitions.—The exact meaning of the terms enunciation and articulation are not agreed upon by phonologists. *Articulation* comes from the Latin *articulare* (to join together) and usually refers to the position the vocal organs assume in speaking; also to the joining together of the elementary sounds, especially consonants, into syllables and words.

Enunciation is a more general term and refers to the distinct utterance of all elementary sounds, especially the vowel sounds.

The words enunciation and articulation are generally used synonymously.

Pronunciation deals with the correct utterance of the elementary sounds, with the proper accent and the syllabification of a word.

Elementary Sounds.—Ordinarily the elementary sounds are divided into vowel (*voco,* to call) and consonant (*consonant,* sounding with).

The *vowel* sounds are made by an uninterrupted flow of the tone. The *consonant* sounds are obstructed and modified by the articulatory organs.

Again, the elementary sounds used in pronunciation may be divided into, I. Tonics or Vocals, II. Subtonics or Subvocals, and III. Atonics, or Aspirates.

Tonics are unobstructed tones. Vowels and diphthongs belong to this class.

Subtonics are tones modified by the articulatory organs.

Atonics are without tone, or are mere breath modified by the articulatory organs.

As to *formation,* consonant sounds may be divided into:

I. Labials, formed chiefly by the lips.

II. Linguals, formed chiefly by the tongue.

III. Palatals, formed chiefly by the soft palate.

IV. Nasals, made by the free escape of vocalized breath through the nostrils.

Tables II and III show the position and shape of the tongue in forming the elementary English sounds. There are nine positions of the tongue—the front, the middle, and back; also high, medium, and low. In giving the sound of "ĕ" in *because,* the front or tip of the tongue approaches the hard palate. In the sound "ĭ" in *it,* it has the same position but it broadens out. In the mixed sound of "ē" in *eve,* it glides from "ĕ" to "ĭ." The sound of "ah" is called natural because the tongue lies in a natural, restful position in the mouth. It is a sound common to all languages; and is one of the first sounds the baby makes—mama, papa, etc.

In all the sounds modified by raising the back of the tongue, the lips are rounded. The lips should not be moved in making the other sounds.

Enunciation.—Clear-cut enunciation is the basis of all effective oral expression, for it is obvious that a reader must first of all be heard. And to be heard, the elementary sounds that make up our language must be brought out clearly. Mere loudness is insufficient, for in nine cases out of ten, when a speaker cannot be heard, it is due, not to weakness of voice, but to weakness of articula-

I. TABLE OF ELEMENTARY ENGLISH SOUNDS

Tonics	Subtonics	Atonics
Single vowel sounds	Labials	

Tonics	Subtonics	Atonics
ă (short) ăt	B ban	P pin
â (before r) fâre	M (nasal) man	F fit
ä (long Italian) äre	V vote	Wh why
a̍ (short Italian) a̍sk	W will	
ą (broad Italian) ąll		
ē̆ (long) bē̆cause	**Linguals**	
ĕ (short) ĕnd		
ê (like â) thêre		
ĭ (short) ĭt	R rate	T tin
ŏ (short) nŏt	L long	Ch church
ŭ (short) bŭt	D do	S sin
o͞o (long) mo͞on	N (nasal) nut	Th thin
o͝o (short) wo͝od	J just	Sh shun
	Z zinc	
Compound sounds, or	Th this	
diphthongs	Zh vision	
ā (long) māde		
ē (long) ēve	**Palatals**	
ī (long) īce		
ō (long) sōle		
ū (long) mūte	G go	K king
ou as in round	Ng (nasal) song	H how
oi as in noise	Y yes	Q queen

ą	(ŏ) whąt	ï	(ē) polïce	ǫ	(o͞o) wǫlf	ṳ	(o͝o) fṳll
ô	(ą) ôrb	î	(ē) bîrd	ȯ	(ŭ) sȯn	ȳ	(ī) flȳ
ę	(ā) ęight	ǫ	(o͞o) dǫ	ṵ	(o͞o) rṵde	y̆	(ĭ) hy̆mn
						ỹ	(ē) mỹrtle

II. TABLE OF VOWEL ELEMENTS

Position and Shape of Tongue

	Front	Middle	Back
High	ĕ bĕ–	ĕ ĕnd	o͞o mo͞on
High and wide	ĭ ĭt		o͝o wo͝od
Glide	ē = ĕ–ĭ ēve	ā = ĕ–ĭ āte	ū = ĭ–o͞o mūte
Medium		ah (natural)	ŭ bŭt
Glide			ō = ŭ–o͞o old
Low		ȧ ȧsk	ŏ ŏn
Low and wide	ă ăt	ä ärm	a̧ a̧ll
Glide		ī = ȧ–ĭ īce	ou = ȧ–o͞o house
Glide			oi = a̧–ĭ voice

III. TABLE OF CONSONANT ELEMENTS

Place of Articulation	Oral				Nasal
	Momentary		Continuous		Continuous
	Surd	Sonant	Surd	Sonant	Sonant
Lips........................	p	b		w	m
Lip and teeth...............			f	v	
Tongue and teeth...........			th(in)	th(y)	
Tongue and hard palate (forward)	t	d	s	z; r	n
Tongue and hard palate (back).	ch	j	sh	zh; r	
Tongue, hard palate, and soft palate....................				y; l	
Tongue and soft palate.........	k	g			ng
Various places..............	h				

tion. Attention has been called previously to the need of cultivating the mouth-opening habit. Besides this, we need an active and precise use of the articulatory organs. We·get into slovenly habits of speech. We cramp the throat muscles and swallow the sound. We mumble. We talk through the nose. We roll the tongue about in the act of speaking—"flannel-mouthed." We close the jaw and talk through the teeth. We close the lips and sputter. "In just articulation," says Gilbert Austin, "the words are not hurried over, nor precipitated syllable over syllable; nor, as it were, melted together into a mass of confusion; they are neither abridged nor prolonged, nor swallowed nor forced, nor shot from the mouth; they are not trailed nor drawled, nor let slip out carelessly, so as to drop unfinished. They are delivered from the lips as beautiful coins newly issued from the mint, deeply and accurately impressed, perfectly finished."

Now, good articulation involves the three processes of (1) sounding distinctly the consonants, (2) separating the syllables, and (3) separating the words.

And first, one must attain power over the consonants. Some one has said, "Take care of the consonants, and the vowels will take care of themselves." The common trouble is, not lack of power over the consonants, but a lack of the exercise of such power. Aside from such real impediments in speech that may need the aid of a surgeon, any one can, by sufficient attention and practice, learn to speak or read clearly, and at the same time naturally. If you lisp, giving the *th* sound for *s*, you must learn to get control of the tip of the tongue, in giving the *s* sound. If you close the jaw and whistle the *s*'s, or do not close the lips in sounding b, p, v, or fail to bring out distinctly the initial or final consonants in a word—whenever any special trouble in articulation is discovered, practice this until the fault is corrected. A little attention to this matter of sounding the consonants will show the number and variety of muscular movements, in and about the mouth, required for the proper enunciation of a word like *civilization*. In enunciating such a word as this, the common fault is lack of time-taking for bringing out the syllables distinctly.

In articulation, then, primary attention must be directed to the syllabication, rather than to the word as a whole. Many syllables are composed of several elementary sounds, although they may strike the ear as a single sound. The word *man* has three and *strands* has seven elementary sounds (elements), and proper articulation requires that each of these sounds be brought out distinctly. Do not say *jography* for geography, *artic* for arctic, *Amerka* for America, *acrost* for across, *genelmun* for gentleman, etc.

Again, the words should be clearly separated. Careless readers and speakers are apt to give phrases or sentences as a single word; "Light and dark" is given as *lighten dark;* "that will do," as *that'll doo;* "Don't you" as *don chew;* and "what are you going to do" as *whachegondo*. Such slovenly articulation is astonishingly common, and, as has been said, it stands in the way of securing the primary requisite of effective utterance, that of being understood. In those rare cases where a child has been trained to articulate clearly, each word coming out clear-cut, like a coin fresh from the mint, how easily is he understood, and with what pleasure he is heard!

In practice for overcoming faults of articulation, as in overcoming any fault, it is well to overdo at first. In the exercises that follow, therefore, be over-precise, if you

please, so that you bring out clearly every elementary
sound. (The elementary sounds in our language have
been estimated as forty-four in number.)

Pronunciation.—While Enunciation refers to distinctness in speech, Pronunciation refers to correctness.
Correctness in speech generally is a recognized mark of
culture. A person often is judged by his pronunciation:
his speech either commends or betrays him. Since pronunciation is a matter of custom, uniform correctness is
rarely attained by any individual, and yet wide departures
from the prevailing usage grate upon the ear, just as mis-
spelled words disturb the eye, and we variously characterize one's pronunciation as "pedantic," "peculiar,"
"provincial," or "bad." These adjectives represent the
two extremes of faulty pronunciation: the careless and
provincial on the one hand, and the unusual and precise
on the other. He who pronounces for as *fur,* since as
sence, window as *winder,* now as *naow,* catch as *ketch,*
from as *frum,* and so on, represents the provincial class
that usually has the further faults of slovenly articulation and bad grammar. On the other hand, we have the
over-precise, affectedly cultured class—not infrequently
represented by the country school teacher—that pronounces neither as *nither,* pretty as *pretty,* nature as
natyoor, laugh as *lawf,* and so on. But while an over-
precise and pedantic pronunciation is a common fault,
carelessness and incorrectness are far more common.

The test of good pronunciation is the common practice of the best speakers. True, this test is not always
easy of application, but with the aid of a modern dictionary, the best usage can be discovered and acquired. As
was remarked above, pronunciation is a matter of custom; it is a matter of having uniformity for the sake of

convenience. While we have in America no one locality that can properly assume to set the standard of correct English pronunciation, we have, after all, a generally recognized standard of speech; and the main point is, our pronunciation should not reveal an ignorance of this standard, especially with respect to words in common use.

EXERCISES

Table I gives the elementary sounds. Tables II and III show the relative position of the articulating organs in the enunciation of each sound. These tables, especially Table II, will enable the pupil who has not a "good ear" for sound to depend on the "feel" of the tongue to aid him in securing a correct enunciation.

Practice on these elementary sounds until the vocal organs assume the proper and natural positions unconsciously. Some students need much practice on certain difficult sounds.

LIST OF WORDS FOR PRACTICE

Long Italian ä

calm	heart	aunt	laugh	lava
palm	father	half	launch	haunt
balm	spar	almond	laundry	flaunt
psalm	car	gape	guard	daunt

Short Italian

ask	grasp	sofa	bath	command
pass	slant	botany	class	America
grass	after	idea	basket	master
cast	pastor	fast	dance	advance

Short ă

at	add	man	pan	bade
cat	fat	ran	can	sad
back	an	rat	cash	bang
am	and	tan	nap	bank

Coalescent ē

her	were	serge	earn	earth
fern	verse	learn	germ	girl
sir	perch	verge	churn	mirth
first	dirty	bird	pearl	certain

Long ū

due	new	Tuesday	dispute	illume
tune	tube	institute	music	pure
suit	tutor	pursue	student	human
lute	duty	tumult	excuse	use

FINAL COMBINATIONS

Bring out very clearly—overdoing it—the final sounds in the following words:

bold	halls	chasm	ample
regaled	fault	schism	topple
gulf	melt	clasp	troubled
wolf	delve	grasp	doubled
silk	revolve	vast	cradled
bulk	claimed	lest	saddled
helm	blamed	fact	canst
film	land	reject	midst
help	hand	open	didst
gulp	bank	weapon	against
tells	link	taken	wouldst
gains	dance	waken	children
runs	hence	brighten	surpassest
streams	want	able	standeth
climes	paint	double	rounded

Syllabification

Bring out clearly and distinctly, the syllables in the following words:

abominably	congratulatory	inviolability
absolutely	constitutionality	irrefragability
accessory	deterioration	justifiableness
accurately	disinterestedly	lugubrious
adequately	disingenuousness	momentarily
angularly	generally	monocotyledonous
apocalyptic	hospitable	multiplication
appropriateness	idiosyncrasy	mythological
authoritatively	incalculably	necessarily
antipathy	incommensurability	pacificatory
articulately	incomparably	substantiate
atmospherical	immediately	susceptibility
chronological	indisputable	superiority
circumlocution	indissolubly	temporarily
citizenship	inexplicable	unintelligibility
colloquially	institution	valedictorian

Difficult Combinations

Articulate clearly the following, with over-precision, if you please, only aim for absolute distinctness:

1. Reading and writing are arts of striking importance.
2. Make clean our hearts.
3. A big black bug bit a big black bear.
4. Bring a bit of buttered brown bread.
5. Bring me some ice, not some mice.
6. Some shun sunshine, but why should you shun sunshine?
7. Accomplished speakers display aptitude in properly applying the principles of aspiration and inspiration.
8. Goodness centers in the heart.
9. He saw six slim, sleek, slender saplings.

10. Henry Hingham has hung his harp on the hook where he hitherto hung his hope.

11. Jasper, the jolly juror, justly joked John, the journalist.

12. Nine neutral nations negotiated numerous nuptials.

13. Obstructionists and oppressors often opposed these operations.

14. Querulous quips were quoted by quiet Queenie Quelp.

15. She sells sea-shells; should he sell sea-shells?

16. They fell like leaves and fill long lists.

17. Milestones mark the march of time.

18. Willow wands waved weirdly in wild wintry winds.

19. Flags fluttered fretfully from foreign fortifications and fleets.

20. Our forefathers fought fearlessly for freedom.

21. Opportunities for benefiting the unfortunate and comforting the afflicted are offered often to affluence.

22. Rejoice with them, though then and there they and theirs will be greater than thee and thine.

23. To-morrow try to talk truly and truthfully.

24. Breathe with care, do not mouth thy words.

25. Both were loath to travel the length of the sixth path to reach the fourth booth.

26. Seated on shore, she sees ships with shining sails on the shimmering sea.

27. The chief cheerfully chose the choicest chair.

28. I did not say, wig, heart, ear, hair, and all, but whig, art, hear, air, and hall.

29. Richard chanted in church like a cherub.

30. The yarns of the ubiquitous Yankee used to be humorous, yet you yawned.

31. Dora, defending sound doctrines, discomfited the disputants.

32. No man need know need in this new nation.

33. Kittens cunningly crept across the cotton coverlet.

34. Little likeliness, laughed the low lawyer, that legibility and liability are linked indissolubly.

35. He spoke reasonably, philosophically, disinterestedly, and yet particularly, of the unceremoniousness of their communicability, and peremptorily, authoritatively, unhesitatingly, declared it to be wholly inexplicable.

36. Taciturn and talkative pupils are troublesome to teachers.

37. The pink flowers grew rank on the dank bank near the river's brink.

38. Rude, rocky, rural roads run round rocky ranges.

39. Round the rough and rugged rocks the ragged rascals rudely ran.

40. A lily lying all alone along the lane.

41. Pillercatter, tappekiller, kitterpaller, patterkiller, caterpillar.

42. How much wood would a woodchuck chuck if a woodchuck would chuck wood?

43. Peter Prangle, the prickly, prangly pear picker, picked three pecks of prickly, prangly pears from the prickly, prangly pear trees on the pleasant prairies.

44.
The Cataract strong then plunges along,
Striking and raging as if a war waging,
Rising and leaping, sinking and creeping,
Showering and springing, flying and flinging,
        Writhing and ringing.
Recoiling, turmoiling and toiling and boiling,
And gleaming and streaming and steaming and beaming,
And rushing and flushing and brushing and gushing,
And flapping and rapping and clapping and slapping,

And curling and whirling and purling and twirling,
And thumping and plumping and bumping and jumping,
And dashing and flashing and splashing and clashing;
And so never ending but always descending,
Sounds and motions for ever and ever are blending,
All at once and all o'er, with a mighty uproar,
And this way the water comes down at Lodore.
—Robert Southey.

The foregoing exercises are intended to bring out an extra effort for precision. But in reading there is such a thing as overpreciseness—the "prunes, prisms, and potatoes" articulation sometimes affected by the country school teacher. In good reading one should never call attention to the articulation as such, but he should, nevertheless, be distinct. Without overpreciseness, now, but at the same time with clear articulation, read the following:

1. Speak the speech, _ pray you, as I pronounced it to you, trippingly on the tongue. But if you mouth it, as many of your players do, I had as lief the town crier spake my lines. —Shakespeare.

2. Nature has proved that the great silent Samuel shall not be silent too long.—Carlyle.

3. From the dark portals of the Star Chamber, and in the stern text of the Acts of Uniformity, the pilgrims received a commission more important than any that ever bore the royal seal.—Everett.

4. When thou wast young, thou girdedst thyself, and walkedst whither thou wouldest; but when thou shalt be old, thou shalt stretch forth thy hands, and another shall gird thee, and carry thee whither thou wouldest not.—St. John, xxi, 18.

5. Thoughts black, hands apt, drugs fit, and time agreeing;
Confederate season, else no creature seeing;
Thou mixture rank, of midnight weeds collected,
With Hecate's ban thrice blasted, thrice inflected,
Thy natural magic and dire property
On wholesome life usurp immediately.—Shakespeare.

6. And the Gileadites took the passages of Jordan before the Ephraimites: and it was so, that when those Ephraimites which were escaped said, Let me go over; that the men of Gilead said unto him, Art thou an Ephraimite? If he said, Nay; then said they unto him, Say now Shibboleth; and he said Sibboleth: for he could not frame to pronounce it right. Then they took him and slew him at the passages of the Jordan: and there fell at that time of the Ephraimites forty and two thousand.—JUDGES, XII, 5, 6.

7. When I consider how my light is spent
   Ere half my days, in this dark world and wide,
   And that one talent which is death to hide
   Lodged with me useless, though my soul more bent
   To serve therewith my Maker, and present
   My true account, lest he returning chide,—
   Doth God exact day-labour, light denied?
   I fondly ask;—But patience, to prevent
   That murmur, soon replies; God doth not need
   Either man's work, or His own gifts: who best
   Bear His mild yoke, they serve Him best: His state
   Is kingly; thousands at His bidding speed
   And post o'er land and ocean without rest:—
   They also serve who only stand and wait.
On His Blindness. MILTON.

8. To an American visiting Europe, the long voyage he has to make is an excellent preparative. From the moment you lose sight of the land you have left, all is vacancy until you step on the opposite shore, and are launched at once into the bustle and novelties of another world.
Sketch Book. IRVING.

9.   Look how the floor of heaven
   Is thick inlaid with patines of bright gold:
   There's not the smallest orb, which thou behold'st,
   But in his motion like an angel sings,
   Still quiring to the young-eyed cherubim,—
   Such harmony is in immortal souls;
   But whilst this muddy vesture of decay
   Doth grossly close it in, we cannot hear it.
Merchant of Venice. SHAKESPEARE,

10. Once more: speak clearly, if you speak at all;
   Carve every word before you let it fall;

Don't, like a lecturer or dramatic star,
Try overhard to roll the British R;
Do put your accents in the proper spot;
Don't—let me beg you—don't say "How?" for "What?"
And when you stick on conversation's burrs,
Don't strew the pathway with those dreadful *urs.*
Urania.   O. W. HOLMES.

Pronounce the following words; note carefully the exact vowel and consonant sounds:

abdomen	address	alternate	asphalt
abject	adept	amenable	associate
abstemious	adieu	aniline	athlete
accept	advertisement	antarctic	Attila
acclimate	again	apparatus	auxiliary
accurate	aggrandizement	apparent	awry
across	ailment	applicable	bade
acumen	albumen	aquiline	balm
adamantine	alias	Arab	banquet
adult	allied	area	bayonet
because	bounteous	candelabrum	chasten
been	bouquet	canine	chastisement
believe	bravado	canyon	Chicago
bestial	brigand	carmine	clangor
betroth	bronchitis	catch	clapboard
bicycle	bulwark	cayenne	clearly
biography	buoy	cello	clematis
bitumen	burlesque	cerement	clique
blackguard	calisthenics	chalybeate	coadjutor
blouse	calm	chasm	cognomen
column	contents	creek	depot
combatant	contrary	Daniel	designate
commandant	contumely	daguerreotype	desperado
comment	conversant	data	despicable
communist	corps	decade	desuetude
compeer	coterie	deaf	detail
composite	courier	decadence	dictionary
condolence	courtesy	defalcate	direct
consummate	coyote	deficit	disciplinary
contemplate	cow	demoniacal	discourse

disputant
divan
docile
dog
dolorous
domain
drama
due
duke
duty

feminine
ferocity
fertile
fetish
fiasco
fidelity

government
granary
gratis
grimace
grovel
gymnasium
harass
hearth
height
heinous

interested
interesting
interpolate
intrinsic
inveigle
iodine
irrefragable
Italian
Iowa
jaunty

magazine
manufactory
maritime
matinée

egregious
education
elongate
encore
enervate
England
English
enquiry
envelope
epoch

finance
financier
flageolet
forensic
fragmentary
frontier

hiccough
hideous
history
homage
homeopathic
horizon
hospitable
hostage
hostile
hovel

jocose
jocund
jugular
just
juvenile
kept
kiln
kinetics
laboratory
lamentable

molecule
municipal
museum
mustache

equitable
escapade
every
examine
excess
exemplary
exigencies
exist
exploit
exponent

forehead
fungi
gape
garage
generic
genial

hover
humble
humor
hygiene
hypocrisy
idea
Illinois
illustrate
imbecile
impious

languor
larynx
laugh
launch
learned
legend
lenient
lettuce
legate
licorice

nephew
nepotism
neuralgia
new

exquisite
extant
eyrie
façade
facet
factory
faucet
February
fecund
feline

gentlemen
genuine
gibbet
gigantic
God
gondola

implacable
importune
incentive
incomparable
indefatigable
indisputably
indissoluble
inexplicable
inquiries
integral

lineament
listen
literature
lithography
livelong
Lodi
lower
lozenge
lugubrious
lyceum

now
oasis
oaths
oath

mediocre
memory
mineralogy
mischievous
misconstrue
mobile

nape
nascent
national
nature
nauseate
necessarily

New Orleans
niche
nicotine
nomenclature
nothing
none

obesity
object
objurgatory
obligatory
oblique
occult

odor
office
often
oleomargarine
on
opponent
orchid
ordeal
ordnance
orgies

ornate
orotund
orthoepy
oust
pageant
palmistry
parliament
patriotism
patron
patronize

peremptory
piano
piquant
plagiarism
plague
pomegranate
prairie
predecessor
preface
precedence

precedents
premature
prestige
pretense
pretty
primarily
principle
progress
proscenium
protestation

puissance
pyramidal
quadrupedal
quay
querulous
quiescent
quinsy
qui vive
radish
rapine

receptivity
recess
recluse
reconnaissance
recreant
refutable
régime
remonstrate
reptile
requiem

research
resource
respite
revocable
rhythm
rid
rinse
Rio Grande
romance
roof

root
route
routine
salutatory
sandwich
sapient
satiety
schedule
secretary
senile

sergeant
serpentine
simultaneous
since
sinecure
sirup
sojourn
solitaire
sonorous
sophistry

soporific
sovereign
splenetic
spontaneity
squalor
St. Louis
stalwart
steady
substantiate
succinct

suite
suggest
supererogatory
superfluous
taunt
tenet
tepid
testimony
tiny
topography

toward
transact
travail
tremendous
tribunal
tribune
trilobite
truculent
truth
tyrannic

umbrella
unanimity
uninteresting
untoward

vehement
veracity
Versailles
verbose

viscount
visor
Wellesley
wharf

wound
Worcester
wrath
wreathe

urbanity	versatile	which	wreak
usage	version	whistle	yacht
usurp	via	whole	youth
vagary	vicar	whooping	youths
vaseline	victory	with	Zaccheus
vaudeville	virulent	wont	zoology

A Test in Pronunciation.—This rather curious piece of composition was once placed upon a blackboard at a teachers' institute, and a prize, a Webster's Dictionary, was offered to any person who could read and pronounce every word correctly. The book was not carried off, however, as twelve was the lowest number of mistakes in the pronunciation made:

A sacrilegious son of Belial, who suffered from bronchitis, having exhausted his finances, in order to make good the deficit, resolved to ally himself to a comely, lenient, and docile young lady of the Malay or Caucasian race. He accordingly purchased a calliope and a coral necklace of a chameleon hue, and securing a suite of rooms at a principal hotel he engaged the head waiter as a coadjutor. He then dispatched a letter of the most exceptional caligraphy extant, inviting the young lady to a matinée. She revolted at the idea, refused to consider herself sacrificeable to his desires, and sent a polite note of refusal; on receiving which he procured a carbine and a bowie-knife, said that he would not now forge letters hymeneal with the queen, went to an isolated spot, severed his jugular vein and discharged the contents of the carbine into his abdomen. The debris was removed by the coroner.

V

MELODY

Definitions.—*Melody* in speech may be defined as a pleasing succession of changes in pitch.

Pitch is a term applied to the position of the tone relative to the key-note. It is dependent on the number of vibrations per second. The greater the rapidity of vibrations the higher the pitch. The number of vibrations is dependent on the tension, thickness and length of the vibrating body.

In the production of vocal sound, our vocal cords vibrate with a certain rapidity. And the pitch of our voice depends on the thickness, length, and tension of these cords. The pitch is also slightly modified by the size of the resonating chambers, but this seldom does more than sharp or flat a certain note.

Compass.—The human voice has a certain range which lies between the highest and lowest limits. In the ordinary individual, this range seldom reaches two octaves. The conventional voice seldom varies more than one octave, and the reading voice is usually limited to a range of two or three notes.

Key.—The predominating tone or pitch of the voice in speaking is called the key. It may also be defined as the average pitch the individual uses; this ordinarily varies from the high soprano voice of girls to the bass voice of boys. Your normal key should be a tone near which you can speak with greatest ease.

Inflection.—Inflection refers to the bend or wave of the voice above or below the key. *The Slide* denotes a prolonged inflection extending over a number of words. *Cadence* is a term usually applied to the inflection at the close of a sentence.

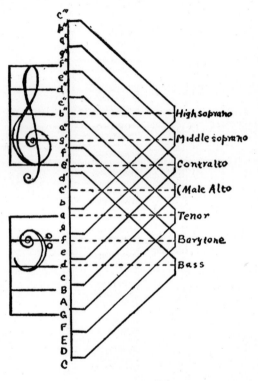

A reader, then, must ask himself, "Do I speak in a key that is most conducive to ease and effectiveness? Can I readily go above or below my normal key?" An habitual key, it should be remembered, is not necessarily a natural one. Many people habitually speak in either a high or a low key, rather than in the middle range. One who

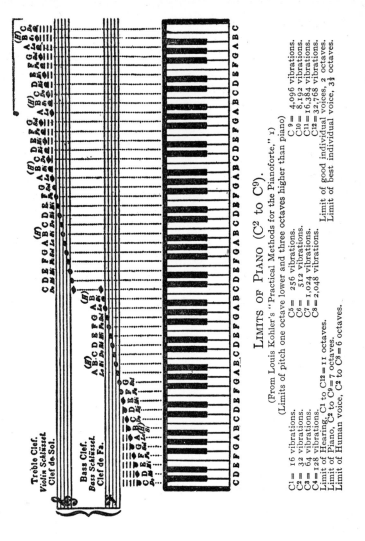

LIMITS OF PIANO (C² to C⁹).

(From Louis Kohler's "Practical Methods for the Pianoforte," 1)

(Limits of pitch one octave lower and three octaves higher than piano)

$C^1 = 16$ vibrations.
$C^2 = 32$ vibrations.
$C^3 = 64$ vibrations.
$C^4 = 128$ vibrations.
Limit of Hearing, C^1 to $C^{12} = 11$ octaves.
Limit of Piano, C^2 to $C^9 = 7$ octaves.
Limit of Human voice, C^2 to $C^8 = 6$ octaves.

$C^5 = 256$ vibrations.
$C^6 = 512$ vibrations.
$C^7 = 1,024$ vibrations.
$C^8 = 2,048$ vibrations.

$C^9 = 4,096$ vibrations.
$C^{10} = 8,192$ vibrations.
$C^{11} = 16,384$ vibrations.
$C^{12} = 32,768$ vibrations.
Limit of good individual voices, 2 octaves.
Limit of best individual voice, 3½ octaves.

Treble Clef,
Violin Schlüssel.
Clef de Sol.

Bass Clef.
Bass Schlüssel.
Clef de Fa.

speaks in a high, thin, squeaky tone, represents the one extreme, while one who speaks as from the bottom of a well, represents the other extreme. Either extreme is a fault. The most pleasing voices use neither the upper register—the "head tone"—nor the lower register—the "chest tone"—to the exclusion of the other, but readily pass from one to the other, as the thought and emotion may require.

Ease, variety, and strength depend on using the middle or average key; we then have a common point above and below which the voice is allowed to play. The importance of this free and easy play of the voice in reading and speaking cannot be overestimated. Inflection, emphasis, climax, and modulation generally depend upon it.

The normal key will vary with the individual. Physiological conditions will determine what the key of one's voice shall be. The point is, are you using to the best advantage the key-range that nature has given you? Probably the more common fault is exhibited by those who habitually use about the highest pitch of their key-range. The high, shrill tone of the average American girl is frequently remarked upon by foreigners. Such voices are not only unpleasant to hear, but they lack strength, "body," and the power of sustained force. If your voice is too high-pitched, you must acquire an habitually lower key. The only way to do this is—to lower it. Find the desired note on a musical instrument and speak to it. Relax the throat muscles and roll the voice out from the chest. *Think* of its coming, if you please, from the diaphragm. Watch yourself in conversation and do not allow the voice to rise into a high, compressed pitch. On the other hand, if you speak down "in the shoes" so that the tone is habitually swallowed, learn to raise the key, project the tone, and get it out.

Again, key should vary with the matter. The manuals of elocution give an elaborate classification of degrees in pitch, with rules as to how matter, expressive of a given function, fits into a certain "degree," but all this is largely dogmatic and artificial. The main object should be to conceive and feel the thought, and then to use the key best adapted for its expression. We know, for example, that in explanatory or narrative matter the key is higher than in the expression of deep feeling. In the one case, the sole object is to get something lying easily in the speaker's mind into the mind of a hearer; in the other case the impression lies deeper, and for its adequate expression a deeper note must perforce be struck. This is a single phase of the matter. On the other hand, uncontrolled mental states—as an outburst of indignation—produce a nervous and muscular tension which naturally results in a high key. Note the difference in the pitch of the tone of a pig that gets his leg caught in a fence, and the pitch of his voice when grunting contentedly in his pen. When you are excited your muscles become contracted, including your throat muscles, your pitch will be high, whether it be grief, joy, or pain. On the other hand, when the muscles of your body are relaxed, the throat muscles will be relaxed, and your pitch will naturally be low. The point is to get control and variety of pitch; the rest can best be left to the requirements of the varied and changing emotions of a given selection.

Old age is frequently characterized by a high, or even falsetto tone. As Shakespeare says,

> His big, manly voice,
> Turning again towards childish treble, pipes
> And whistles in his sound.

There was a time, now happily passed, when it was thought that when a man read the lines spoken by a lady that he must imitate her voice and consequently used the falsetto tone. Sometimes for the sake of ridicule and fun this is still heard in vaudeville acts, but never by those who wish to interpret properly a selection of literature. Neither should one use the high pitched voice of the child in reading what Little Boy Blue said in the following stanza:

> "Now don't you go till I come," he said;
> "And don't you make any noise!"
> So toddling off to his trundle-bed
> He dreamt of the pretty toys.—FIELD.

For convenience it is well to speak of degrees of pitch as *high, middle,* and *low.* There is no absolute standard, for voices vary with different individuals. What would be a low pitch for some would be high for others.

A Few Simple Principles May be of Help

1. The key of a selection does not so much vary with the emotion expressed as with the *degree* of the intensity of the emotion.

2. The greater the degree of the emotion the higher the key.

3. The greater the intensity of a selection the greater the range of pitch.

4. Most narratives, and other selections expressing great enthusiasm require quick and frequent changes in pitch—something on the order of ragtime music.

5. Selections in a "minor key," and those expressing deep and profound emotions or ideas require slow changes. These changes usually demand the slide. Big things do not move rapidly.

6. Variety in pitch, merely for the sake of avoiding the monotone, is not to be encouraged.

EXERCISES

I. Go to a piano and find your normal key. Run up and down the scale and register your range. Refer to the table in this chapter and find out what your singing voice is. If you do not know much about music get some one to assist you.

II. Sing the scale up and down: do, re, mi, fa, sol, la, ti, do.

III. Sing the scale by counting: one, two, etc.

IV. Run the scale by counting. Do not prolong the words as in singing.

```
                    two,
V. Say: One              three,
                              four,
                                   five,
                                        six,
                                            seven,
                                                 etc.
```

```
                  three,
VI. Say: One, two,       four,
                              five,
                                   six,
                                       etc.
```

VII. Continue with a variety of cadence.

VIII. Read the first line of each of these couplets four notes higher than the second:

> I slept and dreamed that life was Beauty;
> I woke and found that life was Duty.—HOOPER.

"O, father! I see a gleaming light; oh say, what may it be?"
But the father answered never a word; a frozen corpse was he.
—LONGFELLOW.

IX. Read the following selections and make an effort to have a difference of at least four notes between the high key and the middle key, and a difference of at least four notes between the middle key and the low key. The aid of some musical instrument will prove serviceable:

HIGH KEY

1.   Ring out, wild bells, to the wild sky,
         The flying cloud, the frosty light;
         The year is dying in the night.
      Ring out, wild bells, and let him die.

—TENNYSON.

2.   Sing loud, O bird in the tree,
         O bird, sing loud in the sky,
      And honey bees blacken the clover seas,
         There are none of you glad as I.

—INA COOLBRITH.

3.
"Be that word our sign of parting, bird or fiend!" I shrieked, upstarting;
"Get thee back into the tempest and the Night's Plutonian shore!
Leave no black plume as a token of that lie thy soul hath spoken!
Leave my loneliness unbroken! quit the bust above my door!
Take thy beak from out my heart, and take thy form from off my door."
        Quoth the raven: "Nevermore!"
The Raven.   POE.

4.
Now glory to the Lord of Hosts, from whom all glories are!
And glory to our sovereign liege, King Henry of Navarre!
Now let there be the merry sound of music and of dance,
Through thy corn-fields green and sunny vines, O pleasant land of France!
And thou, Rochelle—our own Rochelle—proud city of the waters,
Again let rapture light the eyes of all thy mourning daughters:

As thou wert constant in our ills, be joyous in our joy,
For cold and stiff and still are they who wrought thy walls
    annoy.
Hurrah! hurrah! a single field hath turned the chance of
    war!
Hurrah! hurrah! for Ivry and Henry of Navarre!
The Battle of Ivry.   MACAULAY.

MIDDLE KEY

1. To live content with small means, to seek elegance rather than luxury, and refinement rather than fashion; to be worthy, not respectable; and wealthy, not rich; to study hard, think quietly, talk gently, act frankly; to listen to stars and birds, babes and sages, with open heart; to bear all cheerfully, do all bravely, await occasions, hurry never; in a word, to let the spiritual, unbidden and unconscious, grow up through the common. This is to be my symphony.
My Symphony.   WILLIAM HENRY CHANNING.

2.   Oh, if I could only make you see
        The clear blue eyes, the tender smile,
        The sovereign sweetness, the gentle grace,
        The woman's soul and the angel's face,
        That are beaming on me all the while!
        I need not speak these foolish words;
        Yet one word tells you all I would say,—
        She is my mother; you will agree
        That all the rest may be thrown away.
An Order for a Picture.   ALICE CARY.

3.   If I were a man, a young man, and knew what I know
          to-day,
I would look into the eyes of Life undaunted
    By any fate that might threaten me.
I would give to the world what the world most wanted
    Manhood that knows it can do and be;
    Courage that dares and faith that can see
    Clear into the depth of the human soul,
    And find God there, and the ultimate goal,
If I were a man, a young man, and knew what I know to-day.
If I Were a Young Man.   ELLA WHEELER WILCOX.

4.   The little Road says "Go,"
          The little House says "Stay;"

And oh, it's bonny here at home,
    But I must go away.
The little Road, like me,
    Would seek and turn and know;
And forth I must, to learn the things
    The little Road would show!
The House and The Road.   JOSEPHINE PEABODY.

LOW KEY

1.
'Tis midnight's holy hour,—and silence now
Is brooding like a gentle spirit, o'er
The still and pulseless world. Hark! on the winds
The bell's deep tones are swelling,—'tis the knell
Of the departed year.
The Closing Year.   GEORGE D. PRENTICE.

2.   Then, with eyes that saw not, I kissed her;
            And she, kissing back, could not know
        That *my* kiss was given to her sister,
            Folded close under deepening snow.
The First Snow-Fall.   JAMES R. LOWELL.

3.
At last the thread was snapped: her head was bowed;
    Life dropped the distaff through his hands serene;
And loving neighbors smoothed her careful shroud,
    While death and winter closed the autumn scene.
The Closing Scene.   THOMAS BUCHANAN READ.

4. All is peace; and God has granted you this sight of your
country's happiness, ere you slumber in the grave. He has
allowed you to behold and to partake of the reward of your
patriotic toils; and he has allowed us, your sons and countrymen, to meet you here and in the name of the present generation, in the name of your country, in the name of liberty, to
thank you!
Bunker Hill Oration.   DANIEL WEBSTER.

Inflection.—By inflection, in its broad sense, is meant the various bends or waves of the voice above and below the dominant key. Its uses are to aid in bringing out the thought, to express the relationship between the ideas in a discourse, and, in general, to give the "lights and shades" to expression in reading. While the inflections of a well-modulated voice are infinite in number— gradual or abrupt, long or short—the principal movements are as follows: The Falling Inflection (`), the Rising Inflection (´), the Sustained Inflection (-), the Falling Circumflex (∧), the Rising Circumflex (∨), the Falling Slide (\ ), and the Rising Slide (/).

Inflections are not conventional devices, but are expressive of the mind and emotion of the reader or speaker. Now, a given passage may be spoken with different inflections, according to the interpretation of the individual reader, but similar shades of meaning will always find expression through similar inflections. One's meaning is often expressed far more clearly by the inflections used, than by the mere words uttered. If, for example, you see a friend evidently making preparations to leave the house, and you ask, "Are you going to town?" for the purpose of receiving information, you would naturally use a rising inflection on "town." If surprised at your friend's leaving, you would use a still wider rising inflection. If, now, you had asked the question several times and received no answer, and felt impatient thereat and demanded your right to an answer, then, on repeating the question, you would naturally use a pronounced falling inflection—as if to say, "I want to know if you are going to town, and that's all there is to it." Hence the *General Law* of inflection is: *When the thought is complete, the voice falls; when the thought is incomplete, the voice rises.* That is, the completeness or incompleteness of the *thought,* not the form of the sentence or the punctuation, determines the inflection. Nothing could be more misleading than to suppose that the voice always falls at the period, for a sentence may be grammatically complete, but incomplete in thought. However, since the purpose of punctuation is to aid in determining the thought, a period usually denotes that the thought is complete.

Now, there are various applications of the General Law as above stated. Let us notice some of them.

I. The *falling inflection* denotes affirmation, determination, positiveness, assertion—completeness. Such completeness may be either final or momentary. If final, the thought is concluded at that point, and this is indicated by the fall of the voice, as in the following examples:

1. I expect to pass through this life but once`. If there is any kindness or any good thing I can do to my fellow-beings, let me do it now`. I shall pass this way but once`.—WILLIAM PENN.

2. And Morley was dead`; to begin with`.—DICKENS.

3.   Man's inhumanity to man,
         Makes countless thousands mourn`.—BURNS.

4.   If every ducat in six thousand ducats
       Were in six parts, and every part a ducat,
       I would not draw them`: I would have my bond`.
                                              —SHAKESPEARE.

II. *A series of words or phrases equally emphatic in theory takes the rising inflection, except the last.*

Examples:

1. Property', character', reputation', everything was sacrificed.
2. Charity beareth all things', hopeth all things', endureth all things.

III. *Incompleteness of thought arises in a variety of forms.* Generally speaking, conditional, doubtful, obvious, or negative ideas denote incompleteness, and hence should be followed with the rising inflection.

Examples:

1. If we fail, it can be no worse for us'.
2. I will wait for you in the corridor, if you do not stay too long'.
3. It is in studying as in eating—he that does it gets benefit', not he that sees it done'.
4. He may be an honest man'; he says he is'.
5. I cannot promise definitely, but I think you may rely upon getting it'.
6. It is not necessary to be rich in order to be happy'. We are apt to think that a man must be great, that he must be famous, that he must be wealthy. That is all a mistake'. It is not necessary to be rich', to be great', to be famous', to be powerful', in order to be happy'. —Ingersoll.

IV. *A loose sentence is usually delivered with the Falling Inflection at intermediate pauses, except the clause preceding the last, when the Rising Inflection is used.* The reason for this general rule is, that by using the rising inflection on next to the last clause, the effect is to connect all the preceding clauses with the very close.

It is sometimes said that the falling inflection, used at the pauses in the following examples, is a partial fall only, as distinguished from the complete fall that denotes the conclusion of thought. That is, there are degrees of inflection that will represent the various degrees of relationship between ideas. It would be impossible, as well as undesirable, to give an exposition of these various degrees on the printed page. Here again the speaker's mind must be the guide.

EXAMPLES:

1. To-day men point to Marengo in wonderment. They laud the power and foresight that so skilfully planned the battle, but they forget that Napoleon failed; they forget that he was defeated; they forget that a general only thirty years old made a victory of the great conqueror's defeat', and that a gamin of Paris put to shame the Child of Destiny.—ANONYMOUS.

2.
Once to every man and nation comes the moment to decide,
In the strife of Truth with Falsehood, for the good or evil side;
Some great cause, God's new Messiah, offering each the bloom or
    blight,
Parts the goats upon the left hand, and the sheep upon the right',
And the choice goes by forever 'twixt that darkness and that light.
                         —LOWELL.

3. A little consideration of what takes place around us every day would show us that a higher law than that of our wills regulates events'; that our painful labors are unnecessary and fruitless'; that only in our simple, easy, spontaneous action are we strong', and by contenting ourselves with obedience we become divine.—EMERSON.

V. *In a periodic sentence, the Rising Inflection should usually be given at the intermediate pauses.* The construction of a periodic sentence is especially adapted to oratorical discourse, its leading idea, the climax, being reserved till the close. The thought is onlooking, and the rising inflection aids the thought-movement onward to the climax.

EXAMPLES:

1. If men cared less for wealth and fame,
    And less for battle-fields and glory´;
    If, writ in human hearts, a name
    Seemed better than in song and story´;
    If men, instead of nursing pride,
    Would learn to hate it and abhor it´;
    If more relied on love to guide,
    The world would be the better for it`.

The World Would be Better for It. M. N. COBB.

2.

When earth's last picture is painted´, and the tubes are twisted and
    dried´,
When the oldest colors have faded,´ and the youngest critic has
    died´,
We shall rest`, and, faith´, we shall need it`—lie down for an aeon
    or two´,
Till the Master of All Good Workmen shall set us to work anew` !

L'Envoi. KIPLING.

3. It was not his olive valleys and orchard groves that made
the Greece of the Greek´; it was not for his apple orchards or
potato fields that the farmer of New England or New York marched
to Bunker Hill, to Bennington, to Saratoga´. A man's country is
not a certain area of land´, but it is a principle`; and patriotism is
loyalty to that principle`.

Duty of Educated Men. CURTIS.

VI. *In alternative and antithetical expressions, the first
part usually takes the Rising, the second part the Falling
Inflection.* That is, contrasted ideas require contrasted
inflection; and coördinate ideas require like inflections.
However, if the negative part of a contrasted idea comes
last the inflection is usually the same as for coördinate
ideas.

Examples:

1. Shall we fight´, or shall we fly`?

2. For I am persuaded, that neither death´ nor life`, nor angels´ nor principalities´ nor powers`, nor things present´ nor things to come`, nor height´ nor depth`, nor any other creature, shall be able to separate us from the love of God, which is in Christ Jesus, our Lord.—Romans viii, 38, 39.

3. It is sown in corruption´, it is raised in incorruption`; it is sown in dishonour´, it is raised in glory`; it is sown in weakness´, it is raised in power`; it is sown a natural body´, it is raised a spiritual body`.—I Corinthians xv, 42–44.

4. Contrast now the circumstances of your life and mine, Æschines, and then ask these people whose fortunes they would each of them prefer. You taught reading´, I went to school`; you performed initiations´, I received them`; you danced in the chorus´, I furnished it`; you were assembly clerk´, I was speaker`; you acted third parts´, I heard you`; you broke down´, and I hissed`; you have worked as a statesman for the enemy´, I for my country`.
On the Crown.   Demosthenes.

The Circumflexes.—The Circumflexes consist of a combination of the rising and falling inflections on a single syllable or word. We have the Falling Circumflex (∧), where the rising inflection is followed by the falling. The Rising Circumflex (∨), when the falling inflection is followed by the rising. The Double Rising Circumflex (∿), when the falling circumflex is followed by the rising. The Double Falling Circumflex (⋀) is the union of two falling circumflexes.

Usage.—The rising circumflex may be used in expressing emphasis and to point the thought forward, as "You say he is goĭng?" This is equivalent to saying, "You say he is going`, do yoú?" The falling circumflex may indicate delight and surprise, as "Ôh, how are you?"

The circumflex is often used in irony, sarcasm, rail-lery, contempt, duplicity. Beware of one who habitually speaks with a zigzag inflection. His character is no straighter than his accent.

Examples:

1. You think you are smart, don't you?

2. You will send your child, will you', into a room where the table is loaded with sweet wine' and fruit'—some poisoned, some not?—you will say to him, "Choose freely, my little child! It is good for you to have freedom of choice; it forms your character —your individuality! If you take the wrong cup or the wrong berry, you will die before the day is over, but you will have acquired the dignity of a Free child"—Ruskin.

3.   Signior Antonio, many a time and oft
In the Rialto you have rated me
About my moneys and my usuances:
Still have I borne it with a patient shrug;
For sufferance is the badge of all our tribe. . . .
Well, then, it now appears you need my help:
Go to, then; you come to me, and you say,
Shylock, we would have moneys. . . .
What should I say to you? Should I not say,
Hath a dog money? Is it possible
A cur can lend three thousand ducats? Or
Shall I bend low, and in a bondman's key
With bated breath and whispering humbleness,
Say this,—
Fair sir, you spit on me on Wednesday last;
You spurn'd me such a day; another time
You call'd me dog; and for these courtesies
I'll lend you thus much moneys?
        The Merchant of Venice, Act I, Scene III.

The Slides.—The Slides are inflections extended over a number of words. The voice is carried through a series of words, phrases, clauses, or sentences, usually from below the key to and above it, or *vice versa.*

Examples:

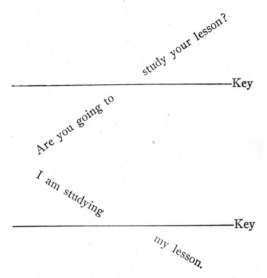

Usage.—The principal uses of the slides are:

I. *A definite question takes the Rising Slide.* A definite question is one that can be answered by *yes* or *no.* A definite question repeated takes the falling slide.

Examples:

1. Are you coming home?

2. Is it that summer's forsaken our valleys,
   And grim, surly winter is here?—Burns.

3. Hast thou forgot me, then, and do I seem
   Now in thine eyes so foul'?—Milton.

4. Are we to go on cudgelling, and cudgelling, and cudgelling men's ears with coarse processes? Are we to consider it a special providence when any good comes from our preaching or our teaching'? Are we never to study how skillfully to pick the lock of curiosity; to unfasten the door of fancy; to throw wide open the halls of

emotion, and to kindle the light of inspiration in the souls of men? Is there any reality in oratory'? It is all real.—BEECHER.

II. *An indefinite question takes the Falling Slide.*—An indefinite question is one that cannot be answered by *yes* or *no*.

EXAMPLES:

1. What can this man say`? What can he do`? Where can he go`?

2. Why was the French Revolution so bloody and destructive`? Why was our Revolution of 1641 comparatively mild? Why was our Revolution in 1688 milder still`? Why was the American Revolution, considered as an internal movement, the mildest of all`?

3. Shut now the volume of history, and tell me, on any principle of human probability, what shall be the fate of this handful of adventurers? Tell me, man of military science, in how many months were they all swept off by the thirty savage tribes enumerated within the early limits of New England? Tell me, politician, how long did this shadow of a colony, on which your conventions and treaties had not smiled, languish on the distant coast?

Melodic Change in Pitch.—In inflection there is a gradual and definite rise or fall of the voice; usually this change is made in a syllable of a word. In reading and speaking it is essential that there be a great variety of changes of pitch in the same sentence, as well as inflectional changes.

Imagine listening to a song that had all whole notes and these all on the same line on the staff! Some people talk like that; many more read like that. When in earnest conversation, we usually have a pleasing variety of pitch, but it is very difficult to secure such variety when reading. In practicing the following, suppose that the space between each line represents one note on the musical staff. It does not matter so much just where the change of pitch comes, but it is very important that you do have a change of pitch of some kind. No two readers

Oral Reading

would wholly agree on the melodic changes in any selection.

EXAMPLES:

```
          Sol-            but
                             ebbs
      like the    way                like
    swells                           its
1. Love                                   tide.
```

```
                                    bi-
          Brutus        was am-
                        he
    But        says              tious.
```

```
      cheer-              em-
                    pre-   i-        use-
          ful              nent-  a    ful
    A         man is              ly      man.
```

```
    All                   all
      the            and   its
        world's            men   women
          a                and      merely
            stage,                   players.
```

foot of thy	
at the	
Break, break, break,	crags, O Sea!

of a day	Will never	
tender grace	that	come
	is	back
But the	dead	to me.

Faults in Speech Melody.—*General Monotone.* The monotone is a comparatively unvarying change of pitch in reading or speaking. It is sticking to one tone all the time. This droning tone is often heard in the pulpit and everybody feels like taking a nap. Cultivate an "agile" tone, not one that is "stiff." Variation is restful to the speaker as well as to the audience. Most of us have been given good voices, but we do not use them. Everything is read and spoken on a dead level. Singing is good practice in learning to get away from the monotone in speaking, but the best way is to *will* to make your voice more agile.

There is no greater fault in reading than the habitual monotone. But do not run up and down the scale as you read or speak just for the sake of changing; let there be a mental reason for the change. The *thought* and *emotion* must determine not only your key, but your change in pitch.

A Monotony of the Rising Inflection.—The effect is a continuous flow of words without any breaks or stops. The audience feels impelled to say "Give us a rest!" It is frequently noticed that this habit is carried to such ridiculous extremes that those speakers who swing into a "ministerial" or "oratorical" tone, will close a speech or address with the rising inflection. The hearers are left suspended, as it were, in mid-air, and must come down of their own accord, after they realize that the speaker has concluded. The habit has its origin, no doubt, in the use of the rising inflection for voicing an appeal—a characteristic of oratory proper. But it is sadly overworked, even by prominent and successful orators. Young would-be orators imitate and perpetuate the fault, just as young preachers imitate the faults of their elders. Avoid it.

A Monotony of the Falling Inflection.—We have seen the use of the falling inflection in expressing "momentary completeness"—in giving added emphasis, strong affirmation, positiveness. For such purposes it is widely serviceable in oratory. But the proper use of the falling inflection is a very different matter from its habitual and almost constant use. Many speakers never seem to see farther than the length of a phrase or clause, and at well-nigh every pause the voice goes down, no matter what the phrase relation may be. This habit gives a scrappy, disconnected, heavy and tedious effect to speech. Avoid it.

Using a Semitone Instead of a Complete Downward Slide at the End of a Sentence.—Speakers, especially ministers, often drop their voices a semitone instead of a full note. This defect is usually accompanied with a prolongation and a rise in pitch on the final sound. There are a number of variations of this fault, but all result in a pathetic, plaintive, wail or whine that is neither pleasing nor effective. Drop your voice at least a whole tone, and make a definite, straight, downward inflection when the thought is complete, or at a full pause.

Dropping the Voice so Suddenly or so Low that the Last Syllable is Husky or Inaudible.—This may arise either from an excessive fall of the voice on the final word or syllable, or from delivering the syllable or word preceding the close in so low a key that there is no room in the compass for a further distinct fall. The fault may be corrected by keeping the voice up—or raising it if need be—on the syllable or word preceding the close, and thus preparing for the complete and normal fall.

The High Pitch.—It is natural to speak in a low key when talking to a friend, and when we address a large crowd we think it is necessary not only to speak louder but to raise the key. This results from the fact that we have only a certain amount of breath to use, and desiring to increase the amplitude of the vibrations of our cords, we bring them closer together so as to vocalize all our breath. This produces a tension on the cords resulting in a higher pitch. But remember that the carrying power of a voice is not dependent on pitch. Again, those who speak in this high key seldom have a great range of pitch at this high level, and this accounts for the lack of agility of tone in so many speakers when before an audience.

EXERCISES

I. Read the sentence, *Do you have your lesson?* first as a rhetorical, and then as an ordinary question.

II. Read the following:

1. *Questioning:* Do you like this book?
2. *Hesitation:* Yes—I—guess—so.

3. *Begging:* Lend me your pencil.
4. *Positiveness:* Yes, I like this book.
5. *Irony:* Give you money? The idea.
6. *Conciliation:* Come, let us be friends.

III. Read the following:

Othello: "Indeed? ay, indeed! Discern'st thou aught in that? Is he honest?"
Iago: "Honest, my lord?"
Othello: "Honest? Ay, honest."

IV. It is said that a certain actor read Iago's part in this manner: "Honest? My Lord!" How does this differ in meaning from this: "Honest, my Lord?"

V. Mark the inflections in Lincoln's *Gettysburg Address.*

VI. Determine the difference in meaning:

1. Shall I tell a story or a narrative?
2. Shall I tell a story or a narrative?

VII. Plot out the melody in the following:

1.　　　　　The mate for beauty
　　Should be a man, and not a money chest!—LYTTON.

2. Be thou as chaste as ice, as pure as snow, thou shalt not escape calumny.—SHAKESPEARE.

3.　　　In the lexicon of youth, which Fate reserves
　　　For a bright manhood, there is no such word
　　　As "fail."—LYTTON.

4.　　　We think our fathers fools, so wise we grow;
　　　Our wiser sons, no doubt, will think us so.—POPE.

5. I find earth not gray but rosy, heaven not grim but fair of hue.
　　Do I stoop? I pluck a posy. Do I stand and stare?
　　All's blue.—BROWNING.

VIII. Tell a short, humorous story. Observe the change of pitch.

EXAMPLES FOR PRACTICE

Determine the proper Key, Inflection, Slides, and Melody in the following:

I. "I've done now," said Sam, with slight embarrassment; "I've been a-writin'."

"So I see," replied Mr. Weller. "Not to any young 'ooman, I hope, Sammy."

"Why, it's no use a-sayin' it ain't," replied Sam. "It's a walentine."

"A what?" exclaimed Mr. Weller, apparently horror-stricken by the word.

"A walentine," replied Sam.

"Samivel, Samivel," said Mr. Weller, in reproachful accents, "I didn't think you'd ha' done it."—DICKENS.

II. Has he maintained his own charges? Has he proved what he alleged?—WEBSTER.

III.　Does the road wind up hill all the way?
　　　Yes, to the very end.
　　　Will the day's journey take the whole long day?
　　　From morn to night, my friend.—ROSSETTI.

IV. I desired Titus, and with him I sent a brother. Did Titus make a gain of you? Walked we not in the same spirit? Walked we not in the same steps?—BIBLE.

V. "Is it possible you can forgive me for the miserable lies I have uttered?" asked John, almost unconscious of the words he was speaking. "Is it possible you can forgive me for uttering these lies, Dorothy?" he repeated.—MAJOR.

VI.　We live in deeds, not years; in thoughts, not breaths;
　　　In feelings, not in figures on a dial.
　　　We should count time by heart-throbs. He most lives
　　　Who thinks most, feels the noblest, acts the best.
　　　Life is but a means unto an end; that end,—
　　　Beginning, mean, and end to all things,—God.—BAILEY.

VII. We are not trying to give an improper advantage to the poor man because he is poor; to the man of small means because he has not larger means, for that is not in accordance with the spirit of this government; but we are striving to see that the man of small means has exactly as good a chance, so far as we can obtain it for him, as the man of larger means— that there shall be equality of opportunity for the one as for the other, because that is the principle upon which our government is founded.—ROOSEVELT.

VIII. Neither blindness, nor gout, nor age, nor penury, nor domestic afflictions, nor political disappointments, nor abuse, nor proscription, nor even neglect, had power to disturb his sedate and majestic patience.—SELECTED.

IX. They tell us, sir, that we are weak—unable to cope with so formidable an adversary. But when shall we be stronger? Will it be next week, or the next year? Will it be when we are totally disarmed and when a British guard shall be stationed in every house? Shall we gather strength by irresolution and inaction? Shall we acquire the means of effectual resistance by lying supinely on our backs, and hugging the delusive phantom of hope, until our enemy shall have bound us hand and foot? Sir, we are not weak, if we make a proper use of those means which the God of nature hath placed in our power.

Liberty or Death. PATRICK HENRY.

FIRST VOICE

X.   "Ah me—the scorching sand!
    The cloudless, burned-out blue!
  The choking air on every hand,
    That the rain drops never through!"

SECOND VOICE

"The oasis was fair,
    The green palm-tree with its dates,
And the breath of the far-off ocean-air
    Where the restful harbor waits."

FIRST VOICE

"Ah me—the weary way!
    The burden heavy to bear!
The short, swift nights that die to-day,
    The silence everywhere!"

SECOND VOICE

"The oasis will rise
    Over the sand-swept ring;
In music under cool, starry skies
    Will ripple the running spring."

FIRST VOICE

"Ah me—the scorching sand!
    The cloudless, burned-out blue!
The choking air on every hand,
    That the rain drops never through!"

The Desert.   ANNA C. BRACKETT.

XI.   I lived first in a little house, and lived there very well,
      I thought the world was small and round, and made of
         pale blue shell.

      I lived next in a little nest, nor needed any other,
      I thought the world was made of straw, and brooded
         to my mother.

      One day I fluttered from the nest to see what I could
         find.
      I said: "The world is made of leaves, I have been very
         blind."

      At length I flew beyond the tree, quite fit for grown-up
         labors,
      I don't know how the world is made, and neither do
         my neighbors!

Bird Thoughts.   AUTHOR NOT KNOWN.

XII.   My home was a dungeon,—how could that be,
      When loftiest ceilings rose stately and free?
      Love roamed in the forest or sat by the sea,
      And through the long hours was nothing to me.

      My home is a palace,—how can that be,
      When through the rude rafters the stars I can see?
      Love knocked at my window and bade me be free.
      I followed him gladly to share this with thee.

Then and Now.   RENA H. INGHAM.

XIII. In 1864 when Lincoln was a candidate for re-election, a friend spoke to him of a member of his Cabinet who was a candidate also. Mr. Lincoln said that he did not concern himself much about that. It was important to the country that the department over which his rival presided should be administered with vigor and energy, and whatever would stimulate the Secretary to such action would do good. "R———," said he, "you were brought up on a farm, were you not? Then you know what a *chin-fly* is. My brother and I," he added, "were once plowing corn on a Kentucky farm, I driving the horse, and he holding the plow. The horse was lazy; but on one occasion rushed across the field so that I, with my long legs, could scarcely keep pace with him. On reaching the end of the furrow, I found an enormous *chin-fly* fastened upon him, and knocked him off. My brother asked me what I did that for. I told him I didn't want the old horse bitten in that way. 'Why,' said my brother, *'that's all that made him go!'* "Now," said Mr. Lincoln, "if Mr. ——— has a presidential *chin-fly* biting him, I'm not going to knock him off if it will make his department go."

—B. F. CARPENTER.

VI

FORCE

This property of voice is dependent primarily on the amplitude of the vibrations of the vocal cords. When a violin string is struck, it makes a sound. If it is struck harder, it will vibrate wth a greater amplitude and make a louder sound. The vocal cords are like the violin strings; the more forcefully the breath is thrown against the cords, the greater the amplitude and the louder the tone.

There are several properties of force when applied to expression—*Loudness, Volume, Intensity,* and *Stress.*

Loudness.—This property is the direct result of the amplitude of the vibration of the vocal cords and proper resonance. As a vocal quality, it is of great importance. Who has not been sadly disappointed in a reader or speaker because of being unable to hear what was said? One extreme is about as bad as another; speak so that you can be distinctly heard, but not too loud. Do not speak with the same degree of loudness all the time. As in pitch, avoid monotony.

Students often ask: "How can I make my voice carry?" The carrying power of the voice does not depend on mere loudness of tone—not alone on the amount of breath that is expended, but also on the amount of breath that still remains in the lungs. The first thing you

81

do in trying to make one hear you at a distance is to take in a deep breath—you instinctively want more breath support.   Hence breathe often and deeply.   When reading, always retain as much air in your lungs as possible.

The degree of loudness is governed by mental concept rather than by emotions.   When the mind contrasts two objects, this contrast may be expressed by using different degrees of loudness.

EXAMPLE:

> From every hill, by every sea,
> In shouts proclaim the great decree,
> "All chains are burst, all men are free!"
> Hurrah, hurrah, hurrah!

The first part should be said in a low tone; the second in a strong, loud tone.

Again, in interpreting a selection, it is necessary to be governed by the meaning to be expressed, as:

> "Halt!"—the dust brown ranks stood fast;
> "Fire!"—out blazed the rifle blast.

The words of command should be spoken louder than the explanations which follow.

A high key and a loud tone frequently go together; they both result from an excited mental state.   Therefore, passions such as æsthetic joy, defiance, alarm, terror, or rage require a louder tone than timidity, contentment, pathos, reverence, or veneration.

EXERCISES IN LOUDNESS

Say *Halt* to one person, to ten, to fifty, to one thousand—as loud as you can.

Soft tone:

I.   Softly! She is lying
        With her lips apart.
        Softly! She is dying
        Of a broken heart.

II.   O balmy breath that dost almost persuade
        Justice to break her sword! Once more, once more.
    Be this when thou art dead and I will kill thee.
    And love thee after. Once more, and this the last;
    So sweet was ne'er so fatal. I must weep,
    But they are cruel tears: this sorrow's heavenly;
    It strikes where it doth love. She awakes.

Othello.   Shakespeare.

III. Jean Valjean listened but there was no sound; he pushed the door with the tip of his finger lightly. He heard from the end of the room the calm and regular breathing of the sleeping bishop. Suddenly he stopped, for he was close to the bed; he had reached it sooner than he had anticipated.

Jean Valjean.   Victor Hugo.

Medium tone:

I.   Whither, 'midst falling dew,
  While glow the heavens with the last steps of day,
  Far, through their rosy depths, dost thou pursue
      Thy solitary way?

      Vainly the fowler's eye
  Might mark thy distant flight to do thee wrong,
  As, darkly seen against the crimson sky,
      Thy figure floats along.

      Seek'st thou the plashy brink
  Of weedy lake, or marge of river wide,
  Or where the rocking billows rise and sink
      On the chafed ocean side?

To a Waterfowl.   Bryant.

II. I honor the man who is willing to sink
    Half his present repute for the freedom to think,
    And who, having thought, be his cause strong or weak,
    Will risk t'other half for the freedom to speak.

                              —Selected.

III. Any one who lays claims to culture should train himself to think on his feet, so that he can at a moment's notice rise and express himself intelligently.—ELBERT HUBBARD.

Loud tone:

I.   Awake, awake!—
Ring the alarum-bell.—Murder and treason!—
Banquo and Donalbain!—Malcolm! awake!
Shake off this downy sleep, death's counterfeit,
And look on death itself! up, up, and see
The great doom's image!—Malcolm! Banquo!
As from our graves rise up, and walk like sprites,
To countenance this horror. Ring the bell.
Macbeth.   SHAKESPEARE.

II.   "Young man, ahoy!"
     "What is it?"
     "Beware! beware! The rapids are below you!"
                             —GOUGH.

III. What ho, my jovial mates! come on! we'll frolic it
     Like fairies frisking in the merry moonshine.
                             —SCOTT.

IV. Meanwhile the criers were calling the defendant at the four corners of the lists. "Oyes! Oyes! Oyes! Richard Drayton, duke of Nottingham, come to this combat in which ye be enterprised to discharge your sureties this day before your liege, the King, and to encounter in your defense Henry Mansfield, knight, the challenger. Oyes! Oyes! Oyes! Let the defendant come."—SCOTT.

Volume.—Technically, volume refers to the relative quantity of breath used in the vocalization of a given word or phrase. It expresses the quantity, fullness or roundness of the tone. A voice of great volume will have an open throat, and as the sound rolls out, it must seem to fill the room.

The volume natural to individual voices differs greatly, but one should learn to use discrimination in this regard, as in other elements of expression. When a word or phrase indicates wide extent or large dimensions, or stands for solidity or weight, we should express this concept of largeness in the delivery. The small, delicate, or trivial is expressed with less volume than the large, ponderous, or expansive. We would, therefore, speak of a mountain daisy in a lighter, thinner tone than in speaking of a mountain.

Increased volume requires a lower key and the chest tone. A pure, clear, full tone is a desirable attribute to a good voice. Practice the following exercises in a loud, clear tone. Be sure that the voice rolls out easily and that the throat is not cramped. Avoid having a breathy tone; vocalize all the breath.

Exercises in Volume

Small Volume:

I.   I have a little shadow that goes in and out with me,
And what can be the use of him is more than I can see.
He is very, very like me from the heels up to the head;
And I see him jump before me, when I jump into my bed.
My Shadow.   R. L. Stevenson.

II. "It's time for me to go to that there buryin'-ground, sir," he returned with a wild look.

"Lie down and tell me. What burying-ground, Jo?"

"Where they laid him that wos good to me; very good indeed, he wos. It's time for me to go down to that buryin'-ground, sir, and ask to be put along with him. I wants to go there and be buried. He used fur to say to me, 'I am as poor as you to-day, Jo,' he ses. I wants to tell him that I am as poor as him, now, and have come there to be laid along with him."—Dickens.

Great Volume:

I.   Holy! holy! holy! Lord God of hosts.

II: Roll on, thou dark and deep blue ocean, roll!
Ten thousand fleets sweep over thee in vain.
                    —Lord Byron.

III.   Thou, too, sail on, O ship of State;
        Sail on, O Union, strong and great.
        Humanity with all its fears,
        With all its hopes of future years,
        Is hanging breathless on thy fate.
The Building of the Ship.   LONGFELLOW.

IV. Lift up your heads, O ye Gates; and be ye lifted up,
ye everlasting doors; and the King of Glory shall come in.
    Who is this King of Glory? The Lord strong and mighty,
the Lord mighty in battle. He is the King of Glory.
                                              —BIBLE.

Intensity.—Force and intensity sometimes are
used interchangeably. Intensity may be said to be that
division of force which manifests the degree of energy
with which we read and speak. Intensity is not limited
physically to the amplitude of the vibration of the vocal
cords, but it is the manifestation of the thought and emotional life as expressed by the entire body. Intensity
of tone is not dependent on mere loudness. One may
speak with the greatest of intensity and not speak above
a whisper.

Intensity denotes strength—a reserve power. Too
often the student speaks as though he spoke from the
"teeth out." This does not indicate strength. There
seems to be nothing back of the voice. It appears all on
the surface. It may be a loud tone, and perchance, have
a great volume, but it is like a drum—all hollow within.

While under great emotional excitement of anger, or
sorrow, the muscles of the body become tense; so do
the muscles governing the vocal cords. These cords may
be so tightly drawn together that they scarcely vibrate
at all.

Intensity is audible earnestness. The student should

never confuse mere loudness or volume of voice with intensity of tone. Guard against restricting the throat when expressing great earnestness. This will cause your voice to "break." A pure, clear tone is far more forceful and powerful and effective than a sharp, squeaky one. Read and speak as though you meant every word you said. Show by your degree of force the tenderness, pity, love, admiration, indignation within you. Get some "pep," as the boys say; wake up; get busy—do not read as though it were a task or as though you were hired to read, or speak. Show animation, life, interest.

The first thing essential is thoroughly to understand the selection read. You must grasp the author's ideas as well as you can, and permit yourself to be moved to sympathy, or hate, joy, or sorrow, as the case may be. To do this it is essential that you know the circumstances under which the poem was written or the speech was made.

A teacher can often, through suggestion, make more definite the purpose of the writer, and throw such sidelights on the selection as will stimulate the pupil's imagination and feeling. For example, the following words were uttered by Henry W. Grady in 1886, in the course of a speech at Boston. Mr. Grady was speaking, if not to a hostile audience, at least to a critical one. There was at that time before Congress a bill that proposed to have the Federal Government take charge of national elections, as was done during the Reconstruction period. The opening quotation in the following selection was taken from a special message to Congress by President Harrison. With all these facts and attendant circumstances in mind, the following becomes charged with more force in the utterance than might otherwise appear:

The question is asked repeatedly: "When will the black man in the South cast a free ballot? When will he have the civil rights that are his?"

When will the black man cast a free ballot? When ignorance anywhere is not dominated by the will of the intelligent; when the laborer anywhere casts a ballot unhindered by his boss; when the strong and the steadfast do not everywhere control the suffrage of the weak and the shiftless. Then, but not till then, will the ballot be free. . . The negro can never control in the South, and it would be well if partisans in the North would understand this. You may pass your force bills, but they will not avail; for never again will a single state, North or South, be delivered to the control of an ignorant and inferior race. We wrested our state government from negro supremacy when the Federal drum-beat rolled closer to the ballot-box and when Federal bayonets hedged it about closer than will ever again be permitted in a free community. But if Federal cannon thundered in every voting district of the South, we would still find, in the mercy of God, the means and the courage to prevent its re-establishment.

Again, force should change with the varied emotions. All force is no force, for herein, as in other elements of expression, a hearer is impressed through contrasts. It is easy for one to acquire the habit of reading everything, regardless of the content, in a general monotone—a habit that is not uncommon even with experienced readers in reading their own productions: some prevailing though indefinite and inappropriate emotion dominates the whole delivery. Sometimes this is due to non-appreciation of the varying emotions of a discourse, and again it is simply a habit. A reader must learn to appreciate and give free expression to the play and interplay of emotions. Of course, the emotions that come during the rendition of a given selection will rarely, if ever, be exactly the same for different individuals. This, however, cannot excuse patent incongruities between the thought and its expression, such as being loud and harsh, rather than soft and tender, expressing anger where pathos is required, or failing to express the transition from one emotion to another. If we remember that emotions come and go, as the ideas march forward; that now one emotion becomes predominant, now another; that at times, in almost any selection, occurs the purely intellectual, where little force is required—we may know that one can rarely render a selection with a single, continuous emotion and read "naturally."

Degrees of Intensity.—For convenience, four degrees of intensity are suggested: Quiet, Moderate, Energetic, and Strong.

In the exercises that follow, remember that only the general "atmosphere" is suggested. This does not mean that every word should be expressed in that degree. Again, remember that strong intensity may be expressed best in a loud tone in some selections, but in others, a very soft tone should be used.

EXERCISES IN INTENSITY

I. Sweet and low, sweet and low,
       Wind of the western sea,
    Low, low, breathe and blow,
       Wind of the western sea!
    Over the rolling waters go,
    Come from the dying moon, and blow,
       Blow him again to me;
    While my little one, while my pretty one, sleeps.
The Princess.   TENNYSON.

II. Not a drum was heard, not a funeral note,
        As his corse to the rampart we hurried;
     Not a soldier discharged his farewell shot
        O'er the grave where our hero we buried.
The Burial of Sir John Moore.   CHAS. WOLFE.

III. Like as a father pitieth his children, so the Lord pitieth them that fear him. For he knoweth our frame; he remembereth that we are dust. As for man, his days are as grass; as a flower of the field, so he flourisheth: for the wind passeth over it, and it is gone; and the place thereof shall know it no more.—BIBLE.

IV.   O sweet and strange it seems to me, that ere this day
　　　　is done,
　　　The voice that now is speaking may be beyond the sun.
　　　Forever and forever,—all in a blessed home,—
　　　And there to wait a little while, till you and Effie come.
　　　To lie within the light of God, as I lie upon your
　　　　breast,—
　　　And the wicked cease from troubling, and the weary
　　　　are at rest.
The May Queen.　　　　　　　　　　　　　　　TENNYSON.

Moderate Degree:

I.　　　　　It's easy enough to look pleasant,
　　　　　　When life flows along like a song,
　　　　　　But the man that's worth while
　　　　　　Is the man who can smile
　　　　　　When everything goes dead wrong.
　　　　　　　　　　　—ELLA WHEELER WILCOX.

II. Is there not an amusement, having an affinity with the drama, which might be usefully introduced among us? I mean, Recitation. A work of genius, recited by a man of fine taste, enthusiasm, and powers of elocution, is a very pure and high gratification. Were this art cultivated and encouraged, great numbers, now insensible to the most beautiful compositions, might be waked up to their excellence and power. It is not easy to conceive of a more effectual way of spreading a refined taste through a community. The drama undoubtedly appeals more strongly to the passions than recitation; but the latter brings out the meaning of the author more. Shakespeare, worthily recited, would be better understood than on the stage. Recitation, sufficiently varied, so as to include pieces of chaste wit, as well as of pathos, beauty, and sublimity, is adapted to our present intellectual progress.—CHANNING.

III.   My doctren is to lay aside
         Contensions, and be satisfied;
         Jest do your best, and praise er blame
         That follers that, counts jest the same.
         I've allus noticed great success
         Is mixed with troubles, more er less,
         And it's the man who does the best
         That gits more kicks than all the rest.
                    —JAMES WHITCOMB RILEY.

IV. Who ne'er suffered, he has lived but half;
      Who never failed, he never strove or sought;
    Who never wept is stranger to a laugh;
    And he who never doubted never thought.
                    —J. B. GOODE.

V.   Flower in the crannied wall,
        I pluck you out of your crannies,
        Hold you here, root and all, in my hand,
        Little flower—but *if* I could understand
        What you are, root and all, and all in all,
        I should know what God and man is.
                    —TENNYSON.

VI. "My boy, the first thing you want to learn—if you haven't learned to do it already—is to tell the truth. The pure, sweet, refreshing, wholesome truth. For one thing it will save you so much trouble. Oh, heaps of trouble. And no end of hard work. And a terrible strain upon your memory. Sometimes—and when I say sometimes I mean a great many times —it is hard to tell the truth the first time. But when you have told it, there is an end of it. You have won the victory; the fight is over. Next time you tell the truth."

Energetic degree:

I.   It was a lover and his lass,
        With a hey and a ho, and a hey-nonino!
        That o'er the green cornfield did pass
        In the spring-time, the only pretty ring time,
        When birds do sing hey-ding-a-ding;
        Sweet lovers love the spring.
                    —SHAKESPEARE.

II.   Blessings on thee, little man,
Barefoot boy, with cheek of tan!
With thy turned-up pantaloons,
And thy merry whistled tunes;
With thy red lip, redder still
Kissed by strawberries on the hill;
With the sunshine on thy face,
Through thy torn brim's jaunty grace.
From my heart I give thee joy;
I was once a barefoot boy!

The Barefoot Boy.   WHITTIER.

III. Oh! when the heart is full—when bitter thoughts
Come crowding thickly up for utterance,
And the poor, common words of courtesy
Are such a very mockery—how much
The bursting heart may pour itself in prayer.

—WILLIS.

IV. Here I stand ready for impeachment or trial: I dare accusation. I defy the honorable gentleman; I defy the government; I defy the whole phalanx; let them come forth. I tell the ministers I will neither give them quarter nor take it. I am here to lay the shattered remains of my constitution on the floor of this House in defense of the liberties of my country.

Invective Against Corry.   HENRY GRATTAN.

V. Suffer not yourselves to be betrayed with a kiss. Ask yourselves how this gracious reception of our petition comports with those warlike preparations which cover our waters and darken our land. Are fleets and armies necessary to a work of love and reconciliation? Have we shown ourselves so unwilling to be reconciled, that force must be called in to win back our love? Let us not be deceived, sir. These are the implements of war and subjugation—the last arguments to which kings resort.—PATRICK HENRY.

Strong degree:

I. Must I budge? Must I observe you? Must I stand and crouch under your testy humor?—SHAKESPEARE.

II. When officers and men have given up all hope of relief, and are bravely awaiting a horrible death, Jessie Brown, a corporal's wife, made doubly sensitive to sound by sickness, hears the far-off music of the Scotch regiments sent to their succor, and shouts:

> The Highlanders! Oh, dinna ye hear
>   The slogan far awa'?
> The MacGregors! Oh, I ken it weel;
>   It is the grandest of them a'.

> "God bless the bonny Highlanders!
>   We're saved! we're saved!" she cried;
> And fell on her knees, and thanks to God
>   Poured forth, like a full flood-tide.

The Relief of Lucknow.   ROBERT T. S. LOWELL.

III.   Dost thou come here to whine?
  To outface me by leaping in her grave?
  Be buried quick with her, and so will I;
  And, if thou prate of mountains, let them
  Throw millions of acres on us, till our ground,
  Singeing his pate against the burning zone,
  Make Ossa like a wart! Nay, an thou'lt mouth,
  I'll rant as well as thou.

Hamlet.   SHAKESPEARE.

IV.   Too hard to bear! why did they take me thence?
  O God Almighty, blessed Saviour, Thou
  That didst uphold me on my lonely isle,
  Uphold me, Father, in my loneliness
  A little longer! aid me, give me strength,
  Not to tell her, never to let her know.
  Help me not to break in upon her peace.
  My children too! must I not speak to these?
  They know me not. I should betray myself,
  Never: no father's kiss for me,—the girl
  So like her mother, and the boy, my son.

Enoch Arden.   TENNYSON.

Stress.—Stress refers to the manner of applying the force to the emphatic syllable or word. There are two main divisions of stress. It is called radical stress when the greatest force is applied at the beginning of the important word, and final stress when there is a gradual increase of force culminating on the last part of the word.

1.   *Boot, sadd*le, to *horse,* and away!
       *Res*cue my *cas*tle before the hot *day*
       *Bright*ens to *blue* from its *silvery gray.*

2. Once *more* into the *breach,* dear friends, once *more.*

Note that in reading the first illustration there was an explosion of the breath on the initial syllable which gradually diminished. The glottis is forcefully kept closed until there is a great pressure beneath it, when it is thrown open like a cork popping out of a bottle.

In the second illustration, the force is applied gradually and finally swells into a strong emphasis.

Radical stress is used in all forms of animated expression; it signifies life and action. It shows decision. Final stress is used in expressing determination and impatience. Sometimes it characterizes a drawling delivery.

Again, this emphasis may be placed in the middle and characterizes the pathetic voice, and the whine. The radical and final may be united into a compound stress which is used to express irony and sarcasm.

Care should be used against overdeveloping this abruptness. This causes a jerky, dogmatic delivery. Practice the following exercises with a view of developing the ability to express the thought appropriately:

EXERCISES

I. Sound "ah" with a Radical stress; with a Final stress.

II. Say "no" so that it expresses an emphatic negative; so that it shows impatience; so that it shows sorrow.

III. Use the word "yes" in the same way.

Radical stress:

I. The charge is utterly, totally, and meanly false!

—GRATTAN.

II. "Now, upon the rebels, charge!" shouts the red-coat officer. They spring forward at the same bound. Look! their bayonets almost touch the muzzles of their rifles. At this moment the voice of the unknown rider was heard: "Now let them have it! Fire!"—CHARLES SHEPPARD.

III. Freedom calls you! Quick, be ready,—
   Think of what your sires have been;
  Onward, onward! Strong and steady,
   Drive the tyrant to his den;
    On, and let the watchword be,
    Country, home, and liberty!

The Polish War Song.   J. G. PERCIVAL.

IV. Sink or swim, live or die, survive or perish, I give my hand and my heart to this vote! Sir, before God I believe the hour is come. My judgment approves this measure, and my whole heart is in it. All that I have, and all that I am, and all that I hope in this life, I am now ready to stake upon it; and I leave off as I began, that, live or die, survive or perish, I am for the declaration. It is my living sentiment, and, by the blessing of God, it shall be my dying sentiment:—Independence now, and Independence forever.—WEBSTER.

V. Stand! the ground's your own, my braves!
  Will ye give it up to slaves?
  Will ye look for greener graves?
   Hope ye mercy still?
  What's the mercy despots feel?
  Hear it in that battle-peal!
  Read it on your bristling steel!
   Ask it,—ye who will.

Warren's Address.   JOHN PIERPONT.

Final Stress:

I. *King Henry.* Once more into the breach, dear friends, once more;

Or close the wall up with our English dead!
In peace there's nothing so becomes a man
As modest stillness and humility:
But when the blast of war blows in our ears,
Then imitate the action of the tiger;
Stiffen the sinews, summon up the blood,
Disguise fair nature with hard-favor'd rage;
Then lend the eye a terrible aspect;
Let it pry through the portage of the head,
Like the brass cannon . . . .
Now set the teeth, and stretch the nostril wide;
Hold hard the breath, and bend up every spirit
To his full height!—On, on, ye noblest English,
Whose blood is fet from fathers of war-proof!
Fathers, that, like so many Alexanders,
Have in these parts from morn till even fought,
And sheath'd their swords for lack of argument. . . .
I see you stand like greyhounds in the slips,
Straining upon the start. The game's afoot:
Follow your spirit; and, upon this charge,
  Cry—God for Harry! England! and Saint George!
Henry V.   Shakespeare.

II.   You've set me talking, sir; I'm sorry;
          It makes me wild to think of the change!
       What do you care for a beggar's story?
          Is it amusing? You find it strange?
       I had a mother so proud of me!
          'Twas well she died before—Do you know
       If the happy spirits in heaven can see
          The ruin and wretchedness here below?
The Vagabonds.   John T. Trowbridge.

III. It is often said that time is wanted for the duties of
religion. The calls of business, the press of occupation, the
cares of life, will not suffer me, says one, to give that time
to the duties of piety which otherwise I would gladly bestow.
Say you this without a blush? You have no time, then, for
the special service of that great Being whose goodness alone
has drawn out to its present length your cobweb thread of
life, whose care alone has continued you in possession of that
unseen property which you call your time.—Buckingham.

VII

MOVEMENT

One great element in reading as well as speaking is *movement.* The two general divisions are *Time* and *Rhythm.*

TIME

Time, as an element in expression, refers to the duration of utterance. The principal phases are: Rate, Pause, Transition, and Quantity.

Rate.—Rate refers to the general rapidity of reading and speaking. Within certain limits this is a matter of relativity. It varies with the individual temperament, and with the subject matter. As to the nature of the selection, three divisions of rate are generally recognized: *Slow, Medium,* and *Rapid.*

> Hear the tolling of the bells—
> > Iron bells!
> What a world of solemn thought their monody compels!

The slow tolling of the bells is in unison with the slow march of the funeral procession. Deliberate movement pervades the entire stanza. To show haste and impatience in such a selection would be very much out of place. Sorrow, gloom, reverence, sublimity, command, calling, usually are indicative of a slow rate.

On the other hand, the lines,

> Hear the loud alarum bells—
>   Brazen bells!
> What a tale of terror now their turbulency tells!

suggest a rapid rate. They recall to our minds the burning of a building, and every one is running and moving rapidly.

The lines,

> Hear the mellow wedding bells,
>   Golden bells!
> What a world of happiness their harmony foretells!

require a medium rate. Everything is as it should be. Everybody is joyous and carefree.

Thus we see that the thought and emotional content of a selection determines the general rate that should be used in reading and speaking.

Haste can frequently be shown without actually reading rapidly. A quick decisive attack on a word and a quick accent will do much to suggest the element of rapidity.

Again, when you have a word picture to present to the audience, do not go too rapidly. Give them time to picture it out in their minds. Do not make the *transitions* rapidly.

Cautions.—I. Over-rapid utterance—usually the more common fault—should be avoided. In the first place, one should read slowly enough to enunciate clearly. Furthermore, reading must be sufficiently deliberate to enable a hearer to get the thought as the reader proceeds. By acquiring the habit of a deliberate, measured utterance, one can often increase many fold his power and effectiveness in oral expression. Time-taking on significant words and phrases is absolutely necessary and essential in order, first, that the reader may express adequately their meaning and emotional content, and also in order that a hearer may comprehend fully and feel the thought and emotion the words are intended to convey.

II. On the other hand, a dragging or drawling utterance should be avoided. Sometimes the expression may be so slow and labored that a hearer must needs wait on the reader and he feels like saying, "Move along." Such a reader must acquire more energy and movement in his rendering.

III. A well-balanced, even movement, whether fast or slow, should be acquired. Reference is now made, not so much to a selection as a whole—for a uniform rate throughout a whole selection is rarely desirable—but rather to proper rate-proportion in sentence-delivery. It is the habit of some readers to give the first part of a sentence with medium or slow rate; then to snap out the closing words—often the most significant part of the sentence—or *vice versa*. The utterance moves by fits and jerks, like a horse that has not learned to pull steadily. A well-timed, balanced movement should be appreciated and acquired.

Pause.—The pause denotes the time spent between syllables, words, phrases, or sentences. Language is made up of groups of words expressing single ideas, and any discourse is intelligible only through its integral ideas. A group of words that expresses a single thought or feeling, describes a single event, or pictures a single scene, is called a *phrase*. Good reading requires that these word-groups be indicated by pausing between them. Phrasing is vocal punctuation (indicated by vertical lines, thus: / ———— /) ; it is usually identical with grammatical punctuation, though not necessarily so. The thought, and not the grammatical construction, determines the pause.

A common fault in phrasing is too frequent pausing. This arises from word-reading, rather than phrase-reading. In word-reading the reader tends to utter a word as soon as he sees it, regardless of its relation to other words in the sentence. But it usually requires several words to express a complete idea or picture. In phrase-reading one looks ahead of the vocal utterance and groups the words for the proper expression of the successive ideas.

Good sight-reading absolutely requires that the eyes always precede the voice by a number of words, so that the mind has time to understand the ideas. Wrong phrasing is also illustrated in the "sing-song" style of reading poetry, where a pause is made at the end of each line, regardless of the sense; and again, when there is little or no pausing between phrases, every sentence being given in a single breath, and hence no discrimination between the ideas. A reader must learn to realize that a pause between the thought-phrases is a necessary part of the thought-expression; that such pause is "a silence filled with significance—a time to reflect upon what is past and to prepare for what is to come." Pauses will vary in frequency and length according to the reader's conception of relationship.

To illustrate: Take the sentence, "John Keys the lawyer says he is guilty." These words can be grouped so as to express at least a half-dozen different thoughts. It usually is a safe plan to take in additional breath at each pause.

Since punctuation marks are used to help the reader

interpret the meaning, they should be observed carefully. Not in the old-time way of counting *one* at a comma, *two* at a semicolon, and *four* at a period; though that rule encouraged a mechanical expression, it was better than the plan used by many to-day—not to pause at all until at the end of the selection. Punctuation marks, especially the comma, are being used less and less. At the present time, they are seldom used unless their omission makes the meaning doubtful.

Many times you must pause where there is no punctuation. To illustrate: In Tennyson's *The Coming of Arthur* we read, "And Arthur rode a simple knight among his knights." This portrays a unique scene, indeed, unless we pause after "rode."

In the lines,

> "And as the greatest only are,
>   In his simplicity sublime,"

"only" modifies "greatest." Hence the group is "And the greatest only," and not "and the greatest only are."

In the lines from Robert Browning's *Home Thoughts, From Abroad:*

> Hark,/ where my blossomed pear-tree in the hedge/
> Leans to the field/ and scatters on the clover/
> Blossoms and dewdrops—/ at the bent spray's edge—/
> That's the wise thrush:

Some never pause until after dewdrops. This makes "clover" modify "blossoms." "Clover" is the object of "on" and "blossoms and dewdrops" are the objects of "scatters"; hence a pause must be made after clover to bring out this correct relationship.

Let the student determine the reason for the suggested

phrasing in the following example, then read by pausing only as indicated:

I.   A thing of beauty/ is a joy forever.—Keats.
      The proper study of mankind/ is man.—Pope.
      The more we work/ the more we win.—Mackey.

II.   Ah, well! for us all/ some sweet hope lies
        Deeply buried/ from human eyes;/
        And,/ in the hereafter,/ angels/ may
        Roll the stone/ from its grave away.
Maud Muller.   Whittier.

III.   If you and I—/ just you and I—/
        Should laugh/ instead of worry;/
      If we should grow—/ just you and I—/
        Kinder and lighter hearted,/
      Perhaps in some near by-and-by
        A good time might get started;/
      Then what a happy time 'twould be
        For you and me,/ for you and me.
                          —Selected.

Transition.—In reading, *transition* refers to the changes in expression that take place in passing from one shade of thought or feeling to another. It is, in a sense, phrasing on a large scale, and requires proper discrimination as to thought-values. The transition from one completed idea to another, from a literal statement to an illustration, from the mental to the emotional, from one part of a description to another—must be indicated distinctly in the delivery. The larger groups, as represented by the paragraph, require transitions of wider intervals. At such places the reader says to himself, "We now take up a new line of thought," or "Here is another phase of this idea," as the case may be. The reader must take time to adjust his mind to the change, and he must in some way indicate the change to a hearer. To accomplish this, the time-element is employed in taking a relatively long pause, aided, usually, by a change in rate, key, and tone. It should be noted that well-marked, easy, natural transitions in reading, besides showing changes in the thought, aid much in breaking up a general monotony.

The disjunctives "but," "if," "however," etc., usually herald a transition. In the sentence, "He is brave, generous, loving, but he is not trustworthy," a pause should be made after "but," the voice lowered in tone and the clause read with a slower movement.

A change in thought must always be accompanied by appropriate voice modulation. Study the following illustrative examples with special reference to the proper expression of the transitions:

I.   "O father! I see a gleaming light, O say what may it be?"
     But the father answer'd never a word, a frozen corpse was he.—LONGFELLOW.

II.   The little toy dog is covered with dust,
      But sturdy and staunch he stands.—FIELD.

III. If you should transfer the amount of your reading day by day from the newspapers to the standard authors—but who dare speak of such a thing.—EMERSON.

IV.   The combat deepens. On, ye brave,
      Who rush to glory or the grave!
      Wave, Munich! all thy banners wave,
      And charge with all thy chivalry!
      Ah! few shall part where many meet!
      The snow shall be their winding sheet,
      And every turf beneath their feet
          Shall be a soldier's sepulcher.
Hohenlinden.   THOMAS CAMPBELL.

V. While all enjoy the balmy air, the bright sunshine, the social pleasantries of wit and humor, and the like; these are not the fundamental impulses of life.—A. TOMPKINS.

Quantity.—This element represents the time given to the utterance of the sounds, syllables, and words of a sentence. For the sake of convenience, three degrees should be recognized:—*Long, Medium, and Short.*

Long quantity is used to express emphasis, reverence, pathos, laziness, and sometimes in expressing an onomatopœic idea. *Medium* quantity is used in ordinary expression. *Short* quantity is used in joy, laughter, commands and ideas of haste.

Note the difference in the *quantity* of the words in reading the following:

I. O, a wonderful stream is the river Time
   As it runs through the realm of tears,
  With a faultless rhythm and a musical rhyme,
  And a boundless sweep and a surge sublime,
   As it blends with the Ocean of Years.
The Isle of Long Ago.   T<small>AYLOR</small>.

II. For the moon never beams without bringing me dreams
   Of the beautiful Annabel Lee,
  And the stars never rise but I feel the bright eyes
   Of the beautiful Annabel Lee.
  And so all the night-tide I lie down by the side
  Of my darling, my darling, my life and my bride,
   In her sepulcher there by the sea,
   In her tomb by the sounding sea.
Annabel Lee.   P<small>OE</small>.

III. I come from haunts of coot and hern,
    I make a sudden sally,
  And sparkle out among the fern,
    To bicker down a valley.

  By thirty hills I hurry down,
    Or slip between the ridges,
  By twenty thorps, a little town,
    And half a hundred bridges.
The Brook.   T<small>ENNYSON</small>.

IV. A hurry of hoofs in a village street,
   And beneath, from the pebbles, in passing, a spark
   Struck out by a steed flying fearless and fleet,
   A shape in the moonlight, a bulk in the dark.
Paul Revere's Ride.   Longfellow.

V. There is a tide in the affairs of men
   Which, when taken at its flood, leads on to fortune;
   Omitted, all the voyage of their life
   Is bound in shallows and in miseries.
Julius Cæsar.   Shakespeare.

VI. Handsome women without religion are like flowers without perfume.—Heine.

Remember, only long vowels and the nasal sounds may be prolonged to advantage.

Cautions.—One thing must be guarded against in reading selections in *slow rate.* Do not overdo the *long quantity* of the syllables. In reading a solemn selection, or one deeply emotional, there is often a prolongation on the sounds, but the greater time consumed in reading a *slow* selection lies in the relative length of the *pause* between the words and phrases, not in the *quantity,* or the length of time it takes to say the words. Avoid a d-r-a-w-l-i-n-g, l-a-z-y tone unless you desire directly to express imitatively this characteristic.

EXAMPLES

Copy the following selections and mark the *pauses* with the bar (/); the long quantity of the sounds, syllables, or words with a dash (—) above them. Also, note the transitions.

Give reasons for the kinds of rate, and for the pause and quantity in the selections.

SLOW RATE

(From 60 to 100 words a minute.)

I. Eternity,—thou pleasing, dreadful thought.—ADDISON.

II. Tears, idle tears, I know not what they mean,
Tears from the depth of some divine despair
Rise in the heart, and gather to the eyes,
In looking on the happy Autumn-fields
And thinking of the days that are no more.
Tears, Idle Tears.   TENNYSON.

III. I had a dream which was not all a dream:
The sun was extinguished;—and the stars
Did wander darkling in the eternal space,
Rayless and pathless; and the icy earth
Swung blind and blackening in the moonless air;
Morn came, and went, and came, and brought no day.
Darkness.   LORD BYRON.

IV. Lord, thou hast been our dwelling-place in all genera-
tions. Before the mountains were brought forth, or ever thou
hadst formed the world, even from everlasting to everlasting,
thou art God.—DAVID.

V. The hours pass slowly by—nine, ten, eleven,—how sol-
emnly the last stroke of the clock floats out upon the still air.
It dies gently away, swells out again in the distance, and seems
to be caught up by spirit-voices of departed years, until the air
is filled with melancholy strains. It is the requiem of the
dying year.—SELECTED.

VI. Farewell, a long farewell, to all my greatness!
This is the state of man; to-day he puts forth
The tender leaves of hope; to-morrow blossoms,
And bears his blushing honors thick upon him:
The third day comes a frost, a killing frost;
And—when he thinks, good easy man, full surely
His greatness is a-ripening—nips his root,
And then he falls, as I do. I have ventured,
Like little wanton boys that swim on bladders,
This many summers in a sea of glory;
But far beyond my depth: my high-blown pride
At length broke under me; and now has left me,
Weary and old with service, to the mercy

Of a rude stream, that must forever hide me.
Vain pomp and glory of this world, I hate ye:
I feel my heart new opened. O, how wretched
Is that poor man that hangs on princes' favors!
There is, betwixt that smile we would aspire to,
That sweet aspect of princes, and their ruin,
More pangs and fears than wars or women have:
And when he falls, he falls like Lucifer,
Never to hope again.

Henry VIII.   SHAKESPEARE.

MEDIUM RATE

(From 125 to 175 words a minute.)

I.   The little gate was reached at last,
          Half hid in lilacs down the lane;
        She pushed it wide, and, as she passed,
        A wistful look she backward cast,
          And said, "Auf wiedersehen."

Auf Wiedersehen.   LOWELL.

II.   I have just about concluded,
            After figgerin' quite a spell,
          That appearances don't govern,
            And that blood don't allus tell.

Appearances Don't Govern.   PFRIMMER.

III. A good life: To think what is true, to feel what is beautiful, and deserve what is good.—PLATO.

IV.   Reason thus with life,
          If I lose thee, I lose a thing
          That none but fools would keep.
                                    —SHAKESPEARE.

V. Give us, oh, give us, the man who sings at his work! He will do more in the same time,—he will do it better,—he will persevere longer. One is scarcely sensible of fatigue whilst he marches to music. The very stars are said to make harmony as they revolve in their spheres. Wondrous is the strength of cheerfulness, altogether past calculation in its powers of endurance. Efforts, to be permanently useful, must be uniformly joyous, a spirit all sunshine, graceful from very gladness, beautiful because bright.

Work.   CARLYLE.

(From 225 to 300 words a minute.)

I.   Pick it up quick, Jack.

II.   Haste, thee, nymph, and bring with thee
         Jest and youthful jollity,
         Quips, and cranks, and wanton wiles,
         Nods, and becks, and wreathed smiles,
         Such as hang on Hebe's cheek,
         And love to dwell in dimples sleek;
         Come, and trip it as ye go,
         On the light fantastic toe.

L'Allegro.   MILTON.

III.   I sprang to the stirrup, and Joris, and he;
       I galloped, Dirck galloped, we galloped all three;
       "Good speed!" cried the watch, as the gate-bolts un-
           drew;
       "Speed!" echoed the wall to us galloping through;
       Behind shut the postern, the lights sank to rest,
       And into the midnight we galloped abreast.

How They Brought the Good News from Ghent.
                                                 BROWNING.

IV. What do you say? "If it's painful, why so often do it?"
I suppose you call that a joke—one of your club-jokes. As I
say, I only wish I'd any money of my own. If there is anything that humbles a poor woman, it is coming to a man's
pocket for every farthing. It's dreadful!—D. W. JERROLD.

V.   The mustang flew, and we urged him on;
     There was one chance left—and you have but one
     Halt, jump to the ground, and shoot your horse,
     Crouch under his carcass, and take your chance;
     And if the steers, in their frantic course,
     Don't batter you both to pieces at once,
     You may thank your star; if not, good-by
     To the quickening kiss and the long-drawn sigh,
     And the open air, and the open sky,
         In Texas, down by the Rio Grande.

Lasca.   DESPREZ.

VI. I just must talk! I must talk all the time! Of course
I talk entirely too much—no one knows that better than I do

—yet I can't help it! I know that my continual cackling is dreadful, and I know exactly when it begins to bore people, but somehow I can't stop myself. Aunt Patsey says I am simply fearful and just like a girl she used to know, who lived down East, a Miss Polly Blanton, who talked all the time; told everything, everything she knew, everything she had ever heard; and then when she could think of nothing else, boldly began on the family secrets. Well, I believe I am just like that girl—because I am constantly telling things about our domestic life which is by no means pleasant. Pa and ma lead an awful kind of existence—live just like cats and dogs. Now I ought never to tell that, yet somehow it will slip out in spite of myself.

The Buzz-Saw Girl. Douglas Sherley.

RHYTHM

The second great division of *movement* is *rhythm*. The universe abounds in rhythm, pulsations, beats; such as the twitter of song-birds, the chirping of insects, the roar of the ocean waves, the throbs of the heart.

This methodic throb of life is expressed both in poetry and in prose, and it must be heard to be appreciated. Rhythm in speech is a more or less regularly recurring accent or impulse of the voice. Loudness, pitch and duration are the three foremost means employed to mark this accent. In music and in lyric poetry these modulations come at regular intervals. In other forms of poetry and in prose it is not so regular.

Rhythm may be likened to waves as they roll toward the shore. They are not all the same height, shape, or distance apart, nor do they move with the same rapidity. This modification has its counterpart in speech, song, and in the written line. The height of the waves, or accent, indicates the degree of intensity. The distance apart, or the duration expresses deliberation and strength. The rapidity denotes the degree of excitement; and the shape expresses dignity if regular, or triviality and instability if irregular.

Note the rhythm in the following lines from Tennyson's *Brook:*

> I slip', I slide', I gloom', I glance,
> Among' my skimming swallows:
> I make' the nettled sunbeams dance
> Against' my sandy shallows;

The rhythm is short, quick, but regular, suggestive of the movement of the brook.

Again, note the rhythm of the following from Wolfe's *The Burial of Sir John Moore:*

> We buried him darkly at dead' of night',
> The sod' with our bayonets turning,
> By the struggling moonbeam's misty light',
> And the lantern dimly burning.

The duration of accent is longer and not regular, indicative of the solemnity and uncertainty of their expedition.

The following lines from Derzhavin's *God* express the reverence, the majesty, and the strength in the long regular rhythm:

> Being above all beings! Mighty One,
> Whom none can comprehend, and none explore,
> Who fill'st existence with Thyself alone,—
> Embracing all, supporting, ruling o'er,—
> Being whom we call God, and know no more!

Suggestions as to Reading Poetry.—Sense must never be sacrificed to sound; however, the sound is more important in poetry than in prose. A few examples must suffice to illustrate.

In the line,

> The minstrel was' infirm' and old',—

there is no accented syllable in the second foot. In reading, this should be touched lightly. If emphasis were placed on "was," it would be mere sing-song.

> The last' of all' the bards' was he'
> To sing' of border chivalry.

The last measure is not complete. It should be somewhat prolonged and a secondary accent given to the *ry,* making it chivalrē. Guard against overdoing this. In,

> The quality of mercy is not strained',

the *ity* cannot be prolonged. When in doubt stick to the sense.

In the lines,

> Work', work', work',
> Till the brain' begins' to swim',

both lines have the same meter; and it should take no longer to read the second line than the first.

But in the lines,

> Break', break,' break',
> On thy cold' gray stones', O, sea'!

the "break" cannot be prolonged. If it is, the meaning is destroyed.

Time of duration is not the only element in rhythm; the degree of emphasis must also be considered. Poetry must be *read,* not sung. To avoid sing-song, subordinate the *meter* to the *idea* to be expressed. Again, the other extreme is often taken, i. e., to disregard the meter altogether.   The union of the *meaning* and the *measure* is the secret of good poetic reading.

Observe the rhythm in the following extracts, and justify the kind used:

I.   Blessed is the man that walketh not in the counsel of
         the wicked,
      Nor standeth in the way of sinners,
      Nor sitteth in the seat of scoffers:
      But his delight is in the law of Jehovah;
      And on his law doth he meditate day and night.
      And he shall be like a tree planted by the streams of
         water,
      That bringeth forth its fruit in its season,
      Whose leaf also doth not wither;
      And whatsoever he doeth shall prosper.

Psalms.   DAVID.

II.   O, how our organ can speak with its many and wonder-
         ful voices!—
      Play on the soft lute of love, blow the loud trumpet of
         war,
      Sing with the high sesquialter, or, drawing its full
         diapason,
      Shake all the air with the grand storm of its pedals and
         stops.   —STORY.

III. Let me live in a house by the side of the road,
         Where the race of men go by—
      The men who are good, the men who are bad,
         As good and as bad as I.
      I would not sit in the scorner's seat,
         Or hurl the cynic's ban;
      Let me live in a house by the side of the road.
         And be a friend to man.

The House by the Side of the Road.   S. W. FOSS.

IV.   The mossy marbles rest
            On the lips that he had pressed
               In their bloom,
            And the name he loved to hear
            Has been carved for many a year
               On the tomb.

The Last Leaf.   HOLMES.

V.   Alas for him who never sees
       The stars shine through his cypress trees—
       Who hopeless lays his dead away,
       Nor looks to see the breaking day
       Across the mournful marbles play;
       Who has not learned, in hours of faith,
       The truth to flesh and sense unknown,—
       That life is ever lord of death,
       And love can never lose its own.

Snow Bound.   WHITTIER.

VI. How often is the case, that when impossibilities have come to pass, and dreams have condensed their misty substances into tangible reality, we find ourselves calm and even coldly self-possessed, amid circumstances which it would have been a delirium of joy or agony to anticipate.—HAWTHORNE.

VII. Some one has said, in derision, that the old men of the South, sitting down amid their ruins, reminded him of "the Spanish hidalgos sitting in the porches of the Alhambra and looking out to sea for the return of their lost Armada." There is pathos but no derision in this picture to me. These men were our fathers. Their lives were stainless. Their hands were daintily cast, and the civilization they builded in tender and engaging grace hath not been equalled. The scenes amid which they moved, as princes among men, have vanished forever. A grosser and more material day has come, in which their gentle hands can garner but scantily and their guileless hearts fend but feebly.—GRADY.

VIII

EMPHASIS

In reading a phrase or a clause, there is usually one word that expresses the central idea; in reading a sentence, one or more words convey the main thought of the sentence; and in reading a paragraph, some one word or sentence usually contains the principal thought of the paragraph. To read with due discrimination, these words that bear the burden of the thought should be pointed out to a hearer through and by the vocal expression. This is the work of *emphasis*. Emphasis, then, is the art of giving the individual words the relative importance requisite to make the thought easy to seize by a listener. Now, to express this relative importance, a good reader will not only emphasize important words, but he will also trip lightly over the unimportant words. It will readily be seen, therefore, that Emphasis is a very essential element of expression. If you take the sentence, *He is going with my friend,* and emphasize by turn each word, as many different meanings will be expressed as there are words in the sentence. The effect of a misplaced emphasis is plainly seen if the word "lies" should be emphasized in the following line from Wordsworth:

Heaven *lies* about us in our infancy.

Where we have no emphasis, we have no interpretation of the author's thought, and also a hum-drum, monotonous reading, which is not uncommon even with many people of intelligence. Too much emphasis, on the other hand, only detracts from the places where emphasis is chiefly needed. Again, many readers use a misplaced or habitual emphasis. This fault frequently appears in the reading of poetry and also in the "sing-song" in prose rendition; the hymn reading of many preachers consists merely in singing all hymns to a single tune.

Now, there are no invariable rules governing the selection of words upon which emphasis shall be placed. Where it shall fall in a given sentence depends upon the interpretation of that sentence by the individual reader. The trouble is, however, that many a reader will fail to use the voice in a way to express the meaning of a passage as he sees it. The common faults that were mentioned in the preceding paragraph suggest that it is of practical importance to learn how to emphasize, and so train the voice to obey the mind. To this end two things are essential to correct emphasis: first, a clear understanding of the thought to be expressed; second, a thorough and practical knowledge of the various modes of emphasis. These modes are often found in combination, but the best results will be secured by practicing them at first separately.

Ways of Emphasizing.—There are many ways of emphasizing a word or phrase; the five principal ones are, (1) by loudness, (2) by intensity, (3) by time, (4) by pause, (5) by inflection.

I. *Emphasis of Loudness.*—Attention can be called to a syllable, a word, or a clause by speaking it more loudly. This is the usual way of emphasizing, and is used so frequently that the term *emphasis* is often associated only with this one form of calling attention to the important words.

II. *Emphasis by Intensity.*—This form is often more effective than the stress-emphasis. It is usually expressed by lowering the voice and at the same time putting more feeling back of it. In the sentence "War is *hell,*" the word "hell" should be emphasized, not by a loud tone, nor by only lowering the voice; but by lowering the voice and hitting it hard. This is more effective than by yelling it at the top of your voice. Take the sentence, "The merchants say to you—the constitutionalists say to you—the Americans say to you—and I, *I* now say, and say to your beard, sir—*you are not an honest man,*" emphasis could be expressed most forcefully by dropping the voice just above a whisper on the last clause and then putting into it much earnestness.

III. *Emphasis by Time, or Quantity.* — Words or phrases carrying the principal idea require relatively more time than do those of less importance. There are times when ideas of magnitude, length, etc., may be most appropriately emphasized by prolonging the important words. In the following sentences note how the thought is brought out by dwelling upon the italicized words and phrases:

1. The youngest son went into a *far* country.
2. He was a *long* way from home.
3. *Five thousand* people were fed.

IV. *Emphasis by Pause.*—This mode of calling attention to a word or phrase is based on the fact that, if a pause is made before the important word which is to be emphasized, the mind will wait in expectancy of the completion of the sentence and will more carefully note that word when it does come. Also, that a pause after the important word will call attention to that word because the mind will have time to think about the word just spoken. The emphatic pause is considered by some the strongest method of emphasis.

Read the following sentences, pausing at the dashes, and note the effect:

1. The one rule for attaining perfection in any art is—*practice.*
2. Quoth the raven—*"nevermore."*
3. In this—*God's*—world, dost thou think there is no justice?
4. My answer would be—a *blow.*
5. *This*—shall slay them both.

V. *Emphasis by Inflection.*—A word is emphasized by inflection when it is inflected in a manner different from the normal. A change in pitch is the chief element in subordination. The mind naturally associates a change of thought relationship with a change in inflection. Either the rising or falling inflection may be used; but the rising inflection is seldom employed. A downward inflection and a pause at the end of the word is not an unusual combination; especially in sentences like these:

1. "Inhuman wretch, take *thàt,* and *thàt,* and *thàt.*"
2. "There wàs a South of *slaverỳ* and *secessioǹ—thàt* South is *deàd.*"

This form of emphasis cannot be used exclusively in a selection as it would render the delivery heavy and jerky. It is best not to let your voice fall from the keynote; it should be first raised so that there can be a longer sweep of the inflection, and a distinct delivery still be maintained.

There are degrees in all methods of emphasis. Some

words are to be merely touched by the voice; others are to be emphasized; and others should be given still greater emphasis. The most effective emphasis is frequently a combination of two or more modes. Such as, Pause and Inflection; Stress and Inflection; Pause and Stress; Pause and Intensity; Time and Stress; Time, Pause, and Stress.

Rules of Emphasis.—I. *The key-word or words of a sentence should be discovered and emphasized.* The following tests should be applied to discover the logical relation of the words: 1. What words are indispensable to the thought? 2. What words *must* a person hear to tell what you are talking about? 3. What words can, by rearrangement, be made the climax of the sentence?

Study the following examples and note the key-words as italicized:

Centuries ago, on the rock-bound coast of Massachusetts Bay, one night there was a *wedding.* The *sky* was the *roof* that covered the high contracting parties, and the *stars,* painted by the finger of God, were the *fresco-work;* the *music* was that of the singing *night-bird* and the surge of the gray old *ocean;* the *bidden guests* were the *Puritan fathers* and the *Puritan mothers;* the *unbidden* guests were the *dusky savages;* the *bride* and the *bridegroom* were the *meeting-house* and the *school-house,* and from that marriage there was born a *child.* They *christened* it *New England civilization.*—Frye.

II. *Subordinate the modifying or qualifying words, phrases, and clauses.* Keep the relatively unimportant ideas in the background; the more important should be made to stand out boldly.

A study in subordination:

Speak the speech (I pray you), as I pronounced it to you, *trippingly* on the tongue; but if you *mouth* it (as many of your players do), I had as lief the *town-crier* spoke my lines. Nor do not *saw* the air too much with your hand, *thus;* but use all *gently:* for in the very *torrent, tempest,* and (as I may say) the WHIRLWIND of passion, you must acquire and beget a *temperance* that may give it *smoothness.* Oh, it offends me to the *soul* to hear a *robustious, periwigpated* fellow tear a passion to *tatters,* to very RAGS, to split the ears of the *groundlings,* who (for the most part), are *capable* of nothing but inexplicable dumb-*shows* and *noise.* I would have such a fellow *whipped* for o'erdoing *Termagant;* it *out-herods Herod:* pray you avoid it.—SHAKESPEARE.

III. *Ideas compared or contrasted should be emphasized.*—This is a very important rule, and should always be carefully observed. Sometimes the antithesis is implied, only one part of the contrast being expressed. The opposing term must be supplied mentally. Note numbers 7 and 8.

Practice the following:

1. Let us be *sacrificers,* not *butchers.*—SHAKESPEARE.

2. I have found you an *argument,* I am not obliged to find you an *understanding.*—S. JOHNSON.

3. Our good business is not to *see* what lies dimly at a *distance,* but to *do* what lies clearly *at hand.*—CARLYLE.

4. It is *sown* a *natural* body; it is *raised* a *spiritual* body. —BIBLE.

5. There are sins of *com*mission; and sins of *o*mission.

6. With *malice* towards *none,* with *charity* for *all,* with firmness in the right, as God gives us to see the right.—LINCOLN.

7. I trust I am speaking to a *gentleman.*

8. He never took a *cold* bath.

IV. *Words once emphasized should not be emphasized again unless repeated for the purpose of emphasis.* When these words are repeated, it is well to vary the mode of emphasis, or else effect a climax.

Examples:

1. I have seen the gleam from the headlight of some giant engine rushing onward through the darkness, heedless of opposition, fearless of danger; and I thought it was *grand*. I have seen the light come over the eastern hills in glory, driving the lazy darkness before it, till leaf and tree and blade of grass glittered in the myriad diamonds of the morning ray; and I thought *that* was grand. I have seen the light that leaped at midnight athwart the storm-swept sky, shivering over chaotic clouds, 'mid howling winds, till cloud and darkness and shadow-haunted earth flashed into midday splendor; and I *knew that* was grand. But the grandest thing, next to the radiance that flows from the Almighty Throne, is the light of a noble and beautiful life, wrapping itself in benediction round the destinies of men, and finding its home in the bosom of the everlasting God.—GRAVES.

2. *They* were *American soldiers*. So are *we*. They were fighting an American *battle*. So are *we*. They were climbing up a *mountain*. *So are we*. The great heart of their *leader* gave them *time,* and they *conquered*. The great heart of our *country* will give *us* time, and *we* shall triumph.—CURTIS.

V. *Distinguish between emphasis of a single word and that which should be distributed to the whole of a phrase or clause.* Throwing the entire emphasis on one or two adjectives, or on the adjective rather than on the noun, is a common fault.

Example:

Our fathers *raised their flag* against a power to which Rome, in the *height of her glory,* is not to be compared; a power that has dotted over the surface of the *whole globe* with her *possessions and military posts;* whose *morning drum-beat,* following the sun and keeping company with the hours, circles the earth with *one continuous and unbroken strain of the martial airs of England.*—WEBSTER.

Climax.—Climax is the artistic building up of a **dramatic** effect by means of increased emphasis. The climactic arrangement of the author's thoughts and ideas affords a very effective means of arousing the emotions. It is often used in oratory in making an appeal. Each succeeding emphasis should be stronger than the last, though all need not be of the same kind.

Appropriately express the thought relationship in the following examples. Be sure that it has an accumulative effect. The Loudness-emphasis is usually used in the climax. Sometimes the Loudness-emphasis is used on all words except the last, Intensity-emphasis being used on the last word or phrase. This is very often very dramatic.

Examples:

1. Mr. Calhoun, while in the Senate one day, made a speech in which he stated that he was Henry Clay's master. Mr. Clay arose, shaking his finger at Mr. Calhoun, and said in tones and looks in which were concentrated the greatest scorn and defiance: "He my master! *He* my master! HE my master! Sir, *I would not own him for my* SLAVE!"

2. If I were an *American* as I am an *Englishman,* and a foreign troop were landed in *my* country, I would *never* lay down my arms. *Never!* NEVER! NEVER!—BURKE.

3. The merchants say to you,—the constitutionalists say to you,—the Americans say to you,—and I, I now say, and say to your beard, Sir,—You are not an honest man.—CURRAN.

4. You remember the story J. Russell Lowell tells of Webster, when we in Massachusetts were about to break up the Whig party. Webster came home to Faneuil Hall to protest. Drawing himself up to his loftiest proportions, his brow charged with thunder, he exclaimed: "Gentlemen, I am a Whig, a Massachusetts Whig, a revolutionary Whig, a constitutional Whig, a Faneuil Hall Whig, and if you break up the Whig party, where am I to go?" "And," says Lowell, "we all held our breath wondering where he could go."
Eulogy on O'Connell.   PHILLIPS.

5. When a wind from the lands they had ruin'd awoke
   from sleep,
And the water began to heave and the weather to moan,
And or ever that evening ended a great gale blew,
And a wave that is raised by an earthquake grew,
Till it smote on their hulls and their sails and their masts
   and their flags,
And the whole sea plunged and fell on the shot-shatter'd
   navy of Spain,
And the little Revenge herself went down by the island
   crags,
To be lost evermore in the main.

The Revenge.   TENNYSON.

A Few Cautions

I. Avoid emphasizing too much, or none at all, or at random.

> That voice all modes of passion can express
> Which marks the proper word with proper stress;
> But none emphatic can that speaker call
> Who lays an equal emphasis on all.—SELECTED.

II. Avoid emphasizing the next to the last word in a sentence irrespective of the thought expressed. This lends to the "ministerial" tone so much disliked.

III. Avoid emphasizing a word at certain regular intervals. This is characteristic of the "darky preacher tone."

IV. Avoid using only one kind of emphasis. Practice all methods. No one mode will be best at all times.

V. Do not pause for emphasis after a preposition, an article, nor the sign of an infinitive.

VI. When emphasizing a phrase, emphasize each word in the phrase.

VII. Time emphasis can only be used in expressing "number," "time" or "space" relationships.

VIII. Avoid a monotonous chant. Plutarch relates that Julius Cæsar, while yet a youth, hearing some person read in a chanting tone, said: "Are you reading or singing? If you sing, you sing badly; if you read, you nevertheless sing."

After all, formal rules are of little value. Unless the reader gets the *thought,* he will be unable to emphasize properly. Still, there are some who may know *when* to emphasize but are unable to pull the right strings so as to manipulate the machinery. But it is very important that we know how to emphasize and that we do emphasize. As Professor S. H. Clark says: "One's emphasis is the gauge of one's ability to understand. Whatever else a man may be he is not a reader if he fails to emphasize correctly. One who emphasizes correctly is more likely to do justice to his author in other regards. Nothing else betrays our ignorance of the text like bad emphasis."

EXERCISES

I. Emphasize the italicized words by (1) by loudness, (2) by intensity, (3) by time, (4) by pause, and (5) by inflection. Then determine which method or methods are the most appropriate.

1. He said, *"Go!"*
2. Farewell! A *long* farewell to all my *greatness.*
3. The only rule for obtaining perfection in any art is *practice.*
4. *Blaze* with your serried columns, *I* will not bend the knee.
5. *Away* with such follies.
6. The *heavens* declare the *glory* of God, and the *firmament* showeth His *handiwork.*
7. He who *fears* being *conquered* is sure of *defeat.*
8. *Idleness* travels very *slowly* and is soon overtaken by *poverty.*

9. *Health* is the *greatest* of all possessions; a *hale cobbler* is better than a *rich king*.

10. *Get thee back* into the tempest and the night's Plutonian shore!

II. Rewrite, underscore for emphasis—one, two, or three lines, and place above the emphatic words the figures, 1, 2, 3, 4, or 5, or a combination of these figures as: 1-4, etc., indicating the method or methods of emphasis to be employed in the following:

1. War! Its glory is all moonshine. It is only those who have neither fired a shot nor heard the shrieks and groans of the wounded who cry aloud for more blood, more vengeance, more desolation. War is hell.—GENERAL SHERMAN.

2. If to do were as easy as to know what were good to do, chapels had been churches, and poor men's cottages princes' palaces. It is a good divine that follows his own instructions; I can easier teach twenty what were good to be done than to be one of the twenty to follow mine own teaching.

The Merchant of Venice. SHAKESPEARE.

3.
　　The night has a thousand eyes,
　　　And the day but one,
　　Yet the light of the bright world dies
　　　With the dying sun.

　　The mind has a thousand eyes,
　　　And the heart but one,
　　Yet the light of a whole life dies
　　　When love is done.

Light. FRANCIS W. BOURDILLON.

Practice the following, using each of the five principal methods of emphasis on as many examples as possible. Then decide which would be most effective.

1.
　　To *be* or *not* to be—*that* is the question:
　　Whether 'tis *nobler* in the mind to *suffer*
　　The *slings* and *arrows* of *outrageous* fortune,
　　Or to take *arms* against a sea of troubles,

Aňd, by *opposing, end* them?—To *die*—to *sleep*—
No more; aňd, by a *sleep,* to say we *end*
The *heart-ache,* aňd the *thousand* natural shocks
That flesh is heir to—'tis a consummation
Devoutly to be wished. To *die*—to *sleep*—
To *sleep?*—perchance to *dream*—aye, *there's* the *rub!*
Fŏr, *in* that sleep of *death,* what *dreams* may come
When we have shuffled off this mortal coil,
Must give us *pause! There's* the respect
That makes *calamity* of so *long life:*
Fŏr who would bear the *whips* aňd *scorns* of time,
The *oppressor's wrong,* the *proud* man's *contumely,*
The *pangs* of *disprized love* the *law's delay,*
The *insolence* of *office,* and the *spurns*
The patient *merit* of the *unworthy* takes—
When *he himself* might his quietus make
With a *bare bodkin? Who* would *fardels* bear,
To *groan* and *sweat* under a *weary* life,
But that the dread of something *after* death—
The undiscovered country, from whose bourn
No traveller returns—*puzzles* the *will,*
And makes us rather *bear* those ills we *have*
Than fly to *others* that we *know* not *of!*
Thus *conscience* does make *cowards* of us *all:*
Aňd *thus* the *native* hue of resolution
Is *sicklied o'er* with the *pale cast* of *thought;*
Aňd enterprises of *great pith* aňd *moment,*
With *this* regard, thĕir currents turn *awry,*
Aňd *lose* the *name* of *action.*

Hamlet's Soliloquy.   SHAKESPEARE.

II. *Talent* is *something,* but *tact* is *everything. Talent* is
serious, sober, grave and *respectable;* tact is *all* that, and more
too. It is not a *sixth* sense, but it is the life of all the *five.* It
is the open eye, the quick ear, the judging taste, the keen smell
and the lively touch; it is the interpreter of all riddles, the sur-
mounter of all difficulties, the remover of all obstacles. It is
useful in all places and at all times; it is useful in *solitude,*
for it shows a man his way *into* the world; it is useful in
society, for it shows him his way *through* the world. *Talent*
is *power, tact* is *skill; talent* is *weight, tact* is *momentum;*
talent knows *what* to do, *tact* knows *how to do it; talent* makes
a man *respectable, tact* will make him *respected; talent* is
wealth, tact is ready *money.*—LONDON ATLAS.

III.   So live, that when *thy summons* comes to join
     The *innumerable caravan,* that moves
     To the *pale realms* of *shade,* where each shall take
     His chamber in the *silent halls* of *death,*
     Thou go *not,* like the *quarry-slave* at *night,*
     Scourged to his *dungeon;* but, *sustained* and *soothed*
     By an *unfaltering trust,* approach thy grave,
     Like one who wraps the drapery of his couch
     About him, and lies down to *pleasant dreams.*
Thanatopsis.   Bryant.

IV.   The Lord is my shepherd; I shall not want.
     He maketh me to lie down in green pastures;
     He leadeth me beside the still waters.
     He restoreth my soul.
     He guideth me in the paths of righteousness for His
        name's sake.
     Yea, though I walk through the valley of the shadow
        of death,
     I will fear no evil; for Thou art with me.
     Thy rod and Thy staff, they comfort me.
     Thou preparest a table before me in the presence of
        mine enemies;
     Thou hast anointed my head with oil;
     My cup runneth over.
     Surely goodness and mercy shall follow me all the days
        of my life;
     And I shall dwell in the house of the Lord forever.
Psalms xxiii.   David.

V. When I came to my castle, for so I think I called it ever after this, I fled into it like one pursued; whether I went over by the ladder as first contrived, or went in at the hole in the rock, which I called a door, I cannot remember; no, nor could I remember the next morning; for never frighted hare fled to cover, or fox to earth, with more terror of mind than I to this retreat.—Defoe.

VI.   I said, "The past is dead,
       I will bury it deep and still
     With a tablet over its head—
       'Of the dead one may speak no ill.'"

I dug down in the loam,
  I sealed up the grave with prayer;
But the past was the first one home,
  And waited to greet me there.

The Past.   JEANNETTE BLISS GILLESPY.

VII. In the following poem, note that the key-word in the first stanza is "arrow"; and in the second "song." In the last stanza, do not omit emphasizing "oak" and "heart of a friend."

I shot an arrow into the air,
It fell to earth, I knew not where;
For, so swiftly it flew, the sight
Could not follow it in its flight.

I breathed a song into the air,
It fell to earth, I knew not where;
For who has sight so keen and strong
That it can follow the flight of song?

Long, long afterward, in an oak
I found the arrow, still unbroke;
And the song from beginning to end
I found again in the heart of a friend.

The Arrow and the Song.   LONGFELLOW.

IX

QUALITY

The three chief characteristics of tone are *pitch, force* and *quality*. The first two have been considered. We have seen that *pitch* depends on the *number* of vibrations per second, and *force* on the *amplitude* of the vibration; *quality* is dependent on the *character* of the vibrations.

Every sound wave has two kinds of vibrations, the fundamental, the vibration of the entire string; and secondary vibrations, the movement of definite parts of the string. The number and arrangement of these overtones determine the quality of the sound.

In the human voice this character is very complex. As we have seen, the voice is not made by the vocal cords alone, but is modified by the resonating cavities. Hence these cavities, to a large degree, determine the quality of the sound. And, thirdly, the texture of the vibrating surfaces aids in modifying the nature of the sound. This is sometimes called "timbre."

The form of the resonating chambers and the texture of its walls can be slightly modified at will; but under normal circumstances this condition remains the same, thus permitting each individual to possess a quality of voice peculiar to himself alone. But if you put a pebble in your mouth or in some other manner change the size or shape of the resonating chambers, your voice will change its character.

Most people can name the kind of instrument when they hear a certain note struck upon it. A note of the same pitch and force played on a violin can easily be told from the same one played on the organ or flute. Why? Even two violins do not have the same quality. A Stradivarius violin has a much sweeter tone than our modern make. The difference lies in the texture of the wood rather than in the size of the resonating surfaces.

A flute is said to have fourteen overtones, a violin twenty-one. This accounts for the richness of the tone of the violin.

The human voice is capable of producing a very great variety of overtones. The character or shape of the secondary vibrations of the voice is modified unconsciously by the emotions. Hence by the *quality* of voice is meant that subtle change in the tone produced sympathetically in expressing the various emotions.

Atmosphere.—By *atmosphere* is meant the general quality of voice used in interpreting a literary selection, or a part of a selection. It is the "setting" or general spirit of the piece as a whole.

Kinds.—Coördinate with the three phases of mental activity—the intellect, the emotions, and the will—we may characterize three main divisions of atmosphere. These three divisions are also coördinate with the three chief purposes in expressing thought. Every sentence that is spoken or written appeals to one or more of these phases of the mind. Every sentence is expressed for the purpose of (1) giving information, (2) awakening emotions, or (3) arousing to action, or the making of a choice—the *volitional* type.

Broadly speaking, the Essay (descriptive, narrative, expository, or argumentative) is a type of the intellectual quality. True literature (poetry and the best of prose) belongs to the second group. The oration belongs to the third division. Frequently a selection will contain all three elements; but usually one predominates. In poetry the emotional element is never wholly absent, even in those poems usually termed "descriptive," e.g., *The Bells*, by Poe.

It might be helpful at times to speak of a selection as having an "atmosphere," or *general tone* of sadness, joy, animation, sublimity, smoothness, meditation, humor, etc. What is called "local coloring" of a selection will aid in determining its atmosphere. Where is the scene laid? What were the circumstances which gave rise to the selection? Is it an expression of the author's own experience? Did he "sing because he was happy," or because he got two dollars per line?

Dominant Voice Qualities.—As the voice is the index of the soul, and since "out of the abundance of the heart the mouth speaketh," we find three qualities of voice to correspond to the three types of expression:

I. The *intellectual* voice is used to interpret the intellectual type of selection. It is used in descriptive matter, in imparting information; it is the didactic voice; it is the voice the teacher often uses in explaining a problem to her class. This quality is characterized by a clear, hard, distinct, metallic resonance. It is often high pitched and lacks agreeable modulations and flexibility. The intellectual voice has been called a "white" voice; it belongs to the analytical mind, and is used much by the debater. The intellectual gestures are used. This quality is used largely in ordinary conversation.

II. The *spiritual* voice expresses feeling. It is characterized by a soft, smooth, musical, and inflectional tone. Literature is read in this tone. It is "colored" and modulated to express the various emotions of the author. Beauty is expressed by the spiritual voice; it is the persuasive tone; it is used in animated discourse, and whenever the heart is touched as well as the mind. The open hand is used in gesturing. A great range of pitch is demanded. A spiritual quality should be cultivated by every one. "Her voice was ever soft, gentle and low,—an excellent thing in woman." An expressive, agreeable, well-modulated voice is a priceless possession. Manliness is not characterized by a rough, grouchy, lion-like, bull-dog voice. The spiritual voice is indicative of refinement and culture.

III. The *vital* voice is characterized by a full, deep, strong, loud tone; the pitch is often low and re-enforced by chest resonance. It is the voice of command, the voice of the leader, the orator. This type is used to arouse; it stirs men to action; but it must not be degraded into a harsh, throaty, raspy, brute tone. It must be clear, pure, powerful, earnest, and express ideas and thoughts of great weight and importance. This quality is used in Carlyle's *The Triumph of Truth.* Most orations contain all three of the general qualities. Gesturing with a clinched hand is not rare; however, the entire body must be systematically expressive of the earnestness of feeling dominated by a strong will.

Intellectual.

I.   Love all, trust a few,
  Do wrong to none; be able for thine enemy
  Rather in power, than use; and keep thy friend
  Under thine own life's key; be check'd for silence,
  But never tax'd for speech.

All's Well That Ends Well.   SHAKESPEARE

II. Truth is always congruous, and agrees with itself; every truth in the universe agrees with every other truth in the universe; whereas falsehoods not only disagree with truth but usually quarrel among themselves.—DANIEL WEBSTER.

Emotional.

I. Is this a dagger which I see before me,
   The handle toward my hand? Come, let me clutch thee.
  I have thee not, and yet I see thee still.
  Art thou not, fatal vision, sensible
  To feeling as to sight? or art thou but
  A dagger of the mind, a false creation,
  Proceeding from the heat-oppressed brain?
  I see thee yet, in form as palpable
  As this which now I draw.

Macbeth.   SHAKESPEARE.

II. We buried the old year in silence and sadness. To many it brought misfortune and affliction. The wife hath given her husband and the husband his wife at its stern behest; the father hath consigned to its cold arms the son in whom his life centered, and the mother hath torn from her bosom her tender babe and buried it in her heart in the cold, cold ground.
                        —EDWARD BROOKS.

Volitional.

I.   Ye sons of Freedom, wake to glory!
    Hark! Hark! what myriads bid you rise!
  Your children, wives, and grandsires hoary,
    Behold their tears, and hear their cries.
  Shall hateful tyrants, (mischief breeding,
    With hireling hosts, a ruffian band),
    Affright and desolate the land,
  While peace and liberty lie bleeding?

The Marseilles Hymn.   DE LISLE.

II. If ye are brutes, then stand here like fat oxen waiting for the butcher's knife; if ye are men, follow me! strike down yon sentinel, and gain the mountain-passes, and there do bloody work as did your sires at old Thermopylæ!—Elijah Kellogg.

Tone-color.—*Tone-color* is the emotional modulation of a pure tone. Since it is related directly to the emotions, it may be well to take a general survey of them.

Emotions.—Our feelings control our actions. We are always in some mood. Life is a succession of emotions. They are the big things. Literature is the expression of the emotions in language. Just what are emotions and how do they come about? Consult some good psychology. However, all that is vital to the reader is *how* to *express* his own. No satisfactory analysis of emotions has ever been made. There are very many and so many degrees of each kind that you might as well attempt to count all the possible colors, shades, and tints used by the artist. Broadly speaking, they may be divided into positive and negative. The positive emotions have a beneficial effect on the system; they cause expansion, quicken the action of the heart, increase respiration and stimulate all normal functions of the body. The effect on the voice is to increase the rate, extend the pitch and brighten and purify the quality of tone.

The negative emotions poison the system, exhaust the nervous supply, and depress all vital functions. They encourage harsh, unpleasant tones, lower the pitch, enfeeble the volume and retard the rate.

Following is a classification of the more common positive emotions, with the corresponding negative:

Positive.	*Negative.*	*Positive.*	*Negative.*
pleasure	—pain	sympathy	—antipathy
		compassion	—disdain
contentment	—discontentment	mercy	—aversion
cheerfulness	—depression	pity	—disgust
merriment	—disappointment	ease	—anxiety
gladness	—sadness	boldness	—timidity
delight	—melancholy	assurance	—alarm
happiness	—sorrow	bravery	—fear
joy	—grief	courage	—cowardice
bliss	—distress	heroism	—terror
rapture	—despondency		
ecstasy	—misery	self-esteem	—humility
		conceit	—modesty
like	—dislike	hauteur	—lowliness
admiration	—scorn	vanity	—meekness
love	—hate	pride	—shame
honor	—ridicule	complacency	—regret
reverence	—abhorrence	elation	—remorse
adoration	—repugnance	arrogance	—dejection
idolization	—profanation	exaltation	—anguish
resignation	—uneasiness	faith	—worry
confidence	—suspicion	hope	—despair
belief	—doubt	triumph	—desperation
trust	—dread		

The following are not contrasted:

Positive.	*Positive.*	*Negative.*	*Negative.*
firmness	longing	annoyance	fury
determination	yearning	vexation	
defiance		indignation	ill-will
	surprise	resentment	envy
attention	wonder	anger	jealousy
interest	astonishment	revenge	greed
enthuiasm	awe	wrath	avarice
desire		rage	

The foregoing lists contain about one hundred and twenty-five emotions. The classification is, of course, far from complete. A single word frequently represents a dozen different shades of emotion. There are at least twenty varieties of love.

In changes in pitch or rate, as we have seen, readers and speakers are usually very monotonous; they do not exercise a great range of voice. In like manner the average person seldom permits himself a great range of emotional life. Stoicism is characteristic of our commercialized nation. No, you must not wear your heart on your sleeve, weep with the trials of a moving picture heroine, or giggle at the funny pictures in the colored supplement of the newspaper so that you can be heard a block away. That, however, is not sentiment, but sentimentalism. It is said that the fountains of joy and of tears lie close together. The man or woman who feels most, lives most. Unless you can experience the emotions of the author, you cannot express them; not any more than you can express the thoughts of the author without understanding them. Vivid imagination will aid you in putting yourself into a proper mood. And when you feel the emotion your voice will naturally assume the right pitch, resonance, and quality, if it is a trained voice. The motto always is, "From within out." If your emotions are not genuine—only assumed—the audience will know you are shamming and you will appear "stagy" and "affected" and "sickly sentimental." For, says Ferdinand Reyher, "There is no art without passion, and man must know passion, suffer under it, or attain it imaginatively, to put it into art." And ever remember that on the platform the adage runs, "Laugh and the world laughs *with* you, weep and they laugh *at* you." You do not gain sympathy by giving way to your grief, but by your struggle to overcome your grief. The audience sympathizes with a man who struggles, not with the man who lets go. In rendering dramatic selections, or when a speaker is about to be overcome with his emotions of sorrow or anger, let him pause until he gets control of himself and his voice. This silence is tremendously eloquent. The trembling voice, with a "tear in the throat" resonance, is an expression of weakness, not of strength. Never use a quivering voice nor prolong the last syllable of a sentence after dropping it a semi-tone. This error is often made by ministers who imagine they have an effective "pleading voice."

External Aids.—Assuming appropriate facial and physical attitudes of emotion you desire to express, will often aid greatly in mentally appreciating that particular emotion. If you desire to express joy, stand erect, chest out, put on a smile, and while in this attitude, *think* the joyous idea you wish to express.

In love, sympathy, devotion, and kindred emotions, the pitch is above normal, with an interested, earnest facial expression. Surprise, wonder, and amazement are portrayed facially by elevated eyebrows, and open eyes and mouth. In sorrow, shame, anxiety, etc., the face assumes a dejected look, the muscles being relaxed or drawn down. Pride, courage, etc., demand an erect head, chest out, body firm, eyes open, and a strong clear voice.

But do not forget that merely assuming these external attitudes is worse than useless unless they are the expression of the mental state within.

EXAMPLES OF TONE-COLOR

Happiness:

> The year's at the spring,
> The day's at the morn;
> Morning's at seven;
> The hill-side's dew-pearled;
> The lark's on the wing;
> The snail's on the thorn;
> God's in his heaven—
> All's right with the world.

Pippa Passes.   BROWNING.

Sorrow:

> My days are in the yellow leaf,
>   The flowers of love and fruit are gone:
> The worm, the canker, and the grief,
>   Are mine alone.

Latest Verses.   BYRON.

Admiration:

> O sacred forms, how proud you look!
> How high you lift your heads into the sky!
> How huge you are! how mighty and how free!
> Ye are the things that tower, that shine,—whose smile
> Makes glad, whose frown is terrible, whose forms,
> Robed or unrobed, do all the impress wear
> Of awe divine.

Tell to His Native Hills.   KNOWLES.

Scorn:

> I did hear him groan;
> Ay, and that tongue of his, that bade the Romans
> Mark him and write his speeches in their books,
> Alas! it cried, "Give me some drink, Titinius,"
> As a sick girl.—Ye gods, it doth amaze me,
> A man of such a feeble temper should
> So get the start of the majestic world
> And bear the palm alone.

Julius Cæsar.   SHAKESPEARE.

Adoration:

Being above all beings! Mighty One,
Whom none can comprehend, and none explore,
Who fill'st existence with Thyself alone—
Embracing all, supporting, ruling o'er,—
Being whom we call God, and know no more!

God. G. R. DERZHAVEN.

Hate:

Thou hast had shelter under my roof, and warmth at my
hearth; thou hast returned evil for good; thou hast smitten
and slain the thing that loved me and was mine; now hear thy
punishment. I curse thee! and thou art cursed! May thy
love be blasted—may thy name be blackened—may the in-
fernals mark thee—may thy heart wither and scorch—may thy
last hour recall to thee the prophet voice of the sage of
Vesuvius.

Last Days of Pompeii. LYTTON.

Pity:

Alas! for the rarity
Of Christian charity
Under the sun!
O, it was pitiful!
Near a whole city full,
Home she had none.

The Bridge of Sighs. HOOD

Disgust:

What, shall one of us,
That struck the foremost man in all the world
But for supporting robbers, shall we now
Contaminate our fingers with base bribes,
And sell the mighty space of our large honours
For so much trash as may be grasped thus?
I had rather be a dog, and bay the moon,
Than such a Roman!

Julius Cæsar. SHAKESPEARE.

Courage:

"Who dares"—this was the patriot's cry,
As striding from the desk he came—
"Come out with me in Freedom's name,

For her to live, for her to die!"
A hundred hands flung up reply,
A hundred voices answered, "I."
The Revolutionary Rising.   READ.

Cowardice:

Sir Lucius—Well, here they're coming.

Acres—Sir Lucius,—if I wa'n't with you, I should almost think I was afraid,—if my valor should leave me!—valor will come and go.

Sir Lucius—Then pray keep it fast, while you have it.

Acres—Sir Lucius,—I doubt it is going—yes my valor is certainly going!—it is sneaking off!—I feel it oozing out, as it were, at the palms of my hands.

The Rivals.   SHERIDAN.

Pride:

Oh, and proudly stood she up!
    Her heart within her did not fail;
She looked into Lord Ronald's eyes,
    And told him all her nurse's tale.

Lady Clare.   TENNYSON.

Regret:

O, Cromwell, Cromwell!
Had I served my God with half the zeal
I served my king, he would not in mine age
Have left me naked to mine enemies.

Henry VIII.   SHAKESPEARE.

Hope:

Be still, sad heart! and cease repining;
Behind the clouds is the sun still shining;
Thy fate is the common fate of all,
Into each life some rain must fall,
    Some days must be dark and dreary.

The Rainy Day.   LONGFELLOW.

Despair:

Oh! somewhere, somewhere, God unknown exist and be!
    I am dying; I am alone; I must have thee.
God! God! my sense, my soul, my all, dies in the cry;—
    Sawest thou the faint star flame and fall? Ah! it was I.

Last Appeal (The Infidel's Prayer).   MYERS.

Defiance:

> But here I stand and scoff you; here I fling
> Hatred and full defiance in your face!
> Your Consul's merciful;—For this all thanks.
> He dares not touch a hair of Catiline!

Catiline's Defiance.   GEORGE CROLY.

Awe:

> O change! O wondrous change!
>   Burst are the prison-bars!
> This moment there so low,
> So agonized, and now,
>   Beyond the stars!

The Pauper's Death-bed.   SOUTHEY.

Anger:

In an absolute frenzy of wrath, I turned at once upon him, who had thus interrupted me, and seized him violently by the collar. He was attired, as I had expected, in a costume altogether similar to my own. "Scoundrel," I cried, in a voice husky with rage, while every syllable I uttered seemed as new fuel to my fury; "scoundrel! impostor! accursed villain! you shall not—you shall not dog me unto death! Follow me, or I stab you where you stand!"

William Wilson.   POE.

Greed:

> Ah! could they see
> These bags of ducats, and that precious pile
> Of ingots, and those bars of solid gold,
> Their eyes, methinks, would water. What a comfort
> It is to see my moneys in a heap.
> All safely lodged under my very roof.
> Here's a fat bag: let me untie the mouth of it.
> What eloquence! What beauty! What expression!
> Could Cicero so plead? Could Helen look
> One half so charming?

The Miser Fitly Punished.   OSBORNE.

Jealousy:

> By the world,
> I think my wife be honest, and think she is not;
> I think thou art just, and think thou are not;

I'll have some proof: My name, that was as fresh
As Dina's visage, is now begrim'd and black
As mine own face,—If there be cords, or knives,
Poison, or fire, or suffocating steam,
I'll not endure it,—Would I were satisfied.
Othello.   SHAKESPEARE.

Word-coloring.—Word-coloring is suiting the sound to the sense of a word or phrase. There are many words in our language which in themselves suggest definite voice modulations. Such as, buzz, swish, hiss, hum, bang, boom, ping-pong, honk-honk, toot, neigh, bow-wow, etc. Give to such words their characteristic vocal color.

Again, there is another class of words that can be expressed emotionally by touching them with appropriate emphasis. Such as far, long, high, wide, etc. These should be give a *time* emphasis, suggesting their appropriate qualities. Words like quick, jerk, kick, should never be drawn out. Tiny, little, narrow, etc., are given a "small" quality of tone, while harsh, angry, rough, etc., suggest a guttural tone. Words like home, God, mother, should be spoken with love, reverence, and veneration.

Thus we see that word-coloring, while it may include onomatopœia, is a great deal more than mere imitation. Its use is to express the emotional significance of words over and beyond their literal meaning. Says Cicero, in his *De Oratore,* "The tones of the voice, like musical chords, are so wound up as to be responsive to every touch, sharp, flat, quick, slow, loud, gentle. Anger, fear, violence, pleasure, trouble, each has its own tone for expression." The quality of the voice should reveal an appreciation of what words mean, as they are uttered. And so with phrases, clauses, and sentences.

EXERCISES

In practicing the following examples, first create the general atmosphere by putting yourself in the proper mental attitude. If *intellectual,* imagine yourself explaining something. If *emotional, feel* the emotions. If *volitional,* seek to stir some one to action.

I. Read the following selections in all three different ways:

1. Whoever you are, be noble;
    Whatever you do, do well;
    Whenever you speak, speak kindly,—
    Give joy wherever you dwell.—RUSKIN.

2. Heaven is not reached by a single bound,
    But we mount the ladder by which we climb;
    From the lowly earth to the vaulted skies,
    And mount to its summit round by round.—HOLLAND.

II. Note how a preacher should vary the general atmosphere with the different purposes during the course of the morning services:

1. (Announcements.) Mrs. Blank will entertain the King's Daughters at her home Friday evening at 8 o'clock.
Mr. Blank will sing a solo at the evening services.

2. (Prayer.) The day returns and brings us the petty round of irritating concerns and duties. Help us to perform them with laughter and kind faces; help us to play the man; let cheerfulness abound with industry. Give us to go blithely on our business all this day; bring us to our resting beds weary and content and undishonored; and grant us in the end the gift of sleep.—ROBERT LOUIS STEVENSON.

3. (Part of sermon.) Remember, Christ will not reject thee; though thou mayest reject Him. There is the cup of mercy put to thy lip by the hand of Jesus. I know, if thou feelest the need, Satan may tempt thee not to drink, but he will not prevail; thou wilt put thy lip feebly and faintly, per-

haps, to it. But, oh, do but sip! and the first draught shall give thee bliss; and the deeper thou shalt drink the more heaven shalt thou know.—CHARLES SPURGEON.

III. Determine the atmosphere of the following, and express in appropriate tone-color. Name the emotions—if any—suggested.

1.
> He that loves a rosy cheek,
>> Or a coral lip admires,
> Or from star-like eyes doth seek
>> Fuel to maintain his fires;
> As old Time makes these decay,
> So his flames must waste away.

Disdain Returned.   THOMAS CAREW.

2.
> Tender-hearted stroke a nettle,
>> And it stings you for your pains;
> Grasp it like a man of mettle,
>> And it soft as silk remains.
> 'Tis the same with common natures;
>> Use 'em kindly, they rebel;
> But be rough as nutmeg-graters,
>> And the rogues obey you well.
>> —*Written on a Window in Scotland.*

3.
> And this man
> Is now become a god; and Cassius is
> A wretched creature, and must bend his body,
> If Cæsar carelessly but nod on him.
> He had a fever when he was in Spain,
> And, when the fit was on him, I did mark
> How he did shake: 'tis true, this god did shake:
> His coward lips did from their color fly;
> And that same eye, whose bend doth awe the world,
> Did lose its luster.

Julius Cæsar.   SHAKESPEARE.

4. If to do were as easy as to know what were good to do, chapels had been churches and poor men's cottages princes' palaces. It is a good divine that follows his own instructions: I can easier teach twenty what were good to be done, than to

be one of the twenty to follow my own teaching. The brain may devise laws for the blood, but a hot temper leaps o'er a cold decree.

Merchant of Venice. SHAKESPEARE.

5.   O wad some power the giftie gie us,
         To see oursel's as ithers see us!
         It wad frae monie a blunder free us,
             An' foolish notion.

To a Louse. BURNS.

6.   I have had playmates, I have had companions,
         In my days of childhood, in my joyful school days;
         All, all are gone,—the old familiar faces.

The Old Familiar Faces. CHARLES LAMB.

7.   Good name in man and woman, dear my lord,
         Is the immediate jewel of their souls:
         Who steals my purse, steals trash; 'tis something, noth-
             ing;
         'Twas mine, 'tis his, and has been slave to thousands;
         But he that filches from me my good name,
         Robs me of that which not enriches him,
         And makes me poor indeed.

Othello. SHAKESPEARE.

8. Few persons have sufficient wisdom to prefer censure, which is useful, to praise which deceives them.

—ROCHEFOUCAULD.

9.   I had a dream, which was not all a dream.
         The bright sun was extinguished, and the stars
         Did wander darkling in the eternal space,
         Rayless and pathless, and the icy earth
         Swung blind and blackening in the moonless air;
         Morn came, and went, and came, and brought no day.
         And men forgot their passions in the dread
         Of this their desolation; and all hearts
         Were chilled into a selfish prayer for light.

Darkness. LORD BYRON.

10.   *Portia* —A pound of that same merchant's flesh is
                 thine.
                 The court awards it and the law doth give it.
         Shylock—Most rightful judge.

Portia —And you must cut the flesh from off his
          breast;
        The law allows it and the court awards it.
  Shylock—Most learned judge! A sentence!
        Come, prepare!
Merchant of Venice.   SHAKESPEARE.

11. Tone-color is essential to the true expression of poetry.
Without this, it speaks to the *intellect only,* not to the *heart.*
If there is word-painting, express this by the tone, but do not
exaggerate. *Suggest* rather than imitate. Where elevation
of thought is required, let it be obtained by elevation of *feeling,*
giving tone-color not by loudness, swagger, or display of art.—
SELECTED.

12. Hark! I hear the bugles of the enemy! They are on
their march along the bank of the river. We must retreat
instantly, or be cut off from our boats. I see the head of
their column already rising over the height. Our only safety
is in the screen of this hedge. Keep close to it; be silent; and
stoop as you run. For the boats! Forward!—KLEISER.

13. "Jo, my poor fellow!"
"I hear you, sir, in the dark, but I'm a gropin'—a gropin';
let me catch hold of your hand."
"Jo, can you say what I say?"
"I'll say anything as you say, sir, for I know it's good."
"OUR FATHER."
"Our Father.—That's very good, sir."
"WHICH ART IN HEAVEN."
"Art in Heaven.—Is the light a comin', sir?"
"It is close at hand. HALLOWED BE THY NAME."
"Hallowed be—thy—name."
Death of Little Jo.   DICKENS.

14.   He that has light within his own clear breast,
        May sit in darkness and enjoy bright day;
        But he that hides a dark soul and foul thoughts,
        Benighted walks under the mid-day sun.
Comus.   JOHN MILTON.

15.   Let me go where'er I will
        I hear a sky-born music still;

It sounds from all things old,
It sounds from all things young,
From all that's fair, from all that's foul,
Peals out a cheerful song.

It is not only in the rose,
It is not only in the bird,
Not only where the rainbow glows,
Nor in the song of woman heard,
But in the darkest, meanest things
There always, always something sings.

The Poet. .   R. W. EMERSON.

16. Do unto another what you would he should do unto you;
and do not unto another what you would not like if done to
yourself. Thou needest only this law alone. It is the foundation and principle of all the rest.—CONFUCIUS.

17. There should be no selfish devotion to private interests.
We are born not for ourselves only, but for our kindred and
fatherland. We owe duties not only to those who have bene-
fited, but those who have wronged us. We should render to
all their due; and justice is due even to the lowest of mankind.
—CICERO.

18.   With klingle, klangle, klingle,
                 Way down the dusty dingle,
                 The cows are coming home;
              Now sweet and clear, and faint and low,
              The airy tinklings come and go,
                 Like chiming from some far-off tower,
                 Or pattering of an April shower
              That makes the daisies grow—
                    Ko-kling, ko-klang, koklinglelingle,
                    Way down the darkening dingle
                    The cows come slowly home.

When the Cows Come Home.   AGNES E. MITCHELL.

19.   You are the evening cloud floating in the sky of my
                 dreams.
         I paint you and fashion you ever with my love longings.
         You are my own, my own, Dweller in my endless
                 dreams.

With the shadow of my passion have I darkened your
      eyes,
    Haunter of the depth of my gaze!
I have caught you and wrapped you, my love, in the
      net of my music;
You are my own, my own, Dweller in my deathless
      dreams.

           —RABINDRANATH TAGORE.

X

VOCAL INTERPRETATION OF LITERATURE

Definition.—Literature in its broadest sense may be said to include all that is written or printed. But in its usual and more restricted meaning, it embodies only the genuine thought life and emotional life of the race. Mr. Arlo Bates says, "Literature is the adequate expression of genuine and typical emotion." It is one of the fine arts; and as such must express the ideal in mankind. To be the highest form of literature, it must be emotional, universal, genuine, sincere, and true to life. In reading literature, we live the life of the race. A selection is beautiful and enjoyed by us only when it expresses a phase of life comprehended within our experience. It must voice *our* thoughts, *our* emotions, *our* experience.

Vocal Interpretation.—To interpret the thoughts, emotions, and the action of others adequately, is impossible through silent reading. We may gather the thought life of the race in this way, but the emotional phase escapes us; and, as we have seen, this is the only expression of true literature. Hence poetry and the best of prose must be read aloud to be appreciated by ourselves, and it is the only way we may be able to interpret it to others.

Classification.—In the study of a selection with a view to its vocal interpretation, the classification on the basis of purpose suggested in the previous chapter, will be adequate for the present. A more detailed classification is presented in Part II, Chapter VI. Through the study of literature the student will have familiarized himself with many other classifications.

Thought Analysis.—The first step in the study of any selection is to understand it; the second step is to reproduce it.

No selection can be read or spoken properly until understood. To determine the author's thoughts is frequently no easy task, if not altogether an impossible one. To reproduce in our own emotional life what the author felt, is still more difficult. Nevertheless, the aim of the reader should ever be to appreceive the author's meaning and feeling and express the same to others to the best of his ability. He should not be content until he has exhausted all resources at his command.

Words on the printed page are meaningless and dumb until the reader conceives and voices the meaning. The reader is the author's interpreter. The first thing, then, is to interpret properly the author's meaning. While it is desirable to acquire facility in reading at first sight, the best interpretative reading, even of the most simple prose, requires close study in advance of oral expression. For a *student* of reading, at any rate, such preliminary study, with a view of comprehending and assimilating the thought and feeling of a selection, should always precede any attempt at the oral expression. This general suggestion is presented in detail in the following directions.

Let each pupil prepare a written report on his analysis of an assigned selection. Each report should be reviewed with its author, and sometimes with the entire class. Such reports should be continued until the class has a thorough grasp of the requirements of thought analysis. Such reports should be required at intervals throughout the year to guard against superficial study. Keep in mind that good reading requires close, accurate, vigorous thinking, and the lack of this care in reading, in turn, gives rise to most of the troubles that pupils have with other studies.

Written Work.—Just how much of the following outline should be required in written form will vary with each selection and with the progress of the class: this must be left to the discretion of a wise teacher. Usually, answers to Section IV and Nos. 5, 6, 7, and 8 of Section VI need not be written. Far better, however, to study only a few selections intensely than to skim over many.

QUESTIONS AND DIRECTIONS FOR A WRITTEN REPORT
PRELIMINARY TO ITS ORAL PRESENTATION

I. THE AUTHOR

1. Who was the author?
2. Tell *briefly* what you know of his life.
3. Name some of his best productions.
4. What was his temperament? Was he thoughtful, melancholy, pleasant, kind, sociable, sorrowful, cynical, optimistic, pessimistic?
5. What were the immediate circumstances in his life that led him to write the selection, or deliver the speech?

II. THE ATMOSPHERE, OR GENERAL SETTING

1. Where is the scene laid? When?
2. Local color,—surroundings, characters interested, etc.

3. When the selection was written or spoken, was the author in a happy mood, or was he sorrowful, penitent, angry, hopeful, or what emotion best describes his feelings?

4. Is the general purpose of the selection didactic, emotional, or volitional?

5. Of what incidents or emotions in your past life does this remind you?

III.   GENERAL ANALYSIS

1. Classify the selection. Is it a lyric poem, essay, oration, lecture, monologue, or what?

2. What is the *theme* of the selection? This frequently is not the subject.

3. What is the embodiment, if any? That is, what mechanism or means does the author use to convey this theme?

4. Do the paragraphs or stanzas mark the natural thought divisions?

5. Determine the central thought in each logical paragraph.

6. Name the rhythm. Is it appropriate? Why?

7. What *general* picture comes to your mind when you read this selection?

8. What scenes can you most vividly imagine? Are they visual, auditory, motor, or what?

IV.   DETAILED ANALYSIS

1. Determine the meaning of each word and phrase; explain all historical, geographical, and classical allusions.

2. Determine the meaning of each sentence. Paraphrase the more difficult sentences.

3. What word, phrase, or clause in each sentence expresses the principal idea?

4. What words or phrases lend themselves to word-coloring?

V.　MECHANICAL AIDS

1. Copy the entire selection, or such parts as may be deemed expedient.

2. What successive words should be grouped together? That is, where should the pauses come?

3. Indicate these pauses by vertical bars (|). This should include stops at the end of the sentence. Use one (|), two (||), or three (|||) bars to indicate the relative length of the pauses.

4. What word, words, phrase, or clause in each sentence conveys the principal idea?-the new idea? the compared or contrasted ideas? Underscore such words. Degrees of emphasis may be indicated by the number of lines used.

5. Recall the various rules for inflection and mark the inflected words appropriately.

6. How many climaxes are there? Are they all of the same degree? Indicate them with this sign: <

VI.　EXPRESSION

1. What is the normal key of this selection? (High, medium, or low.)

2. What general movement is appropriate? (Fast, medium, or slow.)

3. What degree of intensity should be used? of loudness? of volume? Why?

4. What general quality of voice is demanded? (Intellectual, spiritual, or vital.)

5. What changes of pitch are suggested in the various sentences?

6. Indicate changes of thought by changes in pitch, movement, volume, loudness, intensity, quality, etc.

7. Place yourself in the author's position. Use your imagination to place yourself there. Look at the selection from his point of view as much as you can.

8. Read or speak the selection as though you were in the author's place. But do not imitate him. Be yourself. Do not be satisfied with one reading, or with ten. *Master the selection. Reproduce it the best you can.*

A Specific Illustration

(A written report by a pupil)

CROSSING THE BAR

I. THE AUTHOR.

1 and 2. Alfred Tennyson was born at Somersby, England, in 1809; and died at Farringford, Isle of Wight, in 1892. He attended Oxford College, but did not seem to enjoy college life. He began writing poetry at a very early age, and a great future was predicted for him.

3. Some of his best known poems are: *Two Voices, Idylls of the King, The Princess, In Memoriam, Charge of the Light Brigade, Maud,* and *Enoch Arden.*

4. He was always very thoughtful and frequently very sad, though kind and loving. He was not very sociable and had few intimate friends. The people of England loved him as we love our poet, Longfellow.

At the death of Wordsworth (1850), he was made Poet Laureate of England.

5. Illness and old age.

II. THE ATMOSPHERE.

1 and 2. *Crossing the Bar* was written a few years before he died. One October morning in 1889, he drove to Aldsworth by the seaside. There he heard the "moaning of the bar," which was still in his mind when he returned to his home in Farringford. He was not very well and went to bed. His nurse was sitting by his bedside sharing to a degree the general anxiety about the patient when she suddenly said to him, "You have written a great many poems, sir, but I have never heard anybody say that there is a hymn among them all. I wish, sir, you would write a hymn while you are lying on your sick bed; it might help and comfort many a poor sufferer."

The next morning, when the nurse had taken her quiet place at the bedside, the poet handed her a scrap of paper, saying, "Here is the hymn you wished me to write." She took the paper from his hands with expressions of grateful thanks. It proved to be *Crossing the Bar*.

The entire poem had flashed on his mind in a moment. The hymn was sung at his funeral, and he requested that it be always placed at the end of all editions of his poems.

3. Tennyson had gained a great personal victory over doubt and throughout his life had always expressed a profound faith in the immortality of the soul; not a blind faith, but a personal assurance that left not the least doubt in his mind.

4. This hope he desired to impress on all those who were to pass through the "boundless deep" as he had. It is profoundly emotional.

5. I wonder if I am as trusting as Tennyson? I remember once when I was sick and thought I was going to die, etc.

III. GENERAL ANALYSIS.

1. The poem is a philosophical lyric.

2. The theme is Faith.

3. He compares his soul to a ship, which is about to sail into the Infinite Personality. Death is the *Bar;* the moaning is *Fear* and *Doubt;* the Pilot is that Divine and Unseen who is always guiding us.

4. No. All four stanzas may be considered as one paragraph.

5. When I die it will be with the calm assurance that I shall meet God face to face.

6. The meter is in the main iambic tetrameter. The occasional spondaic foot and the irregular number of feet to the verse, and now and then a catalectic verse may be suggestive of the sentiment expressed.

7 and 8. This selection does not lend itself to imagery as many do; but there comes to us a picture of a ship ready to sail, with the waves at rest, and no dashing of angry waves against the shore. Also that of a dying man. The noise of the waves is auditory. The other images are visual.

IV. DETAILED ANALYSIS.

1, 2 and 3. (Obviously a detailed statement is not necessary in this suggestive outline.)

4. Especially the following words and phrases should

be appropriately colored: *Clear call, moaning, moving seems asleep, too full, deep,* and *dark.*

V. MECHANICAL AIDS.

Sunset and evening star,
    And one clear call for me,||
And may there be no moaning of the bar,|
    When I put out to sea.|

But such a tide as moving seems asleep,|
    Too full for sound and foam,|
When that which drew from out the boundless deep|
    Turns again home.|||

Twilight and evening bell,|
    And after that the dark!||
And may there be no sadness of farewell,
    When I | embark;|

For tho' from out our bourne of time and place
    The flood may bear me far',|
I hope to see my Pilot face to face |
    When I || have crossed || the bar. |

VI. EXPRESSION.

1. Low key.
2. Slow movement; and with some passages, as "moving seems asleep," still slower.
3. Medium degree. There is no suggestion of any unusual excitement, agony, or suffering.
4. A spiritual, meditative quality, and with intense tone-coloring.
5. The first sentence has a medium pitch, followed with a long downward slide, including the next two lines. This selection demands a great variety of pitch and long inflectional slides. Appropriately express the triumphant tone in the last two lines.
6. Change of pitch can best be expressed vocally.

(Do not be satisfied with such a selection until it has been thoroughly memorized and read over many, many times in practice by each pupil.)

Some General Suggestions.—If there be adequate analysis of a selection for the thought, the reader should naturally convey the thought without undue effort, or straining for effect, or conscious attention to the mechanism of speech. We are speaking now, of course, of synthetic reading, and not of the preliminary or incidental training for skill and facility in technique. But however much, or little, practice in vocal technique one may have had, good reading, it will readily be granted by all, requires that the reader give us the *thought.* And whenever a pupil does not do that, the teacher must needs recall to his mind this primary requisite by such queries and suggestions as, "What is the thought here?" "You do not make us see this picture." "Explain this to me in your own words, without reference to the language the author uses." Thus must the pupil's attention be directed, again and again, to the fact that words in themselves are meaningless until he gets from them the author's thought, and that even then they are meaningless to a hearer until he (the reader) conveys the meaning.

What test shall be applied in determining if the reader "conveys the meaning"? We say that one should read "naturally." And what do we mean by that? Simply that a reader should use the same meaning of imparting and impressing thought that he uses in ordinary conversation. It should be his best conversation, to be sure, and even then one's "natural" method of talking can be vastly improved; but the point is this: in good reading there should be no noticeable departure from the animated directness, variety, and spontaneity of one's best method of talking. What proportion of our teachers of reading keep this fact in mind as a guiding principle? And is it true as is often asserted, that if a reader comprehends thoroughly the thought to be conveyed, he will read "naturally"? Listen to the college graduate read from a newspaper, or a college professor reading his lectures, or a preacher reading Scripture or a hymn, or an author, it may be, reading from his own works, and note the wide departure from clearness and discrimination, effectiveness and naturalness. And yet, in the cases cited, the readers know, we must assume, the thought they would convey. Mere mechanical reading must be avoided. The mechanics of oral expression must always be used as a means, not an end. Over-much talk about enunciation, inflection, emphasis, etc., is not advisable on general principles. Individual cases need specific remedies. "The trouble with most of our reading is that it dissociates itself entirely from any relation with conversation, whereas it is precisely the same spontaneous thinking that makes both intelligent," says Professor Clark in his treatise on *How to Teach Reading.*

The natural, or conversational method of reading is frequently impeded by the mechanical directions of the teacher. Proper position, however, must not be entirely neglected. The pupil should always face the class. If this practice were begun in the first grades and continued through the high school, stage fright would be a thing of the past. The book should be held easily in the left hand, and held high enough that the head may be held erect. The throat muscles must never be restricted by bending the head over the book. The student should read to the audience and not to himself. His eyes should play back and forth from the page to the audience, not just glance up occasionally, as if to make sure that the audience had not all slipped from the room. The head should be held erect so that in looking straight at the audience, all that is necessary is to move the eye and not the head. This practice will be a great help in carrying out the basic principle that the most effective reading is simply heightened conversation.

The following quotation from Professor Corson from his book entitled, *The Voice and Spiritual Education,* seems very pertinent: "What chiefly affects a cultivated hearer, in 'elocution' is the conspicuous absence of spiritual assimilation on the part of the reader. At best, he voices only what the eye of an ordinary reader should take in, and leaves the all-important part to the face, arms, legs, and various attitudes of the body. But the spiritual in literature must be addressed to the ear. . . . Reading is not acting. It is the acting which usually accompanies the reading or recitation of the professional elocutionist which cultivated people especially dislike. When they wish to see acting, they prefer going to the theater. When they listen to reading, they want serious interpretative vocalization; only that and nothing more is necessary, unless it be a spontaneous and graceful movement of the hands, occasionally, as one makes in animated conversation."

PART TWO

PUBLIC SPEAKING

I

GENERAL OBSERVATIONS

Introduction.—Dr. Charles W. Eliot, President Emeritus of Harvard University, in a recent address said: "The primary characteristic of an educated man is his ability to speak and to write his own language effectively. Never in the history of the country has there been a time when oral address has had so much use and influence as it has to-day."

Two little children if reared alone in a forest would invent some means of communication. Their language, like the language of the savage, would be, for the most part, by means of vocal inflections and gestures; since these have always expressed sensations and emotions. Ideas are expressed by articulate words, and the savage does not have many ideas. We should master at least one language. Some men can write and speak sixty and even seventy languages; but, it is very doubtful if you have ever heard the names of these men. It is far more important that you learn to master *one* language so that you can write and speak it with clearness, force and elegance.

Definition.—Public Speaking differs from Oral

Reading in that the language of the speaker is his own.
The arrangement of the thought expressed is also left to
the speaker.

The first essential is that the speaker acquire and maintain the right notion about speaking—the right mental
attitude toward the message and his audience. Remember that speaking is simply talking to an assembly of individuals. It is presumed that you have something to say
to such an assembly. You must know clearly and understand thoroughly what you have to say and then you
must convey your own thoughts and emotions to the
minds of your hearers. In other words, the same principle that was laid down for reading applies to speaking:
Get the thought, give the thought.

General Preparation. — The ability to get the
thought and to give the thought most effectively does not
come by a wish or the sway of a fairy's wand. It comes
through "inspiration, respiration, and perspiration."
Who has not listened to some eloquent speaker who mastered his audience, held them spellbound by his knowledge and power, and has not said, "Oh, I would give
almost anything if I could only speak like that!" But do
not think for a moment that that man has not passed
through years of preparation. Beecher, when once asked
how long it took him to prepare a certain sermon, replied,
"Twenty years."

Knowledge.—First of all have something to say. Who
cares to listen to a man who does not know what he is
talking about? Socrates struck a fundamental key-note
in delivery when he said, "all men are sufficiently eloquent in that which they *understand.*" Men everywhere
listened to Christ. Wherever he went a multitude followed him, "for he spake as one having authority." The

man who is the greatest bore in modern society is the walking phonograph. All that is necessary to start him going is to touch a spring, and lo, like Tennyson's brook—

> Men may come and men may go,
> But I go on forever.

When he has once said all he knows, he starts all over again. Lowell suggested this addition to the Beatitudes, "Blessed is he who hath nothing to say—*and cannot be persuaded to say it.*"

Vocabulary.—Secondly, an adequate vocabulary is absolutely essential so that this knowledge can be expressed clearly and adequately. Every workman must have good serviceable tools; every orator must, likewise, have his tools—good serviceable words. A large vocabulary is needed to enable the speaker to express shades of meaning and to insure variety and force in expression. Says Professor Palmer in his *Self-Cultivation in English:*

Why, then, do we hesitate to swell our words to meet our needs? It is a nonsense question. There is no reason. We are simply lazy; too lazy to make ourselves comfortable. We let our vocabularies be limited, and get along rawly without the refinements of human intercourse, without refinements in our own thoughts; for thoughts are almost as dependent on words as words on thoughts. For example, all exasperation we lump together as "aggravating," not considering whether they may not rather be displeasing, annoying, offensive, disgusting, irritating, or even maddening; and without observing, too, that in our reckless usage we have burned up a word which might be convenient when we should need to mark some shading of the word "increase." Like the bad cook, we seize the frying pan whenever we need to fry, broil, roast, or stew, and then we wonder why all our dishes taste alike while in the next house the food is appetizing. It is all unnecessary. Enlarge the vocabulary. Let any one who wants to see himself grow, resolve to adopt two new words each week. It will not be long before the endless and enchanting variety of the world will begin to reflect itself in his speech, and in his mind as well. I know that when we use a word for the first time we are startled, as if a firecracker went off in our neighborhood. We look about hastily, to see if any one has noticed. But finding that no one has, we may be emboldened. A word used three times slips off the tongue with entire naturalness. Then it is ours forever, and with it some phase of life which had been lacking hitherto.

Diction.—The workman must have tools, but without a knowledge of the use of these tools he might do more harm than good. Many a man has wounded his friend by speaking a word which he did not know how to use properly; and many a political speaker has harmed his cause more than he helped it, by an improper use of words and combinations of words which were not understood as he intended.

Read the best books and magazines; listen to good speeches; get the dictionary habit; study synonyms; write out *carefully* whatever you put on paper. Accuracy of expression comes only through careful, persistent practice. This is Benjamin Franklin's testimony:

About this time I met with an odd volume of the *Spectator*. It was the third. I had never before seen any of them. I bought it, read it over and over, and was much delighted with it. I thought the writing excellent, and wished, if possible, to imitate it. With this view I took some of the papers, and, making short hints of the sentiment in each sentence, laid them by a few days, and then, without looking at the book, tried to complete the papers again, by expressing each hinted sentiment at length, and as fully as it had been expressed before, in any suitable words that should come to hand.

Then I compared my *Spectator* with the original, discovered some of my faults, and corrected them. But I found I wanted a stock of words, or a readiness in recollecting and using them, which I thought I should have acquired before that time if I had gone on making verses; since the continual occasion for words of the same import, but of different length, to suit the measure, or of different sound for the rhyme, would have laid me under a constant necessity of searching for variety, and also have tendered to fix that variety in my mind, and make me master of it. Therefore I took some of the tales and turned them into verse, and, after a time, when I had pretty well forgotten the prose, turned them back again.

Practice.—Lose no opportunity to speak. Ease, accuracy, force are the result of practice. Whenever called upon, speak. But be sure you are well prepared and stop as soon as you are no longer interesting. Join some literary society and never neglect to carry out your part of the program. Let it be known in your school and community that you are a man that can be depended upon to carry out his share of the program and you will soon have many opportunities to speak.

It was a cardinal principle with Fox that to reach and maintain perfection it was necessary to speak constantly; and referring to this he said, "During five whole sessions I spoke every night but one, and I regret that I did not speak that night too!"

Henry Clay, handicapped in his youth by an imperfect education, attributed his success in life to the habit of daily reading and speaking the contents of some historical or scientific book. "It is to this early practice of the art of all arts," he used to say, "that I am indebted for the primary and leading impulses that stimulated my progress and have shaped and molded my entire destiny."

Sargent S. Prentiss testifies that he owed more to early practice in a debating society than to any other form of discipline. In a letter to his brother he wrote: "Let me particularly recommend you to cultivate the faculty of expressing your own ideas in the best and most effective manner. . . . There are hundreds and perhaps thousands of men in the United States who exceed Henry Clay in information on all subjects; but his superiority consists in the power and adroitness with which he brings his information to bear. I would again praise before any other acquisition that of expressing forcibly and with ease any idea which the mind may contain. This faculty is attained with difficulty in after-life, but with ease at college, and nowhere so well as in the debating societies of such institutions."

Special Preparation.—Never rely wholly on your general preparation. Always make the best special preparation your time and skill will permit. Demosthenes spent so many weeks and even months over his speeches that his enemies said they smelt of the lamp. It was Lincoln who said, "I always assume that my audiences are in many things wiser than I am, and I say the most sensible thing I can to them."

Subject.—When you are given a choice of subject, be careful to select one suited to the occasion, and one you can present creditably to your audience. It should not be too general as, Democracy, Nature, Education, Freedom, etc. It must be within your own experience and the comprehension of the audience. Select a topic of which you already know something; some topic in which you are deeply interested; some topic upon which you can tell something that is new or at least has not been rehashed a hundred times to the same audience. As one social worker advised a young minister when he invited him to address the inmates of a local prison, "Please don't preach on the prodigal son; that is all they have heard for the last six months." If possible, speak on one small phase of a general subject.

Analyze Your Subject.—After having decided on the subject take a mental inventory of what you know about it—*think* it through. Read your own mind before you read what others have said. If you do not you will become a mere parrot. Think out the main divisions of your speech and the subdivisions. *Write them down.* Attempt a logical arrangement when this tentative outline and mental analysis is completed.

Gather Definite Material.—Consult such books and magazines as bear directly on the subject. A modern, standard encyclopedia will be helpful in gaining a general view of many biographical, political, historical, and scientific subjects, but ordinarily an encyclopedia treats a subject only in its broad outlines. The World and Tribune almanacs, issued annually, contain many detailed facts relating to national and state governments, to general, commercial, industrial, and political statistics, and to abstracts of current events and legislation. The *Congressional Record* gives the proceedings of Congress, and Jones's *Finding List* shows where, in the various government publications, different subjects are discussed. On questions of the day, Poole's *Index to Periodical Literature* should be consulted for references to magazine articles, etc.; the *Cumulative Index to Periodical Literature* contains titles of leading review and magazine articles for the previous month; and Jones's *Index to Legal Periodical Literature* contains titles on legal, political, and constitutional subjects.

In the field of history Larned's *History for Ready Reference and Topical Reading* is a very useful compilation of historical and biographical topics; and Channing and Hart's *Guide to the Study of American History* contains a complete bibliography of United States history, together with suggestions to aid the investigator in his search for books pertaining to his subject.

References in the fields of politics, economics, and sociology are Bowker and Iles's *Readers' Guide in Economic, Social, and Political Science,* a classified bibliography of American, English, French, and German works, with descriptive notes; *The Annual Register,* a review of public events at home and abroad, containing summaries of foreign politics; *The Statesman's Year-Book,* a statistical and historical annal of the states of the world; McPherson's *Handbook of Politics,* a record, issued biennially, of important political action, legislative and executive, national and state; and Bliss's *Encyclopedia of Social Reforms,* an exposition of the leading social questions of the day.

In addition to the foregoing, desired statistics on commerce, banks, debts, shipping, taxes, etc., may be found in the *Statistical Abstract of the United States,* issued annually by the Bureau of Statistics, Washington; Poor's *Manual of Railroads* gives statistics of steam and electric railways and railway corporations in the United States and Canada; and Mulhall's *Dictionary of Statistics* is a standard compilation of statistics for the world.

In going through a mass of material the student must learn to discriminate quickly as to what should be read and what should be passed over—to note at a glance what he wants and what he does not want. Some method in note taking should be followed. An excellent plan is to take the notes on one side of uniform slips of paper. These can be arranged later in a logical order. Always put down the page and volume of the magazine or book. You are sure to want to refer to it again.

Final Outline.—After spending all the time you can

afford gathering material, make a complete outline. This outline will vary with the nature of your subject, the kind of public address, the purpose of your speech, the manner of delivering it, etc. Usually you will have an Introduction, a Body, and a Conclusion. If the speech is very brief—a few minutes—and if others have spoken on the same general topic, omit the introduction and conclusion.

Final Preparation.—Next write your speech following closely your outline, or if it is to be extemporaneous, think it through carefully several times, commit to memory the outline, and if you are adequately prepared, dive in; you never learn to swim by walking along the bank.

Writing Your Speech.—Formal addresses should be written and memorized carefully. They are usually very brief. Everybody knows that there are times when one can write better than at other times. You must get into a good mood. The best way is to read some good author whose style you like, just before you start writing your speech. Get up early some morning and write. Follow your prepared outline carefully. Before you get through you will find yourself getting tired and your inspiration leaving you. Stop. Wait a day if you have time, and after hurriedly reading what you have written, complete it. Lay this aside for a few days. Much that you have written will appear trivial to you—leave this out. You may want to take out about one-half. Work it over and over. A winning contest oration should be gone over at least twenty times. When you get through revising, it will not look very much like the first draft. Do not think that "first impressions are best" when you write speeches.

Read it aloud. Note how it *sounds*. You will find that you are violating the principle of euphony in many places; pick out the offending words and by consulting a book of synonyms you will be able to substitute better ones. Read it to a friend. He may be able to see defects that escaped your notice.

After it is as perfect as you can make it, memorize it.

Start Early.—This advice may appear unnecessary; but the fact remains that more poor speeches are delivered and more contests lost because the speaker did not begin in time, than because of lack of ability. Begin as early as you can. Some college students have been known to have begun their orations two years before they expected to enter the contest. Again, some students begin memorizing their speeches three days before the contest and they wonder why they failed! Experience has proved that the man who gets an early start is the man who is most likely to win.

Practical Suggestions.—Some pupils have too formal an idea of public speaking. They imagine that nothing short of a crowded auditorium would do for an audience upon which to practice. But they began extempore, and even the more or less formal ways of delivering a speech, in the kindergarten. When they answered the teacher's questions, they were using the extempore or memoriter method.

Then let it be suggested first of all that the earlier you begin this work the better. Your classmates will make a very good audience. Pupils in reading in the grades should be taught to face the class. If this method were pursued throughout the grades and the high school, boys and girls would not feel embarrassed when they are obliged to appear before a class of students in college. In answering questions in the class, observe all the suggestions in this book—use a clear voice, speak so that you can be heard, speak to the point, use the best style of language you can, and the many other qualities necessary for a good speech.

The teacher will request in connection with your daily recitations in English literature, history, chemistry, etc., that you make reports upon certain specific topics. Make it a point to use this as an opportunity for practice, for effectiveness. Strive to hold the attention of every boy and girl. Make that report as interesting and instructive as you can. In giving these reports always face the class and speak without notes. It is presumed, however, that those who read this book will have a special class in Reading or Speaking. In that event, the exercises following each chapter will be helpful.

Organize and take an active interest in some debating society, or public speaking club. A history club is an excellent thing for high school boys and girls. This will give you an excellent opportunity to prepare and deliver a more elaborate address and to an appreciative audience. Enter all contests in public speaking to which you are eligible. Suppose you do lose out. Try again next time and make better preparation; and if you do the chances will be that you will win. If you win, do not rest on your oars; there are new, greater, and more difficult victories ahead of you; make ready for them. If you lose, whatever else you do, do not become discouraged.

The Length of a Speech.—You may be able to judge accurately the passing of time when some one else is speaking; but you are inclined to forget all about time when you, yourself, are on the floor. Usually, yes, nine times out of ten, the speaker talks too long—he overruns the time set by the program. Make up your mind that you will be the one of the ten who never will.

When you are asked to speak ten minutes, speak ten

minutes; if five minutes, speak five minutes. Go over your speech enough times so that you know precisely what you can say and what you must omit. Again, if you are expected to speak ten minutes, do not say almost anything just to fill out the time. Your aim should be: How much can I crowd into my ten-minute limit? If you desire to be a popular speaker, there are two things you must never lose sight of: (1) observe strictly the time limit; (2) be dependable. If you are scheduled to appear upon a certain program, *be there*. Here are a few commandments for the public speaker:

"Stand up, so you can be seen; speak up, so you can be heard; shut up, so you will be liked."

The second is like unto the first:

"Say it in as few words as you can; when you have said it, hold your tongue."

Stage-fright.—It is quite impossible to diagnose that common malady known as stage-fright. Usually it afflicts the speaker during the first few seconds, or first few minutes, of his speech. Most speakers have it, in varying degrees. Preachers tell us, for example, that even after long experience, they never begin their weekly sermons without the most intense nervousness. True, experiences vary. Gladstone, when asked if he never became nervous before speaking, said that he often did in opening a debate, but never in replying. Says Sir John Byers in *The British Medical Journal* of recent date:

No great orator has ever lived who did not feel very nervous before rising to his feet. I have often seen the legs of one of the most effective and heart-stirring speakers in the House of Lords, to whom that assembly never failed to listen, shake like an aspen leaf during the delivery of the first few sentences of his speech; and should the young speaker feel his tongue grow twice too big for his mouth, and curl itself inextricably round one of his canine teeth, he may console himself with the conviction that he possesses one at least of the characteristic qualities of a great speaker.

An amusing feature of this matter is, that young speakers are apt to think that they are the only ones that become seriously embarrassed. And right here is the lesson: trained speakers learn to control their embarrassment. It should be remembered that a nervous tension, if brought under control, may prove a help rather than a hindrance to the speaker, for it puts a nerve-force into his delivery that might otherwise be wanting. How attain that control? There is no way but through practice in speaking to audiences. Continued practice, if it does not eliminate all embarrassment, gradually does reduce the earlier terrors. The practice should, of course, be directed along right lines. Nervousness may be aided much by a feeling of mental and physical preparedness. Have the speech thoroughly in hand long enough beforehand to give both mind and body a rest. Students often make the mistake of worrying over a speech up to the very moment of its delivery. This method is suicidal. Even speakers of experience sometimes fail to realize how much the success or failure of a speech depends upon physical conditions. To undergo the severe nervous strain of public speaking, mind and body should be fresh. The day preceding an athletic event the trained contestant either rests or exercises very moderately. So, if a speech is to be given at night, say, the speaker should wholly lay it aside during the afternoon and go for a walk or go to sleep—do anything but exhaust faculties that will be needed in the evening.

Control is also effected through the communicative, conversational attitude, as one rises to speak, and by an exercise of the will. A good plan is to take a few deep breaths. Give your nerves plenty of oxygen and you will not feel so shaky. Certain drugs are sometimes prescribed by physicians to steady the nerves by equalizing the circulation, but these should be avoided. Rather cultivate self-confidence.

Ninety per cent of stage-fright is *fear of failure*. Know just what you want to say, and know that you know it. *Thorough preparation* is the best amulet for stage fright. Have confidence in yourself. You are more afraid of yourself than you are of your audience. Encourage a feeling that you and your audience are getting on well together.

Many nervous speakers have found immense relief in a sort of "post self-hypnotic suggestion." As you lie in bed the night before the day you are to speak, and just before going to sleep, repeat over and over to yourself, out loud, "Tomorrow when I make my speech I will not be nervous, I will not be afraid, I know my speech, I will not forget, I will be a success," or a similar litany. This places a thought deep down into your sub-consciousness, and it will have results. The oftener you try this the greater the success. It works through the same laws as suggesting to yourself, just as you go to sleep, that you will wake up at a certain hour in the morning. Stage-fright can be warded off with equal success.

Study and Practice.—Like every other art, public speaking demands long-continued study and practice. The most proficient always feel there is room for improvement; and like other things in life, if one is earnestly striving to reach an ideal, there is hope for him; if he thinks he has reached it, he is lost. The complex art of public address cannot be learned quickly, and should never be taken up as a plaything. If you expect to be a speaker, make a business of the study, as you would of anything else worth learning. Do not dabble in it. A little dabbling with the technique given in this book is useless. It is because we have so many dabblers that we have so many bunglers. And by way of repetition—do not expect to correct in a month a fault that is the habit of years. Certain incurable defects may be fatal, certain natural qualities are desirable, though not indispensable; the rest is work—thorough preparation and continual practice.

The drill on technique and the daily practice on some speech may be irksome, but the student should undertake it as he does any other task—do it and make it count for something. If you have a declamation, an oration, or an argument to deliver, drill on the oral presentation. Speak to an imaginary audience. Invite your friends in and compel them to listen. Do not be afraid of drilling too much. Students often talk about getting "stale" who do not even enunciate clearly. An expert in technique to criticize and suggest is desirable, but not indispensable. Sometimes a friend who is not over-fastidious, has no dogmatic standards, and can judge of general effectiveness, is the most valuable sort of critic. Take all the advice offered and—do not always act on it. A little experience will enable you to judge of its value; you will soon learn to know your leading faults yourself; and unless you are to surrender your individuality, you must be the final judge. And then, when the occasion arrives, put your technique in the background; let mental and moral earnestness be the predominant processes; and let the practice in technique unconsciously repeat itself in the final effort. Do not fail to make conscientious and thorough preparation for all those occasions, so frequent under the conditions of American life and government. when you will be called upon to speak: and thereby make general preparation for those times, unforeseen yet also frequent—those social or political crises in the affairs of a community, a State, or a Nation—when the public speaker must create, mold, and direct public opinion that conduces to right thinking and right acting.

EXERCISES

I. Select five subjects appropriate for addresses to a group of high school boys urging them to attend college.

II. Select five subjects appropriate for addresses to a group of high school girls urging them to attend college.

III. Suppose you were invited to address the Business Men's Club of your city; select five appropriate topics.

IV. Select five subjects for each of the following occasions:

1. A group of high school boys urging them to attend: (*a*) a business school; (*b*) an agricultural college.
2. A group of high school girls urging them to attend: (*a*) a business school; (*b*) a school of household science.
3. The young people's society in your church.
4. The Mothers' Club in your city.
5. The Local Grange.
6. High School Commencement.
7. Soldiers' Reunion.
8. Alumni Association.
9. The County Medical Association.
10. The County Bar Association.
11. The Local Labor Union.
12. The State Bankers' Association.

V. Get twenty references on one of the above subjects from various periodicals and other sources mentioned in the text.

VI. Determine your reading, writing, and speaking vocabulary.

Take a dictionary and count the words on every fiftieth page, 1, those you understand; 2, those you could use in writing; 3, those with which you are very familiar—your speaking vocabulary.

Then multiply each of these by fifty and you will approximate the number of words in your various vocabularies.

VII. Study synonyms. Memorize five synonyms for each of the following words: Answer, apart, ascend, awful, beauty, better, cheer, clear, compel, delight, direct, emerge, hope, infer, inspect, mean, plain, respect, stingy, strong, true, use, vague, wise, wish.

VIII. Memorize five antonyms to each of the words listed in No. VII.

IX. Make another list of twenty-five words and give five synonyms and five antonyms to each of these.

X. Use the following words correctly in sentences:

Anger, fury, indignation; ask, inquire, interrogate; bait, allurement, temptation; begin, commence, initiate; bewail, lament, deplore; bewitch, enchant, fascinate; bid, offer, propose; birth, nobility, aristocracy; blessing, benison, benediction; bloody, murderous, sanguinary; blue, azure, cerulean; body, company, corporation; bold, brave, resolute; boldness, courage, fortitude; boldness, impudence, audacity; bough, branch, ramification; bow, obeisance, salutation; breed, engender, propagate; bright, luminous, incandescent; bright, brilliant, effulgent; bright, cheerful, animated; brink, verge, margin; bulk, size, magnitude; burdensome, oppressive, onerous; busy, engaged, occupied; care, anxiety, solicitude; choice, preference, predilection; cold, indifferent, apathetic; craft, subtlety, artifice; dear, precious, valuable; deem, surmise, apprehend; downfall, destruction, demolition; draw, allure, attract; dread, dismay, consternation; dull, stupid, obtuse.

XI. The first words of the following series are domesticated old words of Romanesque origin, and the last words are Latin and Greek derivatives of recent and scholastic introduction. Let each student be assigned a part or all of this list and (1) state the distinction, if any, in the meaning of each duplicate; (2) decide which word is preferable; and (3) bring in sentences either choosing between the two words or using both in the same sentence.

Adroitness, dexterity; agreed, unanimous; aim, scope; assail, impugn; banishment, exile; box, chest; calm, quiet; calumny, defamation; chain, concatenation; change, alteration; comfort, console; company, society; copy, transcribe; decay, decadence; discern, discriminate; discovery, detection; dissemble, dissimulation; envious, invidious; exact, extort; exact, precise; feign, simulate; guerdon, remuneration; haughty, supercilious; inquest, inquisition; invective, diatribe; leisure, vacation; mean, pusillanimous; number, enumerate; plot, conspiracy; poison, venom; porch, vestibule; praise, eulogy (or panegyric); pray, supplicate; reproach, opprobrium; restrain, inhibit; revere, venerate; revolt, rebellion; sample, example; sense, consciousness; silent, reticent (or taciturn); slander, defamation; training, discipline; try, attempt; unavoidable, inevitable; valid, conclusive; vanishing, evanescent; variety, diversification; venal, mercenary; vex, irritate; vie, emulate; voluble, fluent; wait, attend.

ESSENTIAL ELEMENTS—THE AUDIENCE

There are three distinct factors involved in Public Speaking: (1) The Audience, (2) The Speech, and (3) The Speaker. In other words, The Occasion, The Oration, and The Orator; or to whom you speak, what, and how.

General Characteristics.—The orator prepares and delivers his speech for the sole purpose of influencing a body of men and women. It is, therefore, essential that he have some knowledge of the crowd he expects to influence. The greater the knowledge of the audience, the greater his chances for success. Upon the audience depend both the orator and the oration. The audience is the objective point; it is the determining and guiding influence.

The speaker must know not only human nature in the individual, but human nature in the aggregate. The collective mind has certain attributes which differ from the individual mind. A man in the crowd thinks and acts differently from the man alone. Arguments which might convince a man in the street might be wholly ineffectual when presented from a platform to a large crowd. Men in a crowd think in terms of the race. Like a chemical, the compound is different from the separate elements composing it. Strange as it may appear at first thought, even men and women are not

influenced in the same manner. Women are the con-
servators of the race more than are the men. Each
woman is the embodiment of the specific characteristics
attributed to the crowd. The individual woman is much
more like a crowd all by herself than the individual man.
A man by himself must be convinced, you must reason
with him, and the more intellectual he is the more de-
pendence must be placed on arguments to cause him to
act. Women are by nature more emotional than men,
and when alone can be persuaded to act by arousing the
emotions rather than by appealing to reason. From this
it must be concluded that *whatever would persuade the
individual woman would persuade the crowd.* And it is
generally admitted that this is not an easy task.

A few of the more specific attributes of the ordinary
audience of interest to the orator are:

I. *Conservatism.*—The attitude of the audience
toward a speaker is like that of a man from Missouri—
he needs to be shown. It demands that the speaker
establish his contention. It reserves the right to remain
neutral until convinced and persuaded to think and act
otherwise. From fundamental and basic principles the
crowd is not easily moved, but it can be moved easily
along these lines. Hence the speaker should always
appeal to such basic traditional sentiments as home, love,
life, revenge, the flag, etc. The crowd far more than
the individual is influenced by the unconscious substra-
tum formed by heredity. The crowd delights to hark
back through the ages, and answer the "call of the wild."
The crowd is always a generation or two behind the
reformer.

II. *Irresponsibility.*—The crowd mind does not feel
any individual responsibility. Selfism disappears. **It**

seems to feel that whatever it does will be justified by the community, by society; for the entire community appears to be a common participant.

III. *Suggestibility.*—The audience is usually in a receptive mood and shows a readiness to entertain suggestions from a leader—the orator. What one does, all are likely to participate in. The crowd is as easily led to do heroic deeds as cowardly ones. This mobility is manifest only in transient matters. On hereditary and racial matters it is conservative. The crowd mind, in many respects, resembles a person hypnotized. Suggestion, if properly made, is equivalent to action, especially if made by the operator—the orator; except in matters of traditional and vital importance to the race.

IV. *Intelligence.*—The audience is never so intelligent as the average members composing it. It possesses rather those attributes which might be called the highest common factor of the attributes of the individual members. The crowd reasons very little. The orator must ever remember that the audience never thinks more than is necessary.

V. *Imagination.*—What the crowd lacks in reasoning is supplied by a vivid imagination. Childlike, it reasons little, but revels in the concrete image; it delights in pictures—word pictures. It demands simplicity. Imagery is the key word which unlocks the crowd mind. The tremendous success of the moving picture shows attests this fact. Hence the value of figures of speech in an oration. All things seem possible to the crowd; to a vivid imagination there is no such word as failure. Impossibility is not in the vocabulary of the crowd.

VI. *Exaggeration.*—Because of this power of imagination, the crowd always exaggerates, personifies. It

deifies a hero. It demands virtues in its characters on
the stage that the individual does not demand on the
street. The speaker must satisfy this characteristic of
the crowd by expressing himself with no uncertain emphasis. Actors always "make up" so that under the
glare of the electric lights their faces will appear natural.
So the speaker never hesitates to exaggerate a fact from
the platform. He must paint a crime or a sin in the
most Stygian colors so that it will appear natural to the
audience. This exaggeration from the platform is not
compromising with the truth; of if the plain matter of
fact truth be told from the platform, it will not be truthful when interpreted by the audience—for the crowd
will always underestimate, will always discount what it
hears. The orator should not hesitate to paint evil as
black as possible, nor virtue as white.

VII. *Impatience.*—Childlike, a crowd must do something. It is restless. It demands action, and it desires
an expression of this attribute in the speaker. The
orator must not stop to rest; he must keep his audience
busy. Attention cannot be long sustained on one point.
Variety, therefore, must be the watchword of the
speaker.

VIII. *Leadership.*—The crowd desires to be led, and
cringes at the feet of the dictator. It respects the
strength of a master. The type of the hero dear to the
crowd will always bear the stamp of a Cæsar. This call
for leadership must be supplied by the orator. And the
crowd stands ready to honor the man who will assume
this position. But remember, no weakling need apply.
The speaker must, therefore, prove worthy of this leadership; he must prove himself master; the crowd will
tolerate no other. How may a man qualify for this

position? Follow in the footprints of those who have gone before.

A few of the most prominent characteristics of the crowd have been suggested. Now let us see how this knowledge may be utilized.

When a group of people assemble, they are all individual units. Each is busy with his own thoughts. The speaker must follow a simple pedagogical principle of the class recitation—*make all think of the same thing at the same time*. The speaker must *unify* the ideas of those gathered together. Until this is done, this group of people cannot, strictly speaking, be called a "crowd." This constitutes the first step of the orator.

A number of different methods, or devices, are used to accomplish this. One is to have everybody sit close together. Each person must become aware of the bodily presence of his fellows. If one person must touch another, so much the better. This bodily contact, this subconscious awareness of the presence of other individuals, causes the individual to forget self, and to be absorbed with the common thought of the crowd. The best speaker in the world cannot make much of an impression on an audience composed of a dozen individuals scattered over a room that would hold a thousand.

A second method often used is to have them all join in doing something in concert. Singing a song, reading in concert, is a very common device found in our churches, and always insisted upon by "revivalists." The ritualism used in some of our churches follows this plan.

A third method of creating a "crowd" spirit is to get all the audience to cheer during the first part of the performance. This justifies some speakers in their invariable habit of telling a humorous story, or making some remark "to bring the house down," at the beginning of their speech.

A fourth method is to present to the audience some idea that will strike a "sympathetic cord" and thus create a common feeling; something that will impress all the individuals in the same way. Such ideas and feelings are aroused by using appropriately such words as: Liberty, Democracy, Honest toil, Christ, Washington, etc. To refer to the glories of our republic, the chivalry of the South, the beauty of the ladies present, the grandeur of our great state, will always bring a cheer or some expression of approval from the audience.

By various methods a general audience is molded into a crowd by *unifying* them—having them think of the same thing and do the same thing at the same time.

We cannot enter into a discussion of the psychology of action, except to state that when the mind is in possession of a *single idea* it will act. When two or more ideas are struggling at the same time for supremacy in the mind, there is a confusion and the will refuses to act. Indecision is the result of conflicting images. But if there is only one dominating idea, one that overshadows all others, and thereby practically excludes all others, the result is action. One idea and only one should be the watchword of the speaker.

The man who is hypnotized will usually do what the operator suggests because he has no other thoughts except that one. We often hear people say, "I did so and so because I did not stop to think." The deed was done because there was only one dominant idea and emotion as the result of a single impression. If time for reflection had been taken, the confusion of ideas would doubtless have prevented the act.

The orator must take the crowd, which, like a child, revels in images, draw a picture so lucid and realistic, so clear and natural, that the audience sees but one side of the question at issue. This is frequently accomplished by presenting ideas of home, love, revenge, happiness, virtue, etc. The crowd will always respond to strong emotional impulses such as fear, pride, sorrow, etc. Remember a crowd should be *loved* into doing what the speaker desires. A second thing that the speaker must never forget is that the speaker himself must see the pictures he paints and feel the emotions he expresses.

Kinds.—Besides observing the attributes of the crowd, the orator must consider carefully the various kinds of audiences.

I. *Purpose.*—Crowds assemble for certain definite purposes: (1) to be entertained, (2) to be informed, (3) to be persuaded. Though one purpose predominates, all may be present. In any event, the purpose in assembling must be respected by the speaker.

II. *Quality.*—The speaker must also bear in mind the quality of his audience, such as nationality, occupation, social status, religion, mentality, etc. The message, language, delivery, will vary with each group. Power of adaptation spells success.

III. *Size.*—You cannot speak to a few in the same manner as you can to a thousand. The style of delivery, volume, action—must be appropriate to the number addressed. Preachers often speak to a congregation of fifty in a small church with the same volume as though they were addressing five thousand in the open air.

That may account for the fact that some preachers have only an audience of fifty. Again, some speak to only a handful on Sunday because their voices carry only to about that many.

IV. *Location.*—Gauge your voice by the size and shape of the room and its general acoustic properties. It requires less effort to be understood in the Christian Science Temple in Boston, seating over 5000 people, than in many town halls seating fifty. The building having the best acoustic properties should have the following proportional dimensions: three times the length equaling four times the width equaling six times the height; that is the length, width, and height should be in the ratio of 4:3:2. The interior should be plain.

EXERCISES

I. Study a church audience and report to the class. What ideas moved the audience? What did you remember of the sermon?

II. Study a street crowd. Note all the general characteristics. Report to the class.

III. Why is not the group of boys and girls who gather in a room before school begins a "crowd"?

IV. While waiting for the play to begin, clap your hands. How many followed your suggestion?

V. Why is it difficult to speak when some persons in the audience whisper?

VI. Which is better for the success of a church service, a room that is very warm or one that is very cold?

VII. Why do many political speakers take off their coats when they speak?

VIII. Have you ever heard a speaker use slang? What was the immediate effect on the audience?

IX. Why does an audience always cheer when the speaker says, "There are no better people to be found on the face of the earth than right here in this city"?

X. Why are some men cowards when in camp and brave on the field of battle?

XI. On one occasion, when Hon. W. J. Bryan was speaking to a packed house, the floor began to sink. The crowd was about to stampede from the building when Mr. Bryan told them that the plank which gave way could not have been a Democratic plank or it would have remained firm. The crowd cheered. He then told them to leave the building quietly, which they did. Explain in terms of the psychology of the crowd.

XII. In a murder trial, would twelve educated men give a different verdict from that of twelve ignorant men? Explain.

XIII. Why does a candidate for office say in his campaign speeches, "When I am elected, I'll do so and so"; instead of, "If I am elected I'll do so and so"?

XIV. Why do doctors who are specialists for the insane very frequently become insane themselves?

XV. Why is it that when we read an advertisement a hundred times that X's medicine cures catarrh, we imagine that everybody says so? We thus become convinced and buy for ourselves.

XVI. Account for the widespread adoption of certain hideous and unsanitary fashions.

XVII. Account for the popular belief in the unluckiness of the number "13"; the popularity of "cut it out," "I should worry," and other street terms.

XVIII. Why will all the boys of a school "cut classes" when one boy alone would not be guilty?

XIX. Can a group of high school boys and girls be as easily led to do a good deed as to do a bad one?

XX. Which sermon will bring the largest collection for the poor, a convincing array of statistics, or a vivid picture of poverty taken from life? Illustrate.

XXI. Enumerate all the ways in which a crowd is like a child. Give concrete examples to illustrate your statements.

XXII. A certain political speaker was a candidate for governor of the state. He began his speeches by saying that he was an ordinary man; that he did not consider himself the best nor the worst man in the state; that he had but an ordinary education; was not much of an orator, etc. Criticize such addresses from your knowledge of the characteristics of the crowd.

III

ESSENTIAL ELEMENTS—THE SPEECH

Having a definite audience to address, what shall be said and wherewithal shall it be clothed?

I. Material.—Something to say! This, indeed, is important. The audience will overlook many imperfections and weaknesses in a speaker, if he brings them a message worth while. *Many audiences ought to be able to recover damages from a speaker for having wasted their time!*

The audience has a right to demand four things as to subject matter:

1. *That It Be Truthful.*—A liar on the platform is as little worthy of respect as by the fireside. The audience demands of the speaker a greater degree of virtue than is required from one in private life. It is not what a man *thinks* on the platform, but what he *knows*, that receives recognition. "The orator is thereby an orator, that he keeps his feet ever on a fact. Then only is he invincible," says Emerson. Ex-President F. L. Patton of Princeton suggests the following as the four essentials for a good speech: "Facts, great facts, human facts, related facts."

2. *That It Be Purposeful.*—Have a message. Not every man can originate new ideas; but we do demand that the speaker express himself in a new and original way. A man who can take a commonplace subject and point out to us new beauties, and picture to us new

relationships and clothe them all in an attractive garb will be listened to by the world. "Knowledge is power." Always speak to the point. Stick to your text. Say what you have to stay in the clearest, briefest, most logical manner possible—and then stop. Speakers who aim at nothing invariably hit it.

3. *That It Be Appropriate.*—Carefully select your material. Do not try to crowd all you know into a five-minute speech. Sift out and retain what will be most appropriate to that particular audience. The food that cured the butcher killed the baker. And many a speaker has figuratively killed himself by not selecting carefully ideas adapted to the occasion. Not only must you say what is true, but "how and when and where." If people desire entertainment and have assembled for that purpose, tell them about funny things. If they desire information, satisfy their intellectual thirst. If they are there to be aroused to duty, speak to them concerning those things which will make each man say, as the Athenians said after listening to Demosthenes, "Let us march against Philip."

4. *That It Be Interesting.*—Material well adapted should be interesting. The question to yourself will be, "What is it that these people care to know? Are these boys interested in the story of David and his sling, or in the genealogy of the Gershonites?" Professor J. B. Esenwein relates an incident of the frank expression of a small boy who doubtless voiced the sentiment of the rest, when he interrupted a long, uninteresting Sunday school address by saying, "Oh, pshaw, let's sing number thirty-six." "The virtue of books is to be readable, of an orator to be interesting," says Emerson.

II. Style.—By Style is meant the manner of wording the material of the speech; the diction of the orator. Some of the qualities mentioned in this chapter are not distinctively oratorical qualities, but belong to all forms of written discourse. They are included here for the purpose of comprehensiveness in treatment and by way of review.

There are four principal attributes of Style: *Unity, Clearness, Force, and Elegance.*

1. *Unity.*—This term connotes the general *form* or structure of the speech. In order to insure unity, the following points must be observed:

A. Outline. Outline everything you write. This is the greatest aid in unity. This will insure a logical and climactical sequence. Some students prefer to sit down and begin to write, putting down the ideas as they happen to come to their minds. This haphazard way will never lead to the best results.

B. Proportion. The Introduction should be about one-tenth of your speech. The Conclusion should be about one-tenth. Do not consume a great portion of your time writing or speaking about unimportant matter, so that you will not have sufficient time left for the important things.

C. Sequence. When ideas are arranged in proper order, they are said to possess logical sequence. One idea must naturally grow out of and follow another. Ideas of coördinate rank should be paralleled. Subordinate ideas must be arranged under their proper heads. Without first forming an outline, this is impossible.

D. Coherence.—Not only must the ideas be arranged logically, but they must be properly joined, connected. They must "hang together." Have one central idea in your theme, and never lose sight of it. Do not branch off on another line entirely. Stick to the main track. There should be a continuous thread extending throughout your entire product from the first sentence in the introduction to the last sentence in the conclusion.

E. Transitions.—Do not make the step from one main idea to the other too abrupt. Let one gradually prepare for the next. This is a strong point in unity. Sudden turns of thought are not conducive to clearness.

2. *Clearness.*—This is an intellectual quality. It is an essential quality in all forms of discourse; but especially in the speech. If you do not understand an author the first time you read a paragraph, you can read it again, and even again if necessary. But you cannot say to the orator, "Stop a moment, please, tell that over again. I didn't quite catch your meaning!" And yet how often we are tempted to do so. Senator Beveridge once said, "As to style, seek only to be clear; nothing else is important." "Clearness at any cost" was the motto of the great preacher and thinker, Joseph Cook. Clearness demands:

A. Clear thinking. There can be no clear speaking without clear thinking. When a thought comes to your mind which you desire to express, revolve it in your mind, look at it from all angles; be conscious of the fact that you, yourself, understand it.

B. Simplicity. A simple style lends to clearness. Do not try to show how learned you are by using big words. The result will likely be that you will thereby expose your ignorance. "Never be grandiloquent when you want to drive home a searching truth. Don't whip with a switch that has the leaves on, if you want it to tingle," said Beecher. But it is not always the size of the word that counts. Some long words are more familiar to your audience than some short words. Speak on the level and in the diction of your audience. It is said of Webster that in addressing a jury he never used words he was not reasonably sure they all understood.

"Root, hog, or die," is more effective than "Queen City quadruped, perforate the mother earth with thy proboscis, or forever cease to exit."

In this famous passage of Sterne, which is said to be the most musical in our language, nearly all the words are Saxon:

"The accusing spirit that flew up to Heaven's chancery with the oath, blushed as he gave it in, and the recording angel, as he wrote it down, dropped a tear upon the words and blotted it out forever."

Rev. Billy Sunday uses this pertinent illustration when replying to his critics for the language he uses:

"Where you put salt it kills the bacteria that cause decay. If a man were to take a piece of meat and smell it and look disgusted, and his little boy were to say, 'What's the matter with it, pop?' and he were to say, 'It is undergoing a process of decomposition in the formation of new chemical compounds,' the boy would be all in. But if the father were to say, 'It's rotten,' then the boy would understand and hold his nose. 'Rotten' is a good Anglo-Saxon word and you do not have to go to the dictionary to find out what it means. Some of you preachers had better look out or the devil will get away with some of your members before they can find out what you mean by your sermons."

C. Definiteness. Don't talk all around your subject. Go straight to the point. Be exact. Study synonyms and learn the precise meanings of words. The motto of the speaker must be, "Not that people *may* understand, but that they *must*."

In the present hustle and bustle of American life, we do not feel that we can afford to listen to men who need an hour to say what might be said in five minutes.

The difference between definiteness and circumlocution is illustrated in a conversation between two negroes when one asked the other what "a bawn owater" is? The reply was:

> "Don't you know what a bawn owater is? Why, sah, you and I would say, 'Two an' two mak' fo';' but a bawn owater would say, 'When in de coase of human events it becomes nec'sa' or exped'ent to coalesce two integers and two moh integers, the result—I declah it boldly an' without feah or favah—the result by simple arithmetical calculation termed addition is fo'.' That's a bawn owater, sah."

D. Concreteness. This term is opposed to what is abstract. It usually is the result of the question, "For instance?" When we desire to make our discourse clear, we usually give an illustration. Abstract arguments should always be clarified by referring to some specific example—an incident, a story. Lincoln was very fond of illustrating his points with good stories. Do not indulge continually in "platitudes and glittering generalities." Put your argument into "some hard phrase, round and solid as a ball, which men can see and handle and carry home." Figures of speech are another form of concreteness. Christ often spoke in parables when he desired to make his meaning clear. All oratory should contain figures of speech. Avoid mixed figures. "The metaphor," said Aristotle, "is the orator's figure, the simile is the poet's."

One seldom hears a speech to-day that does not contain from one to a dozen illustrations. Some are well chosen, but many are not appropriate. Use only good illustrations. They may roughly be divided into four groups; named in order of importance: (1) Historical —those centering around some historical person or event; (2) Personal—those arising from the speaker's own experience; (3) Imaginative—those springing from the fertile brain of the speaker—they never have happened, and may be quite improbable, if not impossible; and (4) Magazine—those found in nearly every newspaper and magazine; often coming under one of the three other classes.

Cautions. (1) Illustrations should always be appropriate—they should always illustrate some point, and not merely attract attention to themselves. (1) Remember that illustrations never *prove* anything. The best they can do is to make the point clear. (3) Avoid illustrations that are very common, those found in popular magazines, or those that are familiar or hackneyed, such as Washington and the cherry tree, etc. (4) Your speech should always contain a few, new, brief, and pertinent illustrations.

E. Restatement. Very frequently a sentence may be repeated to advantage by telling it again in different words. However, it is usually a confession on the part of the speaker that he fears he was not very clear in the first place. Yet obscure thoughts may be understood by certain persons if told one way and by others if told in some other manner. Example:

"I do not know where her hair (the hair of a woman of fashion) comes from. I could never find out. That is, her other hair, her public, her Sunday hair. I do not mean the hair she goes to bed with. Why you ought to know the hair I mean. It is the thing she calls a switch and which resembles a switch as much as it resembles a brick bat or a shot gun, or any other thing you correct people with."—MARK TWAIN.

3. *Force.*—Force is an emotional quality. It is the chief element in persuasion. There are a great many rhetorical elements which contribute to Force; but the most important are:

A. Strength. A sentence should be strong. This property is obtained by putting the important idea in the sentence in the most prominent place. This is usually at the end; sometimes at the beginning. The last word in a sentence resounds in the mind of the hearer longer than any other, for there is usually a downward inflection and a pause at the end. Strength is also acquired by choosing words with a definite meaning. The periodic sentence, if not used too frequently, often adds strength.

B. Climax. Words and sentences should be so arranged that the weakest come first. When the weakest and least important come last, we have what is called an anti-climax. Examples:

(*a*) "I not only did not say this, but I did not even write it; I not only did not write it, but took no part in the embassy; I not only took no part in the embassy, but used no persuasion with the Thebans."

(*b*) "He was loyal to his family, loyal to his friends, loyal to his countrymen, loyal to his God."

Arrange your speech climactically. Drive home one truth after another, each more forceful than the last; like one rill after another, and stream after stream, all flowing into a great torrent which bursts into a mighty cataract in your conclusion.

C. Brevity. Brevity is the soul of force. Omit all useless verbiage from your discourse. Still do not trim it so as to make it sound choppy. But remember that "a fool is known by his multitude of words." This is true of the sentence and of the entire speech. Omit conjunctions whenever possible. A short pointed arrow penetrates deepest. Southey said, "It is with words as with sunbeams; the more they are condensed, the deeper they burn." Note the vigor in this line from Browning:

> Boot, saddle, to horse and away.

D. Iteration. When words or sentences are very important they may be repeated often, adding much to the emphasis. It was Mr. Dooley who wrote, "I belave annything at all, if ye only tell it to me often enough." Napoleon said that there was only one figure in rhetoric of much importance—repetition. The thing affirmed comes by repetition to fix itself in the mind in such a way that in the end it is accepted as a demonstrated fact. Iteration may occur in the same sentence, as: To become perfect you must study, study, study, Also,

> Work—work—work
>   Till the brain begins to swim.
> Work—work—work
>   Till the eyes are heavy and dim.
> Seam and gusset and band,
>   Band and gusset and seam,—
> Till over the buttons I fall asleep
> And sew them on in a dream!   —Hood.

E. Comparison. This includes analogy and antithesis. Comparison is also an element of clearness. We are all impressed with resemblances and contrasts. We always reason from the known to the unknown. Objects look blacker or whiter by comparison. Contrasted colors are intensified. Antithesis is most forceful if arranged in balanced form. Example:

I had rather be a doorkeeper in the house of my God than to dwell in the tents of wickedness.—Bible.

F. Direct Discourse. This gives opportunity for action. It eliminates the middleman. A story loses much of its force and humor if removed from its original setting. *He said that he was Cæsar,* is not as strong as, He said, "I am Cæsar."

G. Rhetorical Question. In asking questions, you invite the audience to participate in your discussion. These questions should usually be in such form as to be answered by "yes" or "no," and the answers so obvious that they need not be given by the speaker. They are merely forceful declarations in interrogative form. Example:

How long, O Catiline! wilt thou trifle with our patience? How long shalt thou baffle justice in thy mad career? To what extreme wilt thou carry thy audacity? Art thou nothing daunted by the nightly watch posted to secure the Palatium? Nothing, by the city guards? Nothing, by the rally of all good citizens? Nothing, by the assembling of the Senate in this fortified place? Nothing, by the averted looks of all here present?—CICERO.

H. Interjection. A sudden burst of emotion frequently thrills an audience to the bone. One word is often more forceful than a whole paragraph. Interjections must only be used to express deep feeling.

I. Imagery. Some words and phrases bring to the mind definite images; others do not. Prepositions and conjunctions rarely do. The image is not as clear in general as in particular terms. The word "fruit" does not bring to the mind a definite image, but "apples" does. Such words as "civilization," "house," "evil," are not so forceful as "cities," "plows," "school-house," and "stealing."

For the orator, imagery is power. Let no man aspire

to be an orator who has not a vivid imagination. "Trope and metaphor" must flow readily from his tongue. Slang is a form of abused imagery. Note the force of this figure of Grattan's: "I never will be satisfied as long as the meanest cottager in Ireland has a link of the British chain clinging to his rags. He may be naked; he shall not be in irons!" Note, also, the antithesis and balance in the last sentence.

J. Loftiness. Especially in the oration, when you are speaking of profound, universal principles, your language must harmonize with your ideas. In your sublime efforts never stoop to the sordid and despicable. Slang never finds its way into an oration. Clothe your ideas in appropriate words. A diamond does not show its brilliancy in a clay setting. Do not speak of the "nation's pocket-book," but of a "nation's wealth," not of "houses," but of "homes" and "mansions."

When, however, you desire to be less formal and more pertinent, take off your gloves and go in with bare fists. In a volume, *The Real Billy Sunday,* by Rev. E. P. Brown, is related the reply by Mr. Sunday to some ministers who requested that he tone down his remarks. To them he said, "Why, if I did that I wouldn't have any more people to preach to than you have."

The subject, occasion, purpose, and audience will determine your selection of words and phrases. But, by all means, be consistent.

K. Adroitness. Frequently a speaker can secure his ends by selecting carefully and diplomatically such words and phrases as to express what he desired in a circuitous manner. Members in Congress and lawyers at the bar have been able frequently to indulge in personalities in such a way that they cut deep, and at the same time shielded the author. The real truth penetrates slowly, but when it does, it sinks deeply. Often it might be better and far more effective to tell a man "to join the Ananias Club," or that he is "a lineal descendant of the impenitent man on the cross," or that he has a "brain storm," than to call him a "liar," "a thief," or "crazy."

An implied antithesis suggested by emphasis, a certain inflection or accent, may convey a meaning entirely different, and be much more effective when spoken than if the same words appeared in print; as, "He won't do a *thing* to you. You are such a brave man!" "I did not say that you were a liar, I only said you did not tell the truth."

4. *Elegance.*—This quality of style appeals to the æsthetic sense: man's sense of beauty, of form, and of harmony. It pleases, interests and fascinates; hence is of great value to the orator.

A. Smoothness. Some speakers mar their language by making it jerky. They use too many short sentences; are often too epigrammatic. Cicero, who loved a smooth and copious style, said that he never heard a Lacedæmonian orator. "If there is a tide in his soul, there will be a flow in his eloquence, and he will not dam it up in pools by too frequent periods." Have both short and long sentences. The average number of words at present is about twenty-five. Emerson has about twenty; and Macaulay about twenty-three. During the 15th century sentences often averaged sixty words.

Gravity, sublimity, and the picturesque demand long sentences. Simplicity, passion, assertion, vigor, find expression in short sentences.

B. Rhythm. A periodic recurrence of a beat or accent aids greatly to impress the hearers. The Greek and Roman orators paid especial attention to this point. Quintilian said that some of the ancient orations might be set to music. The student should familiarize himself with the writings of Shakespeare, Milton, Hawthorne, Erskine, Grady, parts of the Bible, and thus mould his style into patterns of rhythm and beauty.

Rhythm has a great emotional value as well as an æsthetic. Audiences are frequently moved profoundly by the rhythmic cadence in the style of some orators.

Rhythm is mainly a matter of judgment and taste, not of rule. Note the difference of rhythm in the following sentences:

> In the afternoon about two o'clock we made ready.
> About two o'clock in the afternoon we made ready.

C. Balance. The word *balance* is self-explanatory. It signifies adjustment, correspondence, poise, sanity. As an element of elegance and effectiveness in literary style, it is very important. It is a great aid to quickness in understanding, for it is a mental law that similarity of thought must be accompanied by similarity or balance in form, as any change of form tends to distract the attention. Antithesis and balance make an effective combination. Examples:

(*a*) The law of the Lord is perfect, converting the soul; the testimony of the Lord is sure, making wise the simple.— *Psalms*, xix, 7.

(*b*) Thus the successors of the old Cavaliers had turned demagogues; the successors of the old Roundheads had turned courtier.

(*c*) What does he do, this hero in gray with a heart of gold? Does he sit down in sullenness and despair? Not for a day. Surely God, who had stripped him of his prosperity, inspired him in his adversity. As ruin was never before so overwhelming, never was restoration swifter. The soldier stepped from the trenches into the furrow; horses that had charged Federal guns marched before the plow; and fields that ran red with human blood in April were green with the harvest in June.—GRADY.

D. Alliteration. This consists in the repetition of the same initial sound in successive words. It is more frequently found in poetry than in prose. Still some of our great modern orators revel in its use—Ingersoll, Beecher, Grady, Prentiss, and many others. To a limited extent it adds a definite and striking beauty not otherwise obtained, but it fails in its purpose if it be overdone. However, without "alliteration's artful aid," we would no more hear the melodious music of the sobbing seas, the whispering winds, the tossing tempests, and our ear might cease to linger lovingly on the words of the orator.

E. Euphony. Sentences should be constructed with due regard to a pleasant effect upon the ear. But do not sacrifice substance to sound. Avoid the use of words or combinations of words which are difficult to pronounce; as, despicable, indissoluble, sufficeth, etc. Collections of harsh, guttural sounds or words, a succession of sibilant sounds, or words beginning with the same sound,—all of these should be avoided studiously. Examples:

(*a*) He spoke in innocent tongues.
(*b*) He seemed to secure such an excess of similar sibilance in his successive sentences that they seldom sounded sufficiently sane.

Do not use words that rhyme when writing prose; as,
Her hair was fair, but she showed little care about the way she would wear it.

Compare the following two lines with respect to euphony:

Drink to me only with thy eyes.
Drink to me only with thine eyes.

Sonorous sounds such as *o, m, n, l,* should be given preference over *t, d, b,* and *s.* Too many s's make too much of a hissing goose out of the orator.

F. Variety. Avoid using the same or kindred words in the same sentence. Study books on synonyms. Enlarge your vocabulary so that you can make appropriate substitutions. Note the following:

The commander ordered the general to order the soldiers to preserve order.

A better way would be:

The commander directed the general to see that the soldiers preserved order.

G. Floridity. This was at one time the mark of the orator. Words bristling with meaning are to be preferred to picturesque and flowing language. Rufus Choate once gave this advice to a student: "You don't want a diction gathered from the newspapers, but you want one whose every word is full freighted with suggestion and association, with beauty and power." "Certainly the greatest and wisest conceptions that ever issued from the mind of man," says South, "have been couched under, and delivered in a few, close, homey, and significant words."

However, there is an unmistakable charm in such orations as those of Ingersoll, Grady, Beecher, Sheridan, who love to revel in metaphoric and melodic expressions, and paint pictures in vivid colors appealing to the senses as well as to the emotions and the intellect. They somehow seize the whole man, body, soul, and spirit, and in some way, we know not why, we are ready to believe and obey. "How was it done? Ah! how did Mozart do it, how Raphael? The secret of the rose's sweetness, of the bird's ecstasy, of the sunset's glory—*that* is the secret of genius and eloquence."

EXERCISES

I. Bring to the class an example secured from your general reading illustrating each of the following qualities of style: Concreteness, restatement, climax, direct discourse, rhetorical question, rhythm, alliteration.

II. Study an oration and note all the qualities of style you can discover.

III. Secure examples of five different qualities of style from next Sunday's sermon or from some other public speech.

IV. What qualities of style are illustrated in the following:

1. He was still handsome, this great-hearted friend of ours, although disease had whitened his face and made necessary a supporting cane. When I came away, he took my hand in his and said, half jestingly, half earnestly, "Good-bye. God bless you!" I tried to smile but couldn't.

2. At Oxford Johnson resided during about three years. He was poor, even to raggedness; and his appearance excited a mirth and a pity which were equally intolerable to his haughty spirit. He was driven from the quadrangle of Christ Church by the sneering looks which the members of that aristocratical society cast at the holes in his shoes. Some charitable person placed a new pair at his door, but he spurned them away in a fury.—MACAULAY.

3. But the gentleman inquires why he was made the object of such a reply? why was he singled out? If an attack has been made on the East, he, he assures us, did not begin it: it was made by the gentleman from Missouri. Sir, I answered the gentleman's speech because I happened to hear it; and because, also, I chose to give an answer to that speech, which, if unanswered, I thought most likely to produce injurious impressions. I did not stop to inquire who was the original drawer of the bill. I found a responsible indorsee before me, and it was my purpose to hold him liable, and to bring him to his just responsibility without delay.—WEBSTER.

4. The last stick on her andirons snaps asunder, and falls outward. Two faintly smoking brands stand there. Grandfather lays them together, and they flame up. The two smokes are one united flame. "Even so let it be in heaven," says grandfather.

5. When dead winter comes, how wondrous look the hills in their white robes! The round red ball of the sun looks through the frosty stream. The far-off firth gleams strange and ghostly with a sense of mysterious distance. The mountain loch is a sheet of blue, on which you may disport in perfect solitude from morn to night, with the hills white on all sides, save where the broken snow shows the rusted leaves of the withered bracken.

6. Mounted in the field and at the head of his troops, a glimpse of Lee was an inspiration. His figure was as distinctive as that of Napoleon. The black slouch hat, the cavalry boots, the dark cape, the plain gray coat without an ornament but the three stars on the collar, the calm, victorious face, the splendid manly figure on the gray war-horse,—he looked every inch the true knight—the grand, invincible champion of a great principle.

7. The lettuce is to me a most interesting study. Lettuce is like conversation: it must be fresh and crisp, so sparkling that you scarcely notice the bitter in it. Lettuce, like most talkers, is, however, apt to run rapidly to seed. Blessed is that sort which comes to a head, and so remains, like few people I know; growing more solid, and satisfactory, and tender at the same time, and whiter at the center, and crisp in their maturity. Lettuce, like conversation, requires a good deal of

oil, to avoid friction and keep the company smooth; a pinch of Attic salt, a dash of pepper, a quantity of mustard and vinegar, by all means, but so mixed that you will notice no sharp contrasts, and a trifle of sugar. You can put anything, and the more things the better, into salad, as into a conversation, but everything depends upon the skill of mixing. I feel that I am in the best society when I am with lettuce. It is the select circle of vegetables.—C. D. WARNER.

8. The maxim that no people ought to be free till they are fit to use their freedom, is worthy of the fool in the old story, who resolved not to go into the water till he had learned to swim. If men are to wait for liberty till they become wise and good in slavery, they may indeed wait forever.

9. Withdraw thy foot from thy neighbor's house lest he be weary of thee, and so hate thee.

A man that beareth false witness against his neighbor is a maul, and a sword, and a sharp arrow.—BIBLE.

10. Let us at least have this to say: We too have kept the faith of the fathers. We took Cuba by the hand. We delivered her from her age-long bondage. We welcomed her to the family of nations. We set mankind an example never beheld before of moderation in victory. We led hesitating and halting Europe to the deliverance of their beleaguered ambassadors in China. We marched through a hostile country—a country cruel and barbarous—without anger or revenge. We returned benefit for injury and pity for cruelty. We made the name of America beloved in the East as in the West. We kept faith with the Philippine people. We kept faith with our own history. We kept our national honor unsullied. The flag which we received without a rent we handed down without a stain.—A. J. BEVERIDGE.

IV

ESSENTIAL ELEMENTS—THE SPEAKER

"Eloquence," said Webster, "must exist in the man, in the subject, and in the occasion." The latter two of these elements of eloquence have been discussed in preceding chapters. The third great factor in public speaking is the speaker himself. A good speech, however well prepared, will be ineffectual unless well delivered. In treating of delivery we must refer, by way of review, to certain matters that were discussed more fully in Part I.

I. Physical Qualities.—"A man may have the bow of Ulysses, but of what use is it, if he has not the strength to bend it to do his will? His arrows may be of silver and gold-tipped; they may be winged with the feathers of the very bird of Paradise; but if he cannot draw them to the head and send them home to the mark, of what value are they to him?" The crowd demands a leader. This leader must always be an embodiment of strength. Elements of strength as related to physical qualities are:

1. *Physique.*—Men of all ages whose tread has made the world tremble with their eloquence have been men with brawny frames, and great power of physical and mental endurance. With few exceptions, those who have not had large physiques have had close-knit ones. Burke, Fox, Mirabeau, Brougham, Webster, Chalmers, Curran, O'Connell, John Bright, Gladstone, Beecher, Bryan— were all men of powerful frames and iron nerves.

If nature has given you a strong physique, make the

most of it; develop it and make it still stronger. However, there have been mighty powers on the platform who did not enjoy this natural advantage. John Randolph had a small, short body perched upon long, crane-like legs; but every one in the House of Representatives listened to him when he spoke. Wilberforce had a dwarfish body and a weak, shrill voice; but he became a power in Parliament. Richard Sheil, the Irish orator, had a pigmy body, and Summerfield, one of America's most magical preachers, was an invalid all his life.

2. *Voice.*—Even more than a powerful frame the orator needs a good voice. Oh, the magic, the charm, the power, in a strong, well modulated voice! Lord Chatham and William Pitt became leaders in Parliament because of their voices. Burke, far more brilliant in intellect, had far less immediate influence because he lacked a good voice. Thomas Jefferson was never considered an able orator because he could not control his voice. Mirabeau, O'Connell, and Webster controlled assemblies by their powerful throats; Gladstone, Bryan, Clay and Grady by their "silver tongues." When Bryan traveled in Japan, a native who could not understand English heard him deliver an address and gave this tribute to his eloquence: "His voice sounded like music."

Since the voice is such an important factor in making a successful speaker, too much pains cannot be taken in cultivating it to its highest possibility. It is to be regretted, to say the least, that among men who depend on public speaking for their bread and for their success—preachers, lawyers, lecturers—so many are satisfied with a poor voice, throaty and harsh, droning and monotonous, with an abominable minor inflection. What a power some men could be, if they only had good voices!

Why do they not cultivate them? This is the answer: Either ignorance or indolence.

But wherein lies the charm of a good voice? The chief elements are:

A. Distinctness. By all means secure a clear, distinct articulation. It is said that Monvel, the French actor, had scarcely any voice, not even teeth, and yet every one in the audience could hear every word. The secret was distinct articulation. Loudness is not distinctness. Many speakers can make themselves heard in every part of the room when they whisper. How did they acquire this ability? By whispering. When in your room imagine you have a large audience. Speak to them just as you would if you were on the platform, only do not use your vocal cords. Make a special effort to make yourself clear. There is perhaps no better method to cultivate distinctness than to practice whispering with an effort to make your words carry. Besides, you will not disturb those in the same building.

B. Purity. This quality is very essential. No huskiness, throatiness, raspiness, breathiness, mouthing, lisping, can be tolerated in a good speaker. The voice should be clear as the tone of a silver bell.

C. Melody. A voice should have modulations in change of pitch, inflections, a pleasing accent, and a musical cadence. Cultivate a range of at least one octave, and use it when you speak. Do not hang on to one note as though fearful that if you once got off you would lose it forever. "Nothing tires an audience more quickly," says Marden, "than monotony, everything expressed on the same dead level. There must be variety; the human mind tires very quickly without it."

D. Loudness. Speak so you can be heard. Some

speakers begin in such a low tone that they are not heard by one-half of the audience. If you are not heard, you cannot be understood; then why speak at all? Gauge your voice so as to make those in the back row hear what you say, then every one between you and the back row will be able to hear you. Do not yell, but speak. Some people imagine that a low, coarse voice like that of a bull or the sound of a bass drum is essential. Not at all. Neither do you want a high, shrill, rafter-splitting scream. A normal voice is best—one that will permit the speaker to raise or lower the pitch, and to increase or decrease the volume. The secret of power in many speakers lies in their ability to adapt the character of their voices to the ideas and emotions impressed; and the range of the emotions is as great as the gamut of human experience.

E. Tone-color, or the emotional modulation of the voice, is the result of harmonizing sympathetically the four elements just mentioned. "Ninety-nine men in every hundred in the crowded profession will probably never rise above mediocrity because the training of the voice is entirely neglected and considered of no importance," wrote Mr. Gladstone.

3. *Personal Appearance.*—It may be difficult and frequently impossible to develop a robust and commanding physique; but there is little excuse for the public speaker to disregard his personal appearance. If the speaker desires to make the best impression, he should make the most of himself. His clothes should be neat, well-fitting and plain. Flashy jewelry should not be worn. Immaculate linen, and care of hands, nails and hair, are matters not too trifling to be scrupulously observed by the speaker.

II. Mental Qualities.—Our great orators were robust physically; they likewise had giant intellects. Some of the mental qualities absolutely essential for a great speaker are:

1. *Memory.*—Facts and figures must be constantly at the speaker's command. Train your memory. Some of our most eloquent men have made it a rule to commit to memory some choice bit of literature every week. When delivering a memorized selection have it so well in mind that you do not need to think of what is coming next. This reaching out after the next thought ruins any delivery. Cultivate a good memory. Much practice and following correct principles will bring wonderful improvement. Here are a few rules on memory:

A. Get rid of the idea that your memory is not as good as it was years ago.

B. Center your thoughts exclusively on the task at hand. Use your will.

C. Repeat often.

D. Learn familiar matter, if not too long, as a whole. Do not take it a line at a time. Many useless associations of ideas are thus formed.

E. Unfamiliar and difficult matter should be repeated until memorized.

F. Use imagery wherever possible, but do not encumber your mind with useless pictures.

G. Rest after work. Allow the mind to rest after a selection is mastered.

H. Use all the avenues at your command. Do not try to learn a selection silently. If it is a reading or an oration, by all means repeat it aloud each time. There is no economy in writing out the selection you desire to memorize.

I. Learn it well before you discard the manuscript. After a wrong word or association is once fixed in the mind, it requires much effort to correct or to eliminate it.

J. Trust your memory and so go on the platform with confidence.

2. *Will.*—The mind as *will* causes you to act or to make a choice. You may be convinced that a thing should be done, and yet not do it. Self as will must be aroused to action. A strong, controlled will power can be developed by *doing* the things you know to be expedient and right. Your reasoning powers decide what is right and then your *will* must compel you to do the right thing. Hence, the necessity for strong will power in every individual, not only to do things that should be done, but to refrain from doing the things that should not be done.

In the first place, you must practice and drill upon the fundamental exercises in this book. You may soon lose interest in them. At first they are new and interesting, soon they lose their novelty and then you must bring the will to bear and compel yourself to keep at it. In the second place, when topics for speeches are assigned to you, your inclination will be to put off from day to day and depend on the spur of the moment for your thoughts. Do not do it. *Get busy at once.* Just say to yourself, "I have a strong will. I can do the things that I should do. I am no weakling. I may not have a giant's body, but I have a strong will. I know I ought to begin at once, and *I will do so.*" It has been said that what we call a strong will power in ourselves, we often call *stubbornness* in others. Stubbornness is a determination to do a thing just to be contrary—usually to keep on doing something after we are convinced that we are wrong.

But that is a very different thing from will power. A fearless determination to do the right thing has made many a speaker a power in his community. This evidence of will power is illustrated in Garrison when he said, "I am in earnest: I will not equivocate—I will not excuse— I will not retract a single inch—and I will be heard." And he *was* heard.

"Nothing is impossible to the man who can will," said Mirabeau. "He who has a firm will," said Goethe, "molds the world to himself."

> Infinite power dawned in man
> When God created Will.
> Eternal growth consumes its plan,
> Details its laws fulfill;
> High purpose vaults life's endless span;
> But all is strength through drill.

3. *Imagination.*—The difference between an indifferent speaker and an eloquent orator depends largely on a difference in imagination. "It is not by naked, bold statement of facts, but by pictures that make them *see* the facts that assemblies are moved." To develop a vivid imagination, think concisely, observe minutely, study the works of imaginative writers, picture to yourself in detail the ideas impressed by these writers.

Imagination is seldom valued at its true worth. Many ascribe to Will when Imagination should have credit. If you imagine you are sick, the chances are that you are sick or soon will be. Imagine that you cannot make a speech and it is extremely doubtful whether you can. On the contrary, imagine yourself making a speech—picture yourself on a platform, saying to your audience what you want to tell them, and in just the manner you want to tell it—if you can imagine this strong enough, or often enough—you will succeed.

To prove that imagination and not will is a powerful factor in preventing or permitting you to do certain things, let us assume a concrete case. Suppose you place a plank four inches wide on supports, six inches from the ground. Can you walk across this plank from end to end without falling off? Yes, of course. Now place it fifty feet from the ground. Can you walk it? No. You would not try. Why? You imagine you cannot perform the act, and that alone renders you helpless. To perform the second act would be as easy as the first if it were not for your imagination.

Impress yourself sufficiently—daily, if necessary—that a certain task *can* be done, *imagine yourself doing it,* and success is assured. It is not always a weak will, but a wrong image that makes for failures.

4. *Sense of Humor.*—"A man without a sense of humor," declares an anonymous writer, "is occasionally to be respected, often to be feared, and nearly always to be avoided." Wit and humor are closely related. Wit is intellectual; humor, emotional; wit is a perception of resemblance; humor a perception of contrast, of discrepancy, of incongruity. Both afford a pleasurable surprise, a gentle shock. Wit, being intellectual, suffers by repetition. Humor is a feeling and can always be revived. A statement that is humorous, when recalled, may provoke as much and often more laughter than when first heard or seen. Humor, it has been said, is laughing *with* the other man; wit is laughing *at* him. We laugh at the *unusual,* but it must contain an element of truth; at *strange combinations*—a cow sitting on a thistle, whistling like a bird; *unusual relationships*—cow jumping

over the moon; at the *unexpected,* a jack-in-a-box; at sudden turns of thought; as, *Teacher* (to a pupil in a class of English History)—"Mr. Smith, who followed Henry VIII?" *Mr. Smith*—"Anne Bolinsky"; at *exaggerations*—a mule with one ear sticking through a tree top and birds sitting on it, the other lopping on the ground and boys skating on it.

The ability to conceive and mentally to construct unusual and unique relationships between ideas is a rare gift. Again, it is not enough to say interesting things, but to say them in an interesting manner. A witty and apt retort, a bit of irony, sarcasm, or ridicule, is at times more effectual than a whole speech. Avoid personal sarcasm. Do not antagonize your audience. You want to win them. "More flies are caught with sugar than with vinegar."

Avoid being funny. Some speakers make themselves ridiculous, yes, at times disgusting, who have no sense of humor and are always trying to say something "cute" or "smart." And yet how we do admire a man who can at least once in a while leave the dry sands of his discourse and give us a cool drink, by permitting us to bring together two ideas not usually associated! Says Goethe: "There is nothing commonplace which could not be made to appear humorous if quaintly expressed."

5. *Common Sense.*—Use good judgment. If you have not good judgment, at least use the best you have. Interruptions will frequently occur while you are speaking. If you exercise good sense, you will not show your annoyance as the preacher did when a little boy in his congregation was attracting attention by rapidly twisting his head from side to side, by saying, "Boy, if you do not quit that I will come down there and twist your head off."

A more sensible retort and surely more effective was spoken by another minister who, while preaching on the text, "Thou art weighed in the balance and found wanting," was interrupted by a number of persons getting up and leaving the church. When the next person arose to leave the speaker said, "That is right—as soon as you are weighed you may pass out." No more left. The average speaker requires not genius, but common sense.

III. Moral Qualities.—"If I should make the shortest list of qualifications for an orator," said Emerson, "I should begin with manliness."

1. *Character.*—It is said of Sheridan, England's most brilliant orator, that he might have ruled Europe had he only possessed a trustworthy character. Do not pretend—be. "Let no sneak try to be an orator," said Beecher. A man who does not back up by his life what he preaches had better plow corn. Had Luther's words been contradicted by his life they would never have rung through the world like the blast of a trumpet. "There can be no true eloquence," says Emerson, "unless there is a *man* behind the speech." . . . Again, "What care I what you *say*, when what you do stands over my head and thunders in my ear so loud that I cannot hear what you say."

2. *Sincerity.*—The word *sincere* was derived from the practice of filling up flaws in furniture with wax, whence *sine cera* came to mean pure, not adulterated. Earnestness is one of the most essential elements in securing power in delivery. *Sincerity is the mental basis of earnestness.* A liar is not believed even when he does tell the truth. If you have no faith in your message, do not imagine for a moment that you can make any one else believe in it. Remember you cannot fool all the peo-

ple all the time. "I have heard," says Emerson, "an experienced counselor say that he never feared the effect upon a jury of a lawyer who does not believe in his heart that his client ought to have a verdict. If he does not believe in it, his unbelief will appear to the jury, despite all his protestations, and will become their unbelief."

3. *Fearlessness.*—Develop a backbone, if you have none. The orator is a leader. A coward can never lead. Be sure that you are right, then maintain your position. A man who swerves with every change of the wind will never become an orator. We enjoy listening to a man who has convictions and is fearless in expressing them. Fearlessness grows out of the conviction that you know that you know, and a conscious approval that your convictions are truths.

4. *Perseverance.*—Our most successful orators have been men of indomitable perseverance and untiring industry. It is perspiration not inspiration, industry not ingeniousness, work not birth, that will make the orator of the future. These are the words of Salvini, the great actor, to his pupil: "Above all, study, *study,* STUDY. All the genius in the world will not help you along with any art, unless you become a hard student."

5. *Trustworthiness.*—Be dependable. There are few things which will detract more from a speaker's success and popularity than faithlessness. Be a man of your word. If you say you will speak at such a time and at such a place, *do so;* be on time and be prepared. The best way to form this habit is to begin now in your class work. If a speech is due, *have it prepared* the best you can. Offer no excuse, make no apologies. "Back of nearly every excuse for work not done, lies, if the whole truth were told, weakness or negligence." After school

days are over you may receive an invitation to speak upon some occasion. You may also be conscious of the fact that you were second or third in choice, and may be tempted to say to yourself, "I don't want a second-hand invitation, I'll not accept it." But don't say it. *Accept.* Do the best you can, though the time for preparation may be short. Sooner or later invitations will come to you first hand. Prove to your community that you are reliable, that you are dependable, that you are a friend indeed because you were a friend in need. These moral qualities have proved an essential factor in the success of many a business and professional man, and they will likewise be of inestimable service to the speaker.

IV. Style of Delivery.—There is no one style of delivery. Each great orator and speaker has had a style all his own, but there are certain underlying principles which govern all styles. A speaker's delivery should be:

1. *Natural.*—Do not be affected, stagy, or act like a mechanically constructed toy;—be natural. This does not mean that you should exhibit all your peculiar eccentricities on the stage that you may show on the street. Do not imagine that when you speak a selection by Webster you must imitate his voice and his mannerisms. If you are rehearsing the production of another, speak it as *you* would have spoken it on that particular occasion. Had John B. Gough tried to imitate the style of Beecher, we would never have heard of Mr. Gough. Do not try to become a Billy Sunday. His style does very well for Billy Sunday, but it is quite possible that you will be able to express yourself on most subjects on a platform less than twenty by forty feet.

Talking through the nose or teeth, or in the throat, or at the walls, may seem natural to many; but these **are** matters of habit rather than of nature. Students who in their school or college course first give attention to the manner of their speech, bring to the study certain habits. These habits may be good or bad. The good habits need developing and strengthening; the bad represent sundry faults, some curable, many needing to be eradicated and supplanted, all capable of improvement. Now, these bad habits are not natural, in the sense that they are true exponents of nature. They are, rather, a cultivated unnaturalness. We must therefore be careful not to confound habit with nature, peculiarity with individuality. On this "being natural" fallacy, Professor Hiram Corson, in his little book, *The Voice and Spiritual Education,* says: " 'Enter into the *spirit* of what you read, read *naturally,* and you will read well,' is about the sum and substance of what Archbishop Whately teaches on the subject, in his *Elements of Rhetoric.* Similar advice might with equal propriety be given to a clumsy, stiff-jointed clodhopper in regard to dancing, 'Enter into the spirit of the dance, dance naturally, and you will dance well.' The more he might enter into the spirit of the dance, the more he might emphasize his stiff-jointedness and clodhopperishness."

Many students seek instruction in oratory who seem to imagine that the teacher can furnish them with some patent device whereby they will become proficient in the art. Banish from your mind any thought that this or that "system," this or that "method," will make you an orator, or even—what is far more to our purpose—an effective public speaker. No method but your own—the expression of your individuality—will ever make you any sort of a speaker other than a parrot or a machine. Be yourself, not a mere imitator. Certain principles are fundamental, but expression will be as varied as individualities. Avoid any "system" that would cast all speakers in the same mold. Aim not to become a Demosthenes or Cicero, a Webster or Clay, but aim for the best and most effective expression of Yourself. Above all, eschew any ambition to become "eloquent," as the term is commonly used—"to soar among the constellations and strew the floor with star-dust." Keep your feet upon the earth, the audience will more likely be able to follow you.

Study the ways and style of delivery of our great orators, past and present; listen to all you possibly can. If a certain minister or speaker pleases you, listen to him, absorb his style, but do not imitate it. Adopt those characteristics which especially please you, reject certain mannerisms which you think detract from his effectiveness. Thus, slowly and surely, you will develop a style, personal, natural, and effective.

2. *Conversational.*—This is a style suitable for most occasions—a straightforward heart to heart talk. Speak with interest, vivacity, earnestness and naturalness, just as you would in animated conversation. This style must be modified and intensified on the platform, just as everything on the platform must be slightly exaggerated; but the point is, that if the audience is to be impressed by your thoughts, convinced of your convictions, and persuaded to your beliefs, its attention should not be distracted by a method of communication outside of ordinary experience. If here and there a speaker who has special qualities of force or attractiveness attains a certain measure of success by another method, it does not affect the truth of this underlying principle.

Then, too, the conversational style of delivery accords with modern taste; for oratory, like other arts, may have a certain type or style, varying with changing conditions. The style of popular oratory has undergone a marked change in this country—from the heavy and bombastic to the simple and direct—within the past twenty-five years. It was Wendell Phillips who more than any other one man first set the fashion which has largely done away with barnstorming and haranguing. George William Curtis describes his manner as that of a "gentleman conversing." Says Colonel Thomas Wentworth Higginson:

The keynote to the oratory of Wendell Phillips lay in this: that it was essentially conversational—the conversational raised to the highest power. Perhaps no orator ever spoke with so little apparent effort, or began so entirely on the plane of his average hearers. It was as if he simply repeated, in a little louder tone, what he had just been saying to some familiar friend at his elbow. The colloquialism was never realized, but it was familiarity without loss of dignity. Then, as the argument went on, the voice grew deeper, the action more animated, and the sentences came in a long, sonorous swell, still easy and graceful, but powerful as the soft stretch of a tiger's paw.

Again, the style of one's speech will vary with the occasion and the audience. One's style of conversation varies with the formality of the occasion and the intelligence of the hearer or hearers. And so it is in public speaking—and especially in extempore speaking. "Personal grapple" with an audience demands a style suited to that particular audience. Hence the power of adaptability needs to be developed. This cannot be attained through rules, but the student should, so far as possible, practice adapting himself to different audiences. The danger of the over-academic style, which frequently prevents the college-bred man from reaching the popular ear, should be guarded against sedulously.

Always speak on a level with your audience; not down to, nor up to, but on a level with—as complete an adaptation as possible. The preacher, for example, who makes a successful after-dinner speech will not deliver a sermon. He will have the purpose of his address in mind, in the one case as well as in the other, but the same style would ordinarily be unsuited to both types of address. The unimpassioned argument that a lawyer might properly deliver to a court would fail to reach the average jury. The scientist addressing a body of fellow-scientists would naturally use a diction ill adapted to speaking on the same subject to a popular audience. The style of a Sunday-school address would rarely be suited to that of a political speech. And so we might go on multiplying illustrations, for they are as numerous as the audiences one may be called upon to address.

3. *Dramatic.*—Some speakers love to energize their efforts until they resemble the actor on the stage. They "act out" their thoughts; their gestures are many and violent. Frequently they stand upon chairs, lie down on the platform, etc. This style is attractive to a majority of the people, especially to the less educated class. But the "artist" in public speaking need not resort to such physical contortions to interest his audience. However, there are times when a touch of "dramatic eloquence" may be made very effective. Even Beecher occasionally resorted to impersonation to make his points clear and impressive. But when the dramatic style is employed, it should always be spontaneous—natural.

V. Power.—What is the secret of power in the speaker? Have you not asked yourself this question, as you listened to an eloquent address which held you spellbound, or to an evangelist who brought thousands of men and women to their knees? What is the secret? Not even the orator himself can explain the secret of his power. This is not only true of the art of speaking, but it is true of music, painting, and even the military art. When Napoleon was once asked how he managed to win so many victories, he replied: "Mon Dieu, it is natural to me; I was made so!" Eloquence is like the wind, we can feel its presence, but know not "whence it cometh nor whither it goeth." A few of the elements of power are:

1. *Personal Magnetism.*—This element to some degree is always present in the orator and effective speaker; but it is difficult to analyze. Professor Kleiser says, "It is a patent influence in swaying and moving an audience, and is associated with geniality, sympathy, frankness, manliness, persuasiveness and an attractive personal appearance. There is a purely animal magnetism, which passes from speaker to audience and back again, swiftly and silently. This magnetic quality is sometimes found in the voice, in the eye, or may be reflected in the whole personality of the speaker." It is found in men who have deep convictions, strong likes and dislikes and are fearless in expressing them. It is found in men of whom we say, "There is a man with a *strong personality.*"

Worry and fear are the greatest foes to securing a strong personal magnetism. A firm, determined will is the greatest help. Any one who will discipline his mind and body may possess personal magnetism, but the discipline must be daily—yes, hourly. Learn to look people in the eyes when you speak to them on the streets or from the platform, and make them look at you; for the eyes— "the windows of the soul"—are a most important factor in the development and the impress of personality. In a recent address to a graduating class, Ex-President

Charles H. Eliot of Harvard University said: "There is a subtle power latent in each one of you, which few have developed, but which when developed might make a man irresistible. It is called personal magnetism. I advise you to master it."

2. *Earnestness.*—The basic element of earnestness is sincerity. Believe what you say and then say it as though you believed it. Earnestness requires (1) a thorough knowledge of your subject, (2) a sincere faith in that subject, and (3) an unswerving determination to implant in others that knowledge and that faith. Betterton, the actor, gave this reason to the Lord Bishop of London, why the clergy had so little influence with the people: "The actor speaks of things imaginary as though they were real; the preacher too often speaks of things real as though they were imaginary." Do not speak "from the teeth outward," but from the heart. Mr. W. Mathews says, "It is not enough that the speaker utter profound or weighty truths; he must show by all possible forms of expression—by voice, looks, and gestures—that they are truths, living, vital truths to *him*."

When rendering the selection of some one else, learn the circumstances which occasioned it. Get the historical setting, if you can. Try to identify yourself with the speaker and the occasion. Your imagination must be called upon to aid you in this. Picture to yourself as vividly as you can the scenes you describe; do not speak mere words. Unless you see the picture and feel the emotions you will never get your audience to see nor to act. Do not forget that the thought must be clear and vivid in the speaker's mind *at the moment of utterance*. Effective speaking is simply the science and art of thinking out loud. Reverend Joseph Parker, the great London preacher, was once asked by a clergyman to aid him in getting a charge. Mr. Parker asked him to preach a sermon. In the midst of its delivery he was interrupted with the pertinent comment, "Now, I know why you do not have a parish; you are speaking to get something off your mind and not *into mine.*" The trouble with many speakers who excuse themselves when their delivery is poor, by saying that they did not get into their subject, is that the subject did not get into them. Luther said that he could never preach nor pray unless he first became indignant. It is often necessary to be provoked or antagonized before one is stimulated into doing one's best. Some students are very poor speakers until they become angry, and then they have a remarkable command of language and speak with great force.

The audience is often an added inspiration to earnestness. It is difficult to do your best without some inspiration from a sympathetic audience. But in your practice do not depend upon this. Imagine that you have a large audience; speak as though you are commanding one, and some day you may. Forget self. Be conscious only of your subject and a desire to get the subject into your audience. Do not let your earnestness depend upon the occasion, but master the occasion through earnestness. Be prepared; be confident that you have your speech well in hand. Speak it as though you meant it. Loudness is not earnestness. Talma, the French actor, said that he had studied forty years to be energetic without noise.

3. *Progress.*—Get somewhere. Say something worth while each moment, or quit. Get at your point, make it, then stop.

Begin in a tone just loud enough to be heard by every one in the audience. But be sure that you are heard. It is said of Henry Grattan that he "could not utter a half dozen sentences without getting into such a passion and indulging in such violent gestures that it was quite unsafe for any member to sit within reach of his right arm." Such violence, especially at the beginning, is not recommended. Dr. Leifchild's rule is a better one, "Begin low; go on slow; rise higher; take fire." It is natural that you should take some time to get warmed up, but be sure that you do get a little fire in you and let it burn brighter and brighter until you close. In the delivery, as in the composition, everything must be done climactically. Your enthusiasm must be on the increase until you close. In a long speech you may have a number of climaxes, but the close of each succeeding climax should find you more in earnest, more enthusiastic. Get somewhere; never let the interest in your speech fag for a moment. This does not mean constant pounding under a running fire. Interest and attention can be secured only by appropriate *transition*. At the beginning of each main division there should be a lull, not unlike a well-ordered conversation, when the subject under discussion :s changed. The speaker starts out with about the same composure and deliberation he did at the beginning of his speech. Short periods of silence, rising from a transition of ideas, are incident to a normal conversation and are an important factor in holding the attention of the audience.

4. *Control.*—"He who reigns within himself, rules his person, desires, and fears, is more than a king." Emotions must be checked, not choked. Power is not expressed by ranting, by a loud, tearful, tremulous voice, by abundant gesticulations, by sobs, nor by uncontrolled expression of the feeling within. Power *is* expressed by

exhibiting a reserved strength. Like an army, its strength is shown by the men in reserve, not the number on the picket line. The audience sympathizes with a man who *struggles,* not the man who *gives up. Control* your passions, your anger; hatred, sorrow, joy, and sympathy; let it be seen in your eyes, the lines in your face, the color of your cheek, the trembling of your body. The Bible speaks of "unutterable joy" and "voiceless prayer." Those persons who themselves are cool when at white heat, are most likely to set the audience on fire. The three friends who sat down by Job for seven days and nights without uttering a word were more eloquent in their silence than all the subsequent complainings and lamentations.

Mathews says, in his *Oratory and Orators,* "When a speaker who is deeply moved, using a gentler mode of expression than the facts might warrant, appears thus to stifle his feeling and studiously to keep them within bounds, the effect of this partial concealment is to give them an appearance of greater intensity and strength." Silence is often more eloquent than words. That man has the greatest expression of power who does not express all of it, and lets the audience feel that there is still more in him. What the audience sees is merely the overflow. Still waters run deepest; and an empty vessel makes most sound.

5. *Physical Expression.*—This element, mentioned here for completeness in classification, is of such importance to the speaker that a separate chapter will be devoted to it.

EXERCISES

I. Select similar stanzas from some long poem and experiment on yourself as to the best way to memorize it.

1. Read it over silently.
2. Read it silently but move your lips.
3. Read it aloud.
4. Have a friend read it to you.
5. Read it silently but repeat each line until committed, memorizing it sentence by sentence.
6. Write it over and over.

II. Let each member of the class tell a funny story. Let the class tell whether it illustrates Wit or Humor.

III. Look steadily at an object for three minutes.

IV. Let each member of the class relate his efforts in trying to look into the eyes of some person to whom he will speak to-morrow.

V. Select some good oration and practice it in a direct, conversational, natural style.

VI. Describe ten scenes which made you laugh while observing moving pictures.

VII. Describe five scenes that made you feel sad.

VIII. Why do you laugh when one man accidentally steps on the corns of a fellow actor on the stage?

IX. What emotions are aroused in you when an actor sings a parody of *Home, Sweet Home?*

X. Make a full report on the next great speaker who comes to your town. What features impressed you most? What were his main faults?

V

PHYSICAL EXPRESSION

Definition.—Physical expression, or gesture, is any movement of the body that expresses the thoughts and emotions of the individual. It is a myological language, a silent, visual, powerful auxiliary to the human voice.

All movements of the body are not gestures. Such mechanical movements as breathing, walking, buttoning one's coat, "babbling with the hands," and scores of other movements arising from physical necessity, mental embarrassment, or bodily discomfort are ordinarily not auxiliaries or substitutes for the voice; but are premeditated, voluntary, muscular actions that always detract from delivery.

Gestures, then, may be said to be those spontaneous, involuntary movements of the eyes, forehead, lips, head, arms, hands, feet, chest, trunk, or any part or parts of the body that aid in expressing the thoughts and emotions of the speaker. These physical manifestations are always soul-inspired and should always re-enforce vocal delivery.

Purpose.—As articulate speech antedated writing, so the muscular language preceded articulate speech. Delsarte states that thoughts are expressed by articulate speech, feelings by inflections, and emotions by gestures.

The mentality of animals and savages is limited, for the most part, to feelings and emotions. Their expression is likewise limited to vocal inflections and physical action. As races rise in intelligence, their articulate language becomes more developed, and inflections and gesticulation decrease. The Chinese language, for example, is very inflectional. One word may have a dozen different meanings, depending on how it is pronounced. Savages have only a few hundred words in their vocabulary, but have an elaborate myological language. When civilized men permit their emotions to dominate their intelligence, they resort to many, and violent physical expressions. Observe a man when he is angry, happy, in despair, or in pain.

Gesture, then, is primarily the language of the emotions. And as emotions are a large factor in influencing the crowd mind, the orator who desires to persuade his audience can ill afford not to master and use this valuable language. Again on the thought side, gesture is an inestimable auxiliary. The speaker should, as a rule, exhaust his vocal resources to make his meaning clear before resorting to gesture. But as words are seldom adequate to express our thoughts and certainly are weak instruments to convey our emotions, the orator should never hesitate to call to his aid, "all the resources of the living man."

Demosthenes epigrammatically said that the first three qualities of the orator were "action." It is said that the Greeks were so adept in the use of their facial muscles when speaking, that jurists are known to have requested the advocates to wear masks or speak in a dark room so that the bench might not be persuaded to decide a case as the result of this emotional expression instead of being convinced by the logic of their arguments.

Every speaker who is energetic, earnest, and enthusiastic is bound to expend some of this energy in physical action. Again, if he has an impression, it will seek expression in some way; if his thoughts will not form into words readily, this energy is diffused over the body, resulting in the many meaningless and involuntary movements of the body. Why not direct and develop these detracting movements, these useless and undesirable exhibitions of nervousness, and this surplus energy into actions that are mighty auxiliaries to the human voice?

Universality. — The fundamental principles of physical expression have been the same for all ages and for all races. Heart throbs have found expression in sculpture and painting, and we read the history of civilization in these silent but unmistakable memorials. Human emotions have but one expression. The leprous beggar in the streets of Damascus holds out his hand in just the same way as does a New York rent collector; and the unfriendly demonstration of a worm-eating Bushman is as easily interpreted as the same inhospitable salutation of a Broadway policeman.

In 1893, the year of the World's Fair in Chicago, a number of Hottentots were brought from Africa. Being unable to find an interpreter who spoke their language, which consists of only a few hundred words, they were sent to the Baltimore (Maryland) Deaf and Dumb Asylum. The result is corroborated by reliable authority that the students in the asylum and the savages had little difficulty in understanding each other, and all engaged in a very animated conversation.

It is said that a barbarian prince, after seeing a Roman play, begged the Emperor to permit him to take with him the leading actor, as a silent interpreter to the many visitors he was obliged to entertain but could not converse with.

To become a master of this silent coadjutor to the living voice has been the ambition of every speaker of note throughout the history of the world.

The Source of Information.—Why not present "cut and dried" formulæ for every thought and emotion as many elocution manuals try to do, which tell us just where the feet should stand, how the fingers kink, where the palm should land, and when the eyes should blink? Physical expression is not learned in that way. But fine speakers and actors were developed by such systems? Perhaps. But have you ever seen a patent medicine that did not have some "restored" patient who loudly proclaimed the curative virtues of the nostrum?

Physical expression is an art—a fine art, and it can best be taught, like all other arts, not by memorizing rules, but by the sound pedagogical principle of Comenius: *"We learn to do by doing."* Gesture must be a spontaneous, involuntary expression. If too circumscribed and prescribed, it becomes mechanical, affected, and non-expressive.

But the novice in this art, like the young painter or sculptor or musician, must have some guide, some pattern, some aid, some criticism. This is very true. Then how and where may this be obtained? Observe. Study. Learn. Study the works of our great painters and sculptors who have expressed on canvas and in bronze and stone the emotional life of the human race. Observe nature, animals, children, men, and women when they express their heart throbs, unpolluted and unveneered by the formalities of social conventions. If you wish to study the expression of sorrow, follow a widow to the newly heaped grave of her only son. Would you secure the physical expression of anger, study a dog fight or observe the physical expression of two "back-alley brats" settling their disputes by resorting to primitive methods; if you desire to know how joy may be objectively expressed, watch the victorious fans at a football game. Delsarte formulated his great principles of physical expression by visiting, not the fashionable boulevards of Paris, but the poor tenement homes and the hospitals where men were dying and where nature comes into her own.

But many do not have the opportunity to get information first hand, and many more who are already victims of the American hot-house system of education, want a short-cut route to the fundamental principles of this universal language, and desire definite rules and suggestions to guide them in correcting wrong habits already formed. And, if we seem to be inconsistent and appear to deviate from merely stating general principles and suggest a few detailed directions, it is for the purpose of aiding the latter.

Natural Gestures.—Frequently the statement is heard,—*gesture naturally.* This advice needs modification. Gestures must be natural in that they must be spontaneous, and have their origin from a mental desire to call on the body to aid the voice. They must be genuine, for gestures made by rule or by rote will never result in grace, beauty, or effectiveness. On the other hand, since frequently the natural gesture merely follows the line of least resistance, it is usually very awkward and inartistic. It is not nature, but nature perverted. Little children gesture spontaneously and naturally, but seldom gracefully. The shoemaker when making a speech will *naturally* permit his arms to swing upward and outward—the direction his hands daily take when pulling the thread through the leather. The blacksmith will naturally gesture with a measured downward stroke of the clenched fist. A young minister was observed having but one gesture when enthused—his right hand made a short quick pass from right to left in front of his body. It was learned that his early life had been spent in the cotton field. The arms of the pugilist take the character of a punch rather than the stroke of the carpenter. Many of the circular, base-ball, full-arm swings of Rev. Billy Sunday will always be a link connecting him to his early profession. Natural gestures are seldom examples of grace and beauty. As in the voice, so with the gesture—if nature is correct, good; if not, proper modifications and changes must be secured through training.

Classification.—Numerous classifications of gestures are extant. The following is brief, useful, and comprehensive:

I. *Intellectual.*—These aid in expressing the thought, and will be considered under 1, Descriptive, 2, Locative, 3, Emphatic, and 4, Question.

II. *Emotional.* These aid in expressing the emotions, primarily, and are sometimes called emotionally-manifestive. There are as many forms as there are distinct and separate emotions that are physically expressive.

Intellectual Gestures—1. *Descriptive Action.*—The use of this gesture is to stimulate the imagination, both of the speaker and of the hearer, in more clearly perceiving objects or scenes spoken of, but not present to the view. The first essential is that the picture he describes be very vividly outlined on the canvas of the speaker's own imagination; second, that he be true to this scene, consistent in his delineation; and, third, that it be suggestive and not literal. Each one of these points will bear some amplification.

You cannot tell what you do not know, express what you do not understand; neither can you portray a scene that is not minutely and distinctly photographed on your own mind.

Be consistent. Suppose you are describing a battle scene. Do not place the cavalry on top of the infantry, but somewhere beyond; and when in the progress of battle, do not have the cavalry on one side charge upon its own infantry. Lay the scene, if possible, on the platform a little to your right or left and a little in front of you—at an angle of 45 degrees. Avoid placing your scene in the audience or back of you. If you are following the eagle in its flight, point up and out at the same angle. Scenes that take place at a distance demand that you do not point to them as though they were within three feet of you. Again, do not combine impersonation with description. When you are impersonating some one, you may act as he might under the circumstances, but when you are telling what he *did,* you must portray the scene at some distance from you, where both your audience and you may look at it. When you call the attention of the audience to an object, your eyes will first move in that direction; immediately your head, body, and hand must follow your eyes. You *must* look in the direction you point, but do not continue to do so; your eyes must turn back again to the audience. Remember you are speaking to the audience and wish to call their attention to your picture. Your eyes may flit back and forth a few times between them and your object. In description *never call attention to yourself*. When you do that, the audience sees you and loses sight of the picture. For example, when describing the flight of an eagle, do not flap your hands as though they were wings and you the bird. The imagination of your hearers will create a better eagle with you out of the picture. Neither do as the boy did, when telling about the mouth of a hydra-headed monster, by pointing to his own mouth. Although telling how Napoleon walked along the banks of the Seine with his hands behind his back, you have not the liberty to play the part of the Emperor by folding your hands behind you. It is possible that our imaginative picture of Napoleon might lose some of its majesty by your impersonation.

Descriptive gestures should be suggestive. In tracing the history of gestures, we find first what may be called the *colossal* or *effusive* age, when gestures were many and elaborate. Then came the *realistic* age—the period of realism, when everything was to be true to nature, and every gesture literal. We have now advanced to the *suggestive* age, when a few waves of the hand are, frequently, all that is needed to present the basic outline of the picture, leaving the details to the imagination of the crowd; like a modern school of painters, who make a few fundamental strokes with their brushes, and behold! a picture is before you. Your imagination has supplied the details.

Sometimes a scene may be presented in detail by a speaker, making it dramatic and very effective. It is absurd, however, to "act out" the literal meaning of figurative language. In the statement "Go back with me to the commencement of this century, etc.," do not turn around and point backward. A prospective orator at a recent declamation contest was observed to trace with his hands the circumference of an imaginary circle parallel with the floor when he recited the words, "He ascended the ladder of fame *round by round.*" When speaking of love, do not place your hand on your heart.

2. *Locative Gestures.*—These are used to point out or refer to persons or objects that actually may be seen by the audience, or in suggesting geographical directions. For the former, the index finger is appropriate. For the latter, the open hand may be used. Example: "Thou art the man." The index finger would be used. "To the south of us lies Mexico, perhaps the home of the brave, but not the land of the free." Here the open hand would be appropriate.

3. *Emphatic Gestures.*—Gesture for emphasis is most commonly used by the public speaker. It aids the vocal expression by impressing upon the eye as well as the ear the important parts of a sentence. The essentials are a quick downward stroke of the arm and hand. The length of the stroke depends on the amount of emphasis; it usually does not proceed below the waist line. There should be no rebound, a habit of many speakers. When you make an emphatic gesture, do not permit your body to be pulled over to one side. Remain erect. Both hands may be used when great emphasis is desired. If only a few gestures are made, use the right hand only. The Greeks did not use the left hand independently of the right. In fact, the left was merely used as an aid to the right, when used at all. Their form of dress— a cloak thrown loosely over the left shoulder and arm —prevented a free use of this arm for expression. We

are not so handicapped. Do not indicate emphasis by pounding the desk or striking the fist of one hand into the palm of the other. "Let your moderation be known unto all men."

4. *Question Gestures.*—Frequently a rhetorical question or a direct question is asked of the audience. The desired gesture is made by extending the right hand or both hands as you would if you were asking for the loan of a dollar and expected to get it. The palm of the hand should be up and the gesture should be completed on the important word of the question, usually the last word. The appeal is a modification of this gesture, often made with both hands.

Emotional Gestures.—These express the feelings and emotions of the individual; their office is "the revelation of hidden meanings." Words feebly express emotions, yet this important mental condition must be expressed in some way.

Your first expressive gesture was a smile, in response to a smile that was just as sweet. It was an expression of contentment, of satisfaction with your early environment. From that day to this you have daily made manifest the emotional life within you. Now, you lowered your eyebrows, pulled down the corners of your mouth, pressed your teeth tightly together, doubled up your fists, took one step forward—to show to your friends that you were angry. At another time, your eyebrows were raised, your eyes were opened wide, your mouth ajar, your hands partly raised, your body bent backward—to express your great surprise or astonishment.

On or off the platform you are continually exhibiting your moods and feelings; and doing it more truthfully than with your tongue. You may say you are brave, but the trembling lip, the quaking knee, the haunted eye, the nervous step,—prove that you are *not* brave. We often read where young maidens when asked if they loved, said, "No," with their lips, but their eyes said, "Yes."

On the platform you cannot fool an audience. You may say you are sincere, in earnest, and deeply concerned: but unless you really are, insincerity and indifference speak from every muscle of your body, and far more loudly than your words. When you are really sad, you will naturally take on the physical signs, or external manifestation. No one needs to tell you how to twist your mouth or curl your nose. Nature will take care of that, if you will permit her to do so. Again, it is important to note that the rule works the other way. If you wish to be sad, assume the physical attitude, and you will soon feel the emotion. In a dark night, just start to run and imagine something is after you, and see how long it will be until you *feel* frightened.

General Principles—I. *From Within Out.*—All gestures must have their impulse in the mind. Never permit yourself to "beat the air" or go through all kinds of contortions in a vain attempt to express what you do not understand or feel. You must *want* to gesture. Any gesture stuck into a speech at regular intervals because your teacher told you to do so, is artificial, unnatural, ineffective, and never reinforces the delivery. However, slight impulses should at times be encouraged and developed into a graceful coadjutor to delivery.

II. *Gestures Should Be Made from the Chest as a Center.*—The impulse must originate in the mind, and as it struggles for expression through the hand, it must travel through the shoulder, arm, wrist, hand, fingers, consecutively. This impulse should be observed to pass as a wave along the arm. Again, the gesture is made outward, not toward the chest; also, downward and upward from the chest.

III. *The Curve Is the Line of Grace and Beauty.*— Avoid angular movements. The preparatory movements should always be in a curved line. The downward stroke of the emphatic gesture may be quite direct. The stroke departs from the curve and approximates the straight line in proportion to the force of the gesture used. Avoid the pump-handle movement of the arm and an inflexible wrist. Do not extend your arms at right angles to your body, like a clothes rack.

IV. *A Gesture Either Precedes or Accompanies the Vocal Expression.*—Descriptive and locative gestures usually precede the vocal expression. Example: "I bid you, Go!" The force of the gesture is increased if the finger points to the open door prior to the utterance of the word "Go." The added force is the result of the mental suspense. The emphatic and the question gestures are usually given simultaneously with the vocal utterance, since they are only auxiliaries to the voice.

V. *Every Part of the Body Must Act Harmoniously.* —The eye must not say one thing and the hands another and the feet something else. Neither can one part act alone. Each division of the body must play its part in every gesture no matter how trivial. You cannot stand like a drunkard and look and speak like a king. The width of your "base" must be in proportion to the scope of your gesture.

The Mechanics of Gesture.—There are three parts to most gestures: (1) the Preparation, (2) the Execution, and (3) the Return. These divisions are best explained by taking an example: "They were souls that stood *alone.*" In wishing to emphasize the word "alone," with a downward stroke, the preparation consists in first conceiving the idea; the entire body must join the hand in preparing for this gesture. As the impulse travels down the arm, the arm takes on life at the shoulder; the elbow is bent, the fore arm curves slightly inward and moves upward, the wrist leading; the hand, with fingers slightly curved, is raised about on the level with the head. This is the *preparation.* The *execution* comes with a quick, straight downward stroke, until the hand is on a level with the waist line. In this stroke the wrist stiffens and the entire arm becomes quite rigid. The impulse goes out through the fingers, which straighten out. This final *ictus,* or kick, of the fingers must not be omitted. Remember that the impulse is to be sent out to the audience, and not lodged in the elbow or wrist, with a resulting lifeless hand. The hand should be opened toward the audience,—palm, thumb, and fingers—neither perpendicularly nor horizontally, neither rigid nor lifeless. In the *return* the muscles of the arm and wrist are relaxed and the arm falls back to the side of the body in a natural position. The return must not show a "lifeless" arm. It must not fall so as to slap against the side of the body, and jingle the keys or coins in your pocket.

The preparation should be slow and begin on the first word, "They," and rise until the word "stood" is reached. There will be an emphatic pause before the word "alone;" during this pause the hand must be poised in the air; in the execution of the stroke the word "alone" is spoken with emphasis.

The question gesture is made in about the same way

except that the arm is not raised on high and the hand is turned supine while being extended. These gestures are not easy in execution and require much practice to attain grace and ease.

Time well the *preparation*. Most novices begin too soon and raise the hand too rapidly. There should be no "rebound" on the stroke. One gesture can often be used as a preparation for a second. Thus one gesture may be made to glide into another. Seldom should the arm or hand remain suspended in the air for any length of time. Keep your hands in motion or let them hang quietly by your side.

The preparation is important and is in itself significant. Roosevelt, in using this gesture, slowly raised his hand above his head, making a long preparation; and during this period the audience held its breath because that hand must come down, and it usually did very forcefully upon some very important and emphatic phrase.

Planes of Gestures.—Three horizontal planes are usually recognized: 1. Elevated plane with the head as the center; 2. The Horizontal plane with the chest as the center; and 3. the Downward plane with the waist line as the center.

Vertically, nearly all the gestures should be made midway between the front and side. The question gesture is made more directly in front.

On the Platform.—You are seated on the platform, or, perchance, you may be called from the audience. In either case, the moment you rise from your seat, you begin to speak—with your body. It is possible that while still seated upon the platform, you expressed your personality; and impressed the audience favorably or prejudiced them against you. Sit erect in your chair, feet flat upon the floor, knees close together. Do not show the soles of your shoes to your audience. Gentlemen may put one knee over the other, but not the ankle of one foot on top of the knee of the other leg. Practice getting out of your chair gracefully. Usually just after rising, make a slight bow to the presiding officer and at the same time say, "Mr. Chairman." The chairman remains standing until he has acknowledged your salutation. Should the chairman call you to the platform from the audience, it is sometimes best not to address the chair until after you are in position to speak.

Walk easily, spiritedly, and quietly to the center of the stage, and, ordinarily, stop when about three feet from the front edge. Do not walk in a straight line, but curve slightly inward, so as to approach the front of the stage directly from the rear. Guard against overdoing the curve. Do not march like a soldier on parade, nor, cat-like, tiptoe to your position.

You are standing before the audience; shall you bow? Not unless you are a celebrity and you are greeted with "prolonged and enthusiastic applause." When the applause ceases, or if there is no applause, as soon as you find yourself in a position to speak, wait a second, take a good, deep breath (it will relieve your embarrassment), and take a good look at your audience. Stand erect, chest out, head up, hands hanging loosely by your side, one foot slightly in advance of the other—and you are ready to say, "Ladies and Gentlemen," in a pure, clear, deliberate, intelligent and respectful manner. *Never* begin speaking before you are in position. *Always* face your audience squarely. Do not present a side view. Avoid turning your head from side to side without turning your entire body, including your feet. Avoid keeping your feet still and swaying your body from side to side, like a little school girl who swings her body in unison with the rhythm of her selection. This swaying is encouraged when neither foot is in advance of the other. Do not shift too often, neither should you stand like a wooden Indian before a cigar store. When you come to a transition in your thought, indicate this by changing your position. If your right foot is in advance of the left, step forward with your left foot, or step backward with your right. One step is usually sufficient. Take two steps for a very important transition. Your weight should be on your rear foot when delivering unemotional matter, but when you become in earnest always move your weight to the front foot.

When addressing the right half of the audience, it is well to face the far corner of the room. Your right foot should be in advance of the left and you will gesture with your right hand or with both hands. When in this position, *never* gesture toward the *left* half of the audience. This compels the right hand to cross in front of the body and also makes you twist your body, presenting a side view to the audience.

Do not hang on one hip, leaning over like a tired horse. Avoid raising both heels from the floor at the same time, or bending your ankle and standing on the edge of your foot. The most difficult task the young speaker has to accomplish is to keep his hands in view of the audience. His feet seem to him conspicuous enough; but his hands! He just must do something with them, so he puts them in his pockets, behind his back, folds them in front of him, twists the lapel of his coat, or his watch chain—instead of letting them fall where the attraction of gravity will take them.

It has been well said that no man can consider himself a speaker until he can stand still. Stand quiet until the motion of your body directly aids your vocal expression; and when that time comes, do not give a "hunch" with your shoulder, or a jerk with your hand, but let that impulse develop into a graceful and helpful gesture.

The number of gestures depends on your temperament, your earnestness and the nature of the thought or feeling you desire to express. But by all means seek a variety of gestures. Do not use the same one a number of times in succession.

Your action should not be so distinctively individualistic and eccentric as to identify you whenever you speak.

Do not pace the platform. Those who do, have the appearance of a tiger trying to get out of his cage. But if you find it necessary to take a few steps, be sure that it is done while you are speaking, or "walk on the lines" as the actors say; but do not take your eyes from the audience to look where you step. Do not lean on the desk beside you. But it is permissible to rest lightly one or both hands on a table or desk when it gives you a "restful" appearance.

If you want your coat buttoned, attend to it before you get on the platform; and do not change your mind about it after you begin speaking. If you must use your handkerchief, take it from your pocket or from the desk while you are speaking, calling as little attention to it as possible. Remember that *any motion that does not directly aid you detracts from your effectiveness.*

When you have completed your speech, make a *slight* bow to your audience and quietly resume your seat.

A Closing Word.—Some will say that all such

minute directions are nonsense. "If I have anything to say, I get up and say it; and if I must remember all the mechanical rules suggested while on the platform, I couldn't think of anything to say." That is the greatest deception on the American platform to-day. Students appear before the public to speak before they have mastered the first principle of public speaking, and some even think themselves adepts. The same logic would place before a suffering public young musicians before they had mastered their first lesson on the piano, or before they could sing the scale. Usually in music we are willing to drill upon fundamental technique until it becomes automatic, until our fingers unconsciously go to the right key as soon as the eye sees the note. He who desires to become a speaker must master the simple rules of the platform and practice them until *they* become automatic; and when he has done that, he is ready to devote *all* his time to the thought side of his speech and his *action* on the platform will be properly performed; and he will then be on the right road to becoming a successful speaker. If you could see yourself, while on the stage, as others see you, you would be more willing to improve your physical expression.

The intellectual gestures, which are more mechanical than the emotional, may well be practiced before a mirror for the attainment of graceful and effective movements. Delsarte, physical culture, gymnastic exercise, are valuable to practice in your room, to make your body more flexible, graceful, and powerful; but do not impose these physical calisthenics upon the audience while speaking.

After all, the training of students in physical expression should, for the most part, be negative. Tell them what to avoid—what not to do. Direct their movements; do not create them. Ideal bodily expression is suggested in the lines:

> "His pure and eloquent blood
> Spoke in his cheek, and so distinctly wrought,
> That one might almost say his body thought."

CALISTHENICS PREPARATORY TO GESTURE

I. Stand erect, chest prominent, body in easy poise.

II. Dangle the hands, and shake the arms freely from the shoulders (a) at the side; (b) held horizontally in front, and (c) horizontally at the side.

III. Rotate the body on the hip-joints, letting the arms and hands swing freely. Begin slowly, turning the trunk and head as much as possible, then gradually accelerate until the movement is as rapid and energetic as possible.

IV. Raise the upper arm slowly, the forearm and hand trailing. Now unfold the arm and hand by consciously vitalizing in turn the forearm, wrist, palm, fingers, the hand opening at about the level of the hips and midway between the front and side. Practice this with the right arm and hand, then the left, then both together.

V. The same as No. IV, except that the hands are to be unfolded at about the level of the shoulders.

VI. Practice the foregoing unfolding movement, first with one arm and hand, and then with both together, the hands unfolding directly in front at first; then, in succession, during five or six repetitions, end the movement at varying angles between the front and the side.

VII. Move your arm and hand up and down, your

wrist preceding, letting your hand and fingers bend as the hair of a brush when painting.

VIII. Imagine you are raising a pound ball held in the palm of the hand; raise it to a level with the head, then cast it down, letting it roll out of the palm and over the fingers.

IX. Practice turning from side to side. First turn your eyes to the right, then turn your face in that direction, step back with the right foot and as you do so swing your body toward the right and at the same time turn the left heel outward.

X. Turn toward the left in a similar manner.

EXAMPLES FOR DRILL IN MECHANICS OF GESTURE

I. *Descriptive Gesture:*

1. The hawk swooped down to the ground and carried away a little chick.

2. Two armies were encamped on opposite sides of the river. The Federals here, the Constitutionalists, there. A mile down the river was a lake. Overhead the sun looked down on the silver stream as it flowed peacefully towards its goal.

3. I had rather have lived in a hut with the vines growing over the door and the grapes growing purple in the kisses of the autumn sun, with my loving wife knitting by my side as the day died out of the sky.
Happiness and Liberty.   INGERSOLL.

4. The assassin enters, through the window already prepared, into an unoccupied apartment. With noiseless foot he paces the lonely hall half-lighted by the moon. He winds up the ascent of the stairs and reaches the door of the chamber. He enters and beholds his victim before him. The face of the innocent sleeper is turned from the murderer, and the beams of the moon, resting on the gray locks of the aged temples,

show him where to strike. The fatal blow is given. The murderer retreats, retraces his steps to the window, passes out through it as he came in, and escapes.
The White Murder Trial. WEBSTER.

5. She cut his bonds. He stood upright, looked round with a laugh of wild exultation, clapped his hands together, sprang from the ground as if in transport on finding himself at liberty. He looked so wild that Jeanie trembled at what she had done.

"Let me out," said the young savage.

"I wanna, unless you promise—"

"Then I'll make you glad to let us both out."

He seized the lighted candle and threw it among the flax, which was instantly in a flame. Jeanie screamed and ran out of the room; the prisoner rushed passed her, threw open a window in the passage, jumped into the garden, sprang over its inclosure, bounded through the woods like a deer, and gained the seashore. Meantime, the fire was extinguished; but the prisoner was sought in vain.
The Heart of Midlothian. SCOTT.

6. The dog now aroused himself and sat on his haunches, his ears moving quickly backward and forward. He kept his eyes fixed on me with a look so strange that he concentrated all my attention to himself. Slowly he rose up, all his hair bristling, and stood perfectly rigid, and with the same wild stare. I had no time, however, to examine the dog. Presently my servant emerged from his room; and if I ever saw horror in the human face, it was then. He passed by me quickly, saying, in a whisper, "Run, run! it is after me!" He gained the door to the landing, pulled it open, and rushed forth. I followed him into the landing involuntarily, calling him to stop; but, without heeding me, he bounded down the stairs, clinging to the banisters, and taking several steps at a time. I heard, where I stood, the street door open,—heard it clap to. I was left alone in the haunted house.
The Haunted and the Haunters. POE.

7.   A granite cliff on either shore:
       A highway poised in air;
    Above the wheels of traffic roar;
     Below, the fleets sail fair;—

And in and out, forever more,
   The surging tides of ocean pour,
And past the towers the white gulls soar,
   And winds the sea-clouds bear.

The Brooklyn Bridge.   PROCTOR.

8.   "And now depart! and when
    Thy heart is heavy, and thine eyes are dim,
    Lift up thy prayer beseechingly to Him
      Who, from the tribes of men,
    Selected thee to feel his chastening rod,
    Depart! O leper! and forget not God!"

The Leper.   WILLIS.

II. *Locative Gesture:*

1. Go! you will find the door open.
2. I mean you, and you, and you.
3. Do you see the bird on that twig?
4. The South is the land of promise.
5. Thou art the man.

III. *Emphatic Gesture:*

1. I demand to know the *truth*.
2. Jack, you are not my *friend*.
3. I love him because he is *truthful*.
4. I will never *stoop* to conquer.
5. *Too low* they build who build beneath the stars.
6. This restless world is full of *chances*.
7. My answer will be a *blow*.
8. The motive is *unworthy*.
9. Truth gives *wings* to strength.
10. *Trust men* and they will be *true* to you

IV. *Question Gesture:*

1. Must I stand here and *beg?*
2. Is wisdom better than *rubies?*
3. Is *wisdom* the principal thing?
4. Have I not *proved* this proposition?
5. Must I lend *you* a dollar?

V. *Emotional Gesture:*

1. Let a number of students get on the stage and look intently at some object. Have criticisms come from the class.

2. Bring to the class a written report of your obervations of the "foot work" of some speaker.

3. Observe a group of children playing. Imitate before the class the physical expression of some one child and have the class determine the mood illustrated.

4. Have each student in turn express bodily certain general types of emotions, as: Joy, Grief, Love, Hate, Courage, Fear, Hope, Despair, Defiance, Anger, Surprise.

VI

FORMS OF PUBLIC ADDRESS

Numerous and varied have been the classifications of public addresses. The classification here used is both historic and psychologic. Public speech is primarily a mental process—one mind must influence other minds. The method employed is largely dependent on the *purpose* of the address: what is the main object of the speaker in making the speech? And this chief purpose must never be lost sight of by the speaker. The speaker may desire (1) to give information; (2) to arouse the emotions; (3) to move men to action, or to make a choice; or (4) a combination of these purposes.

I. The Essay.—This form of public speaking is primarily *intellectual*. It is that form of public address wherein is used such material, style of composition, and manner of delivery as will best convey to the minds of the listeners the information the speaker has to impart. The purpose is to convince. The essay is usually read from a manuscript; however, the *purpose* of the address, not the manner of delivery, determines its classification. It may be 1, descriptive; 2, expository; 3, narrative; or 4, argumentative. It is *descriptive* when it delineates the attributes of an object with respect to some one period of time. It is a vocal photograph. The description may be so vivid, so artistic as to arouse various emotions and actions; but that is a secondary effect, not a primary purpose. It is *narrative* when it relates the succession of events. The purpose is to tell what happened. It is *expository* when some subject is outlined and developed. It formulates a logical definition, describing its limitations, and is usually applied to some abstract subject. Exposition explains and teaches. It is *argumentative* when its aim is to take certain facts and principles to discover other facts and principles not yet known. It is a process of reasoning used to convince the mind of the truth or falsity of a certain proposition. Argumentation is the process of reaching out after the unknown, a search after the truth. The evidence used, the process employed, and the resulting conclusion or inference is called proof. The argumentative essay usually will have for its introduction a definition of terms, a history of the question under discussion, and the partition or general divisions. The body consists of an outline of the merits and demerits of the proposition. The conclusion should state the writer's final convictions in the matter and a brief summary of the points which determined his decision, or the conclusion he has reached after a thorough and impartial investigation.

The argumentative essay is not unlike a debate, but both sides usually are presented by the writer. Remember when writing an essay always to have a definite audience or a particular class of readers in mind.

II. The Oration.—The purpose of the oration is to move the *will*. When the will is stimulated, it functions in two ways—through action and by choosing. The orator's duty is not completed when he has convinced his hearers or aroused their emotions; he must persuade them to act or make a decision. Now, the will is moved through the medium of the emotions; the emotions are excited by ideas operating on the mind. Any idea clearly, concisely and fully comprehended by the intellect awakens in the individual certain emotions which correspond to that idea. When the emotions dominate the will, expression of the idea is attempted if possible; if an objective expression is not possible at that time, a resolution is formed to carry out that impulse at some future time. Thus we see that the oratorical process is indirect, intricate, and difficult.

The definite means employed by the orator will be discussed in other chapters. But it should be borne clearly in mind that the presentation of a convincing array of facts, the portrayal of vivid pictures, the tapping of the fountains of the emotions, the swaying of the crowd from joy to tears, from tears to joy, from anger to humility, from humility to anger, adding fuel to fire, compelling the crowd to see but one definite picture and to feel one definite emotion at a time, until the cumulative effect is manifested in positive voluntary action,—this is the task of the orator. All this and nothing less. "Oratory," says Beecher, "is the art of influencing conduct with truth sent home by all the resources of the living man." There is, perhaps, no better model of oratory, also illustrating the sequel of a successful effort in this field, than the funeral oration of Mark Antony over the body of Julius Cæsar. About all the "resources of the living man" were utilized, and the result proved the wisdom of the means employed when the mob, overwhelmed by the single idea of revenge, carried out the wishes of the orator.

Suggested Outline.—First of all, when you attempt to write an oration, do not write an essay; remember that an oration appeals to the will through the emotions, and that it is not primarily argumentative. In writing an essay, you describe, narrate, or explain; in a debate, you argue, prove, and convince; but when you deliver an oration, you assert and persuade. Remember, again, that the orator is a leader, and as such the people have confidence in him; that when a statement is made, it is presumed that the orator has thought out the whole problem, considered all sides of the question, and is now giving the result of his deliberation; and the audience does not care to be carried through all the diverse and devious ways along which the speaker himself passed to arrive at the conviction which he now holds, but is ready to listen to his conclusions.

Subject.—An oration should be written upon some fundamental and universal subject, some theme which will move men to action. You can write an essay on "Radium," "Flying Machines," etc.; but for an oration you want a subject like "Child Labor," or "The Influence of the Mother." It must be some phase of Duty, Happiness, or Virtue. If you write on a subject like "Robert E. Lee," be careful not to make it biographical. Your oration for contest purposes should be typical, and therefore should be patterned after the other forms of orations.

The model oration must have an appropriate introduction, in length about one-tenth of the entire production. It may be a general statement bearing directly on the theme, or it may present an interesting, graphic picture germane to the subject. In this the oration and essay differ little.

The body of the oration, about eight times the length of the introduction, should be divided into two parts:

1, the problem; 2, the solution. The problem deals with some present need, something which formerly existed or which should now be changed, some wrong that should be righted. It presents a dark picture, and the blacker this can be painted the better. The solution solves the problem; explains the remedy for the past or present ills. It portrays a bright picture, the whiter the better. The conclusion is an appeal to the audience to accept the orator's solution of the problem.

To illustrate: Suppose the subject is "George Washington." The introduction will dwell on heroes, the value of great men, etc.; or, perhaps, will present a picture of a young surveyor, or a description of a vine-clad mansion on a Virginia plantation. Since the purpose of an introduction is to gain the good will of the audience and to arouse interest, the particular type is not essential. The problem might narrate the critical political situation of the Colonists at the beginning of the American Revolution, and the dangers threatening the new Federation. The solution would explain how Washington solved this problem, overcame the existing evils, and became a mighty factor in establishing the United States, discussing especially such traits of Washington as were exercised in solving the problems before him. The conclusion would be an appeal to the audience to accept the judgment of the orator in his selection of those characteristics, and an encouragement to cultivate similar virtues in solving their own problems.

Again, "An Unknown Hero." Problem; The awful condition of the lepers on Molokai Island, and their need of a friend. Solution: Father Damien's sacrifice in going to their assistance and ameliorating their condition. Conclusion: "Go thou and do likewise" to fellow-beings in distress, and exercise the virtues of the Unknown Hero.

Again, take some social, economical, or political subject; as, "Modern Moloch." Problem: Frightful condition of child labor. Solution: Appropriate legislation, or Socialism, or any other remedy which may seem adequate. Conclusion: Vote right, or apply the remedy suggested.

Time usually permits of but one big problem and one appropriate solution. There can be no fixed ratio relative to the problem and solution. Sometimes the problem is by far the more important; sometimes the problem may almost be conceded; it may be an evil so prominent that it is universally recognized and admitted, hence should be touched on lightly. Again, the solution may often be granted if the problem is manifest. However, an appropriate problem and adequate solution must always be in evidence in some degree.

Since an oration is designed to persuade the hearer to perform some act, there must necessarily be something to be changed. The will is not stimulated to activity without an incentive. The audience must be made conscious that present conditions are not satisfactory. But this is not sufficient. A reasonable remedy must be advanced or the will still refuses to act. The appeal must strike home; to be effective, it must be made as personal as possible.

Orations may be given the following subdivisions:

1. *Forensic.*—The term "forensic" comes from the Latin "forensis," the forum, or market place; the courtroom where every Roman could speak in defense of himself or his friend. It is usually an attempt to arrive at some conclusion concerning facts that have occurred

in the past. Hence it is often called the oratory of the bar, and is to some degree argumentative in character. However, it is the purpose of the lawyer to persuade the jury or judge to vote in favor of his client. The final result is immediate action. Study in this connection Daniel Webster's "Jury Address" and Robert Emmett's "Vindication."

Formal debating, separately treated in Chapter IX, is a special form of forensic oratory and has for a long time been recognized as a very important phase of public speaking. It is an intellectual battle, and most of our great speakers received their early training in debating societies.

2. *Deliberative.*—The oratory of the assembly. Any speech made with the purpose of inducing an audience to accept or reject a given policy for the future may be called a deliberative speech. This includes not only speeches made in congressional and parliamentary assemblies, but in all deliberative bodies such as synods, conferences, and other public meetings. Examples: "Freedom or Slavery," by Patrick Henry; and "Gettysburg Address," by Abraham Lincoln.

3. *Pulpit.*—This is the oratory of the Church. More sermons are delivered in the United States in a week than any other form of public address. Most of the preaching to-day is expository in outline; but most of the evangelical sermons follow this plan. That is, "Christ" is the subject for each sermon. After an appropriate introduction some form of *sin* is the theme, which is the *problem.* After this has been denounced in no uncertain terms, the *solution* is advanced. Christ came to save men from sin. In the conclusion we have an appeal to the audience to accept the solution to the

problem; and they are urged to receive Christ into their own lives to cleanse them from their sins. Examples: "The Evil That Men Do Lives After Them," by Phillips Brooks.

4. *Demonstrative,* or Occasional, includes a miscellaneous group of public addresses dealing with affairs of the present time. The principal subdivisions are: A. Eulogy, B. Commemorative Address, C. Political or Campaign Speech, D. Short Address, or informal "talks," and E. After-Dinner Speech.

A. The Eulogy. This is a very common form of address. Be careful that the eulogies are not made too biographical. They are in the main a recount of such qualities of a great man as served to make him famous. Remember that the general setting or the atmosphere of the Eulogy must harmonize with the occasion. Death is an occasion for kind words and lofty, reverential ideas. Your style need not be direct nor commonplace, but should be chaste, lofty, and beautiful.

B. The Commemorative Address. These occasional addresses are very popular and sometimes quite formal. Under this heading may be grouped the following divisions:

a. Anniversaries. Commemorating such events as birthdays of great men, noted battles, important discoveries, national holidays, etc.

b. Dedications. These addresses are given at the laying of the corner stone of buildings, celebrating the completion of a church, a monument, or a hall, etc.

c. Unveilings. These are occasioned by the presentation of a statue, a fountain, or a painting, to the public or to some organization.

d. Commencement Address. This is a very familiar

form of public address delivered to graduating classes and their friends.

e. Miscellaneous Types. Speeches of Welcome, of Farewell, of Introduction, of Acceptance, Nomination, and many other forms may be enumerated.

The style of composition does not differ greatly from that used in the Eulogy. The diction should be exalted, and in keeping with the occasion. Two main lines of thought are usually followed, (1) An exposition or a narration of the events, and (2) An estimate of the significance and importance of the occasion.

C. The Political Speech. This form is familiar to every boy and girl. It is the "stump" speech heard with biennial regularity. The purpose is to secure the votes of the people at the next election. Since the election does not take place at the close of the speech, this form is more argumentative than sermons or most jury addresses. Though appeals to the emotions are not lacking, vivid pictures fade as days pass by; but good, sound reasoning, plain, solid facts invite thought and stand the test of time. It enables the voter to compare the arguments advanced by the various candidates at his leisure. If the voter is a man of judgment and not too biased, he must eventually decide to vote for the man presenting the most plausible argument, and not for the "barn stormer" and the "spellbinder." The following illustration from an article in the *Reader Magazine,* by Mr. Herbert Quick, in October, 1907, needs no comment:

This "natural orator" [speaking of a gubernatorial campaign in Georgia] was the handsome, eloquent, convivial, jovial, and kind-hearted lieutenant governor, Dr. R. M. Cunningham, who challenged Mr. Comer to a joint debate, and fared as did the first opponent of Tom Johnson, of Cleveland, in Johnson's first campaign. In both cases it was a spellbinder against the man with the bludgeon of facts. Dr. Cunningham felt at once that new standards of discussion had been set up. His eloquent tributes to the beauty of Alabama's women and the chivalry of her sons were as fine as heart could wish. Comer stuck to freight rates. Cunningham cried out in polished periods for good roads. Everybody is for good roads, said Comer, but how about the pass evil and the lobby? Cunningham drew tears as he spoke for the "old veterans." Comer replied that he was one of them, while Cunningham was not; but how about reciprocal demurrage? Then Cunningham came over to Comer's platform, and demanded more reform than did Comer. Comer, clinging to his man like a bulldog, replied that this was unconstitutional nonsense. Gradually it dawned on the spellbinder that something was walking remorselessly over him, trampling out his political life, and that the something was Braxton Bragg Comer, the man who could not make a speech. Comer carried sixty of the sixty-seven counties of the state, and won by twenty thousand votes.

D. The Short Address. Many informal talks are made every day—five- or ten-minute speeches. These, as a rule, have brief introductions and conclusions. The object is to present in as brief and succinct a manner as possible some one point. These short speeches have become of the utmost importance in our busy life. Legislation is decided in committee rooms, not on the floor of our legislative halls. So important, indeed, is this type of address that the next chapter treats of it exclusively.

E. After-Dinner Speeches. If you are going to take a leading part in the community in which you live you frequently will be called upon to give an after-dinner speech.

To give a speech of this character is no easy task. Study carefully some good after-dinner addresses. Henry W. Grady, Mark Twain, and Henry Van Dyke are good speakers to follow.

It is presumed by all on such an occasion that everybody is contented, happy, and in a jovial mood. Do not preach to your hearers. They expect to be entertained and amused. They do not care to do any hard thinking. So give them something light and diverting, but do not be silly. Many begin with a story. Some end with a story; some have nothing but stories all the way through. Suppose you vary this program a little. Begin without a story. You might have a few appropriate ones to illustrate a point now and then, but be sure they are not too familiar. Nothing else that you can say would be quite so complete a failure as to have your speech filled with stories that everybody knows. A good story is not easy to find, and very difficult to tell successfully. Watch the magazines and newspapers for good jokes; keep a number on tap; they will be of great service to you as a speaker on various occasions.

Though you do not want to give anything heavy at such a time, do, by all means, say something worth while; but tell it in a pleasing way. To speak briefly, to make a good point, to be entertaining, are the essentials of a good after-dinner speech.

5. *Contest Orations.*—These orations are so widely different from the other groups that they constitute a distinct and separate class. (1) They partake of all the other forms; they represent the essence of the other four groups. (2) They are prepared for an exceedingly formal and typical occasion. (3) Though they resemble a real oration, the ultimate purpose is to win the vote of the judges. (4) But while the occasion is a contest in excellence, it should be remembered that the judges must be won as part of the audience.

Follow the general outline suggested in this chapter under the topic, THE ORATION.

III. The Reproduction.—In this group are placed those forms of public address that are delivered by some one other than the author; though sometimes a writer "speaks" his own selections, or "stars" in his own plays. The purpose of this group is to arouse the *emotions.* Our literary masterpieces are used for this purpose.

The subdivisions are 1. *declamation,* 2. *story-telling,* 3. *reading;* dramatic monologue where one person takes the part of a number of characters, 4. *dramatics,* or *acting;* plays where each person represents a single character.

IV. The Popular Lecture.—This is sometimes called the Chautauqua lecture. It is frequently didactic in the main; but in order to draw and hold a crowd, the lecturer presents his thought in a popular style, interweaving bits of humor, interesting anecdotes, some poetry, appealing to the emotions, and often makes a direct attempt to reach the will. The successful popular lecture may be said to have a *variety* of purposes, and appeals to the intellect, the emotions, and the will.

EXERCISES

I. Distinguish between the Essay and the Oration. Between the Lecture and the After-Dinner Speech. Between the various kinds of orations.

II. Write a descriptive essay of 500 words characterizing in the blackest terms a man who deserves all you may be able to call him.

III. Write a descriptive essay of 500 words characterizing a man of the opposite type—praise him in the most flattering terms.

IV. Write a eulogy of a man or woman you have intimately known.

V. Have each student be prepared to tell two good

pointed stories. Have them first name the point they wish to illustrate with the stories. Both stories to illustrate the same point.

VI. Have each student give a three-minute talk on "The Need of Orations To-day."

VII. Have each student prepare a contest oration of 1000 words of some national character of his own choosing—observing the suggestions made in this chapter concerning the Introduction, Problem, Solution, and Conclusion.

VIII. Write an oration on one of the following subjects:

1. International Peace.
2. Need of Modern Business Ethics.
3. The Tongue of the World.
4. The Voter Who Does Not Vote.
5. The Voice of the People.
6. Tammany.
7. Africa in America.
8. Waste in Education.
9. Political Machines.
10. Child Labor.
11. Law Enforcement.
12. Politics in Education.
13. The Spirit of Cæsar.
14. Penniless Criminals and Justice.
15. Shall an Unjust Law be Enforced?
16. House Divided Against Itself.
17. A Federated Europe.
18. A World Citizen.
19. As a Man Thinketh.
20. Moral Leadership.
21. The Power of a Purpose.
22. The Measure of a Man.
23. The Four-Square Man.
24. Theodore Roosevelt.
25. Iago.

VII

METHODS OF PREPARING AND DELIVERING A SPEECH

When a man is called upon to make a speech—whether he fortunately has something to say or unfortunately has to say something—he has a selection of five ways:

I. It may be written and then read.
II. It may be written and memorized.
III. It may be spoken extempore.
IV. It may be partly written and partly extemporized.
V. It may be impromptu.

I. Reading a Speech—*Advantages.*—On occasions when the speaker must be exceedingly careful what he says and how he says it, this is the safest plan. He cannot then be misquoted, whether intentionally or carelessly. The inexperienced speaker had better write out his speech and learn to read it well than to attempt any other method and fail. This method is the easiest. Usually speeches read from manuscript are worth listening to, as they have been very carefully prepared. Scientific discoveries are usually thus presented to the public.

Disadvantages.—It is difficult to interest an audience when reading a paper. In the first place, a reader is hampered in adequate physical expression. Again, he cannot adjust his speech to the tenor of the audience. To be a success, he must be able to judge accurately his audience before he speaks. Certain events may occur after the writing of his paper and before its reading which necessitate a change in manuscript on short notice; or part of it may be wholly inappropriate.

Caution.—If reading from manuscript seems necessary or advisable, cultivate the ability to read well. Look at your audience as much as possible while reading, and for as long a time as possible. Hold up your manuscript almost on a level with and within easy distance from your eyes, so that you can look at your audience by merely turning your eyes slightly upward. In short, make your reading a personal message, and allow the manuscript to interfere as little as possible with a personal grapple with your audience.

11. Speaking Memoriter — *Advantages.* — This method gives the most artistic results. It is a safe and popular method for beginners. It has all the advantages of the first method and only a few of the disadvantages. This method was and is used by some of our most able orators. Demosthenes used it whenever time permitted. Cæsar used it at the trial of the friends of Catiline; Webster used it in his Plymouth and Bunker Hill orations, and in his Eulogy on Adams and Jefferson. Everett and Wendell Phillips wrote many of their orations and memorized them.

Disadvantages.—It is an enormous tax upon the memory. It takes much practice to "speak" a selection creditably. Even the best memories are at times treacherous.

Cautions.—Commit the idea and thought as well as the words. Deliver your speech as though it were extemporaneous—do not let the audience know that it is memorized. Do not use this method except when you have plenty of time and the production is not too long. Avoid repeating it so often that the delivery becomes mechanical and lifeless.

III. Speaking Extempore — *Advantages.* — This form of speaking requires careful preparation, a memorized outline, leaving the exact language for expression "upon the spur of the moment." This permit a hand-to-hand grapple with the audience. The speaker can take advantage of any circumstances requiring a modification of his prepared material. He must *think* as he speaks, thus avoiding a mechanical repetition of words. If his speech has not been well adapted to the audience, he can modify it as the occasion demands. He can take advantage of opportunities to speak when he might not have time to prepare a manuscript. We are living in an age when a short, business-like speech is most in demand. The extempore method also permits the orator to profit by the inspiration of the audience. Most of our gems of oratory were produced in this way; flashes of brilliant eloquence come, as Webster said, "if they come at all, like the outbreak of a fountain from the earth, or the bursting forth of volcanic fires, with spontaneous, original, native force." The extempore method cultivates definite thinking and accurate speaking. Become a good extempore speaker.

Disadvantages.—Extempore speaking is likely to be ill-prepared, repetitious. Beginners frequently have their minds and vocal powers practically paralyzed when they appear before an audience—they can neither think nor speak. Many students while thinking of *what* to say have very little time left to garb their thoughts properly; hence their diction and style are poor. Not following a carefully constructed outline, they wander "like the chaff before the wind."

Cautions.—Prepare about four times as much material as you think you will need. Have a well prepared and thoroughly memorized outline. *Never carry a scrap of paper before your audience.* Do not think that all you need is a "gift of gab;" many a speaker is more wordy than brainy. Speak slowly at first; construct your sentences carefully. A large, ready vocabulary is absolutely essential. *Practice,* PRACTICE.

IV. Combined Method — *Advantages.* — There are a number of combinations: (1) To read part of the speech and to give from memory the most important portions. (2) To read part and to extemporize part. (3) To memorize the introduction, conclusion and a few choice paragraphs in the body of the speech and to extemporize the rest. This last combination has been used with remarkable success by many of our most brilliant speakers: Cicero, John Bright, Pitt, Gladstone, Beecher, and many others. It carries with it about all the advantages enumerated under the first three methods.

Disadvantages.—It requires great skill to pass from the extemporized to the memorized portions without being detected by the audience. The speaker usually "recites" in a quality of style different from that in which he "speaks."

Cautions.—Begin by committing the introductions and conclusions; then memorize large bits of your written speech. Memorize choice extracts from noted authors— a few lines of descriptive matter, a choice combination of effective adjectives, etc. You can often use these to advantage. Cultivate a fluent and graceful transition from the one style to the other.

V. Speaking Impromptu — *Advantages.* — Speaking without any special preparation is not an easy task. It demands a broad general preparation. But he who has this foundation frequently can make effective speeches when others are obliged to keep silent. To be able to analyze quickly and to marshal your thoughts together at a moment's notice is a power admired and longed for by all public speakers. Few, however, reach the point where they care to rely upon their general preparation on important occasions. Preachers and other speakers who are frequently called upon for a sermon or speech on short notice should carry a few good outlines for addresses continually in mind.

Disadvantages.—The impromptu method has too many disadvantages for enumeration. Those who wait for the "inspiration of the moment" find out when too late that the moment has come without the inspiration. Special preparation should always be made if time permits. You have no right to impose on the audience in this way. The people in the audience have a right to the best you can give them.

Cautions.—Always keep a few good speeches "on tap." You often are called upon when you least expect it. Keep a few good stories, a few salient ideas, a paragraph from some good speech, which with little modification you can adapt to meet many emergencies. Many a man has been admired for his ability to extemporize or speak impromptu when he was speaking a set speech or repeating a partly memorized prayer. However, the speaker is not always conscious of doing this. Choice bits of your own composition may have been memorized years ago and these will naturally and spontaneously come to your mind; and all you need to do is to recall the thought and they will clothe themselves in the same choice language as upon a previous and more formal occasion. Channing said, "The day of inspiration has gone by. Everything which I have ever said which was worth remembering, was all carefully prepared."

VIII

EXTEMPORE SPEAKING

Quintilian said, "the richest fruit of all our study, and the most ample recompense for the extent of our labor is the *faculty of speaking extempore*. Not that I make it an object that an orator should prefer to speak extempore; I only wish that he should be able to do so."

Since the ability to speak extemporaneously is considered the best all-round method, and since it is demanded especially in our day and time, let us give it a little more detailed attention.

Extempore Speaking in Secondary Schools.—Can extempore speaking advantageously be taught to pupils in high schools? Yes; but, of course, any plan adopted must be suited to the ages of the pupils. The reason that many teachers who try to teach this method do not succeed as well as they should like, is largely due to their lack of faith in this manner of speaking. They give up too soon. Results do not appear at once. Like the cultivation of all life habits, it takes time. The ability to think logically while before an audience, and to select automatically and instantaneously the right words to express one's thoughts does not come "overnight."

Can Extempore Speaking be Acquired?—Can this method of speaking be taught at all? Or is it a gift, a natural endowment, like brown eyes? Here is some testimony. Professor Bredif says that "Pericles never wrote his orations. Like Aristotle, Themistocles, and other ancient orators, he improvised after laborious meditation." Cicero usually used the memoriter method, but when pressed for time resorted to the extempore.

Of the group of famous parliamentary orators in England during the eighteenth century, William Pitt, Lord Mansfield, and Charles James Fox all used the extempore method. Mr. Pitt, along with his gifts, natural and acquired, had a marked susceptibility for being aroused by the occasion. His overwhelming spontaneity and high personal character swept everything before him. It is said that such was the excitement when he spoke that it was impossible to report him, and the speech which in its delivery and publication overthrew Walpole's ministry was reduced to writing by Dr. Johnson.

Mansfield was preëminent as an extempore speaker. At an early age he gave promise of that ready command of his mother tongue which was later shown in his speeches. This was secured by a constant translation and retranslation of Greek and Roman orators, which also gave him a knowledge of the principles of eloquence, a study which he began to pursue with all diligence upon his entry into the university. This he continued after beginning his law studies, especially in the practice of extempore speaking, for which he prepared himself with such fullness and accuracy that his notes were useful to him in after life, both at the bar and on the bench.

The fame of Fox as a parliamentary orator and debater is well known, although he began awkwardly and abounded in repetitions. He was an extempore speaker solely. Oratorically, Fox's ambition was to become a powerful debater, "one who goes out in all weathers," instead of carrying with him to the House a set speech drawn up beforehand. In this course he persevered until he became the acknowledged leader of the Whig party in the House of Commons. He answered well to his own definition of an orator—"one who can give immediate, instantaneous expression to his thoughts." He mastered his subject and accumulated facts. How he used these facts depended upon the mood of the assembly that he rose to address. Burke affirmed him to be "the most brilliant and accomplished debater the world ever saw."

Of English parliamentary orators, the two most illustrious examples are: John Bright and William Gladstone. Bright began by committing his speeches to memory, but he soon abandoned this method as both clumsy and exhausting.

Turning now to American orators, we find that the most famous representative of the early period of our history, Patrick Henry, never wrote a line of his speeches. The sparks of his eloquence flew hot from the anvil of his thought. He owed his success to early practice in conversation and public speaking, and to the courage and readiness with which he met a crisis.

We are apt to think the great triumvirate—Calhoun, Clay, and Webster—as less ready in purely extemporaneous speech than the average legislator of to-day, and yet each of these three great orators showed a gradual development in facility as extempore speakers. Calhoun cultivated extempore speaking with great success while in the law school at Litchfield, and he pursued this method in the "iron logic" of his speeches in Congress. Clay, too, early practiced the extempore method in a debating club at Richmond, and his yet earlier practice with cornfield or woods as an audience is well known. Webster, "a steam engine in breeches," often prepared his speeches with great care; but when pressed for time, as in many of his great cases at the bar, he spoke from carefully prepared notes.

Sargent S. Prentiss, "the most eloquent of all Southerners," says Wendell Phillips, was at his best only when speaking extempore. Wendell Phillips himself was an adept at the art; so was Henry Ward Beecher.

Here is the testimony of four modern speakers:

Hon. B. R. Tillman, United States Senator from South Carolina: "I get chock full of ideas and facts, and then turn loose without much thought or preparation. I very often think over what I am going to say, and then, when I get on my feet, never think of what I intended to say. Practice has enabled me to speak with more ease and without getting excited, but I doubt if my speeches are as effective as when they are belched forth like lava from a volcano."

Hon. William J. Bryan: "I first read all I can on the subject to be discussed, examining the question from all standpoints; then prepare an outline dividing the subject into heads and subheads; then fill in the details. I seldom write a speech complete. Where I have the subject thoroughly in hand, it is easier to use the language which comes at the moment than to remember set phraseology."

Dr. Lyman Abbott in a number of the *Outlook* states that there were two literary societies at New York University. He and his brother belonged to one of them. "It was here," says Dr. Abbott, "I first learned to think upon my feet, and so laid the foundation for my lifelong habit of extemporaneous speech. For the essential condition of really extemporaneous speech is ability to think upon one's feet. Without that ability the extemporaneous address is either a memoriter, though unwritten, oration, or a rambling and discursive talk unfreighted with any thought. The value of the old-time debating societies in village, school, and college appears to me to be under-estimated in our times. 'In the Westminster debating societies,' says Alfred Austin in his autobiography, 'I at least acquired a facility, sometimes an extemporaneous facility, of utterance that has been useful to me, I think, all through life.' "

But, says the student, these are great orators. That is true, but they acquired their power through a long course of practice. So may you. Some have an easier task than others, but often those who have the most to over-come have become the most proficient in the art. If you cannot become as brilliant as Webster, as powerful as Mirabeau, as fluent as Grady, or as eloquent as Ingersoll, *become the best you can.*

Outline.—The special preparation for a speech, discussed in a former chapter, should be followed in pre-paring to deliver a speech extempore. Here is a sug-gested outline:

   I. Introduction
      1. . . . .
      2. . . . .

 II. Discussion
      1. . . . .
        a. . . . .
        b. . . . .
        c. . . . .
      2. . . . .
        a. . . . .
        b. . . . .
        c. . . . .

3. . . . .
    a. . . . .
    b. . . . .
    c. . . . .

III. Conclusion
   1. . . . .
   2. . . . .

In preparing an outline for a speech, use only a few subdivisions. Do not subdivide and re-subdivide *ad infinitum* for an extemporaneous speech. Remember the outline *must be memorized.* Use, therefore, only words, phrases, or short sentences. Such an outline is not a brief, such as you prepare for a debate, which requires each subdivision to be a complete sentence.

Introduction.—An appropriate introduction is essential. The purpose of an introduction is two-fold: (1) To gain the good will of the audience, and (2) to arouse an interest in your subject. This may be accomplished by any of the following ways:

1. *Personal.*—Begin by telling the audience something about yourself—an expression of appreciation of the honor that has been conferred on you by being permitted to speak, etc. But never, *never* offer an apology for not having prepared a good speech.

2. *Anecdote.*—Tell some *appropriate* story, but never tell a story for amusement only.

3. *Illustration.*—Describe some scene, or narrate some incident which makes a direct and adequate setting for your speech.

4. *Quotation.*—Quote a few lines from some great writer, or a stanza of some poem which is connected directly with your theme.

5. *General.*—Speak of your subject in very general terms; as you often do in writing an expository essay.

6. *Explanatory.*—Tell how you intend treating your subject; what the divisions are, etc.

7. *Purpose.*—Explain why you intend speaking. This is a very usual beginning.

Discussion.—The main speech should be arranged logically and climactically, and should contain *one central idea*. It must have unity, order, and movement. Make your point. Beecher once said, "I always aim at somebody in my audience; I may not always hit him, but I try to hit something." Continually ask yourself: What is the purpose of this speech? What do I expect to accomplish by it? What reason is there for my speaking at all? Have I a definite message? Am I saying something or am I talking beside the subject? Is the audience interested in what I say? What can I say that will make a *definite impress* on my hearers, and what will they remember of my speech to-morrow? Would the great majority of my hearers agree, when I have finished as to the one central point I wished to make?

Conclusion.—The aim of the conclusion is *completeness* and *strength*. Every speech should appear complete, rounded out, not just sawed off. On the other hand, do not just talk until some one tells you to stop.

The conclusion may be:

1. *Personal,* 2. *Summary,* 3. *Quotation,* or 4. *Hortatory.*

Memorize Your Outline.—Think through the speech silently. Fix in your mind just what you desire to say upon that particular subdivision. Do not refer to your notes while on the platform, except for statistics;

and even then it is never wise to repeat a long array of figures while speaking. If you use figures, give them in round numbers. Say there are over twelve thousand; do not say there are eleven thousand, eight hundred and twenty-seven. When you get through about all the audience remembers will be "Twenty-seven." Colonel Higginson says:

"Never carry a scrap of paper before an audience. If you read your address altogether, that is very different. It is the combination that injures. So long as a man is absolutely without notes, he is not merely thrown on his own resources, but his hearers see and know that he is; their sympathy goes along with him; they wish him to go triumphantly through. But if they once see that he is relying partly on the stilts and leading strings of his memoranda, their sympathy languishes. It is like the difference between a man who walks a tight rope boldly, trusting wholly to his balance pole, and the man who is looking about every moment for something by which to steady himself. What is the aim of your notes? You fear that without them you may lose your thread, or your logical connection, or some valuable fact or illustration. But you may be sure that neither thread nor logic, fact nor argument is so important to the audience as that they should be kept in entire sympathy with yourself, that the magnetic contact, or whatever we call it, should be unbroken. The chances are that nobody will miss what you leave out, if you forget anything; but you will lose much if you forego the continuous and confiding attention given to a speaker who is absolutely free."

SUGGESTED OUTLINES

I. Announcements

1. Salutation.
2. Command attention with a brief striking statement.
3. State concisely what is to take place.
4. Refute at least one main objection.
5. Mention the place.
6. State the time.
7. Say "I thank you," and sit down.

II. Presentation of a Gift

1. Tell how you came to know the person or persons to be honored.
2. Tell how worth was discovered.
3. Give immediate reasons for presentation.
4. Explain the nature and purpose of the gift.
5. Show its appropriateness.
6. Call the donee to the platform. Make a formal presentation of the gift and in a few words summarize the reasons for the presentation.

III. Acceptance of the Gift.

1. Express your appreciation for the gift.
2. Express your surprise in having been made the recipient of the gift.
3. Disclaim your worthiness stated by the giver.
4. Contribute as much praise as possible to the coöperation and support of others.
5. Speak of your intentions for the future.
6. Express once more your thanks for the gift.

IV. Nominating Speech

1. Gain permission to speak from chairman.

2. Define the type of man needed for the office.

3. Show that your candidate possesses these requirements.

4. Place your candidate in nomination. The name of the candidate should be the last word spoken.

V. After-Dinner Speech

The purpose of an after-dinner speech is to say something worth while in a humorous way.

1. Be brief.

2. Do not begin by saying that you are not prepared, or are surprised, or embarrassed.

3. Do not begin with a story. (Be original).

4. If possible make local references.

5. Do not ridicule any person present.

6. Do not extol yourself.

7. Speak optimistically.

8. Speak to the topic assigned.

9. Develop a climax.

10. Tell a *new, appropriate, humorous* story *well.*

VI. Sales Talk

I. Introduction, or Approach.
  1. Attract favorable attention.
  2. Arouse interest.

II. Discussion, or Demonstration.
  1. State proposition briefly and clearly.
  2. Create a demand.
  3. Explain the virtues of your stock, beginning with the greatest.

    4. Overcome chief objections.

    5. Give picture of possession.

    6. Cite testimony.

    7. State price.

III. Conclusion, or Securing Order.

    1. Take for granted sale is closed.

    2. Arrange details.

EXERCISES

It is a very wise plan to permit pupils, as far as is practical, to correlate their work in Oral English with the other branches they study, or to connect the voice technique in Part I of this volume with exercises in extempore speaking. Suppose you are reading a selection from Browning, assign to students certain topics for oral reports as:

I. A brief sketch of the author's life.

II. A character study.

III. Anecdotes of the author (short talks by two or three students).

IV. Memoriter recitation of selections from the author's works (by different members of the class).

V. If the reading lesson is a selection from a longer story or poem, let one pupil give an abstract of the whole, with illustrative quotations.

VI. Short quotations from the author, by various members of the class.

The topics are merely suggestive. Definite assignments and other topics can be worked out readily by the teacher.

Topics for Extempore Speeches.—It is well to limit these to three minutes or five minutes. Never permit a pupil to "ramble" in his speeches. Encourage him to crowd the best he has into a few minutes. Also, in this way more will be able to speak in a day. It is well at times to have general criticism from the class after each speech.

The pupils should be prepared to answer the following questions about each speech: 1. Was it effective? 2. Did he hold your attention *throughout?* 3. What was his purpose? 4. What was his central idea? 5. Was it appropriate for the audience he imagined? or was it appropriate to the class as an audience? 6. If argumentative, what main objection did he overcome? 7. What item in his speech was the best, cleverest, most appropriate, most interesting, etc? 8. What part was not well prepared? What would he have better said? 9. How about the composition of the speech? 10. What were the good qualities, and what were the defects in his delivery?

I. Suggested Topics

1. Give a short talk to the students of the class urging them to continue their work, (1) in college, (2) in a business school.

2. To a group of high school girls, urging them to go to a Ladies' Seminary.

3. To a group of farmers, urging them to send their sons (1) to college; (2) to an agricultural school, (3) to a business school.

4. To a mothers' club, urging the members to send their daughters to (1) the state university; (2) to a denominational school; (3) to a "finishing" school.

5. To a group of business men urging them to send their sons (1) to college; (2) to a business school.

6. To a group of town boys urging them to join the Y. M. C. A.

7. To a group of town girls urging them to join the Y. W. C. A.

8. To a meeting of the W. C. T. U. on the subject of cigarettes.

9. To a group of prisoners in the county jail.

10. To the students urging them to join a literary society.

Remember that the arguments which might convince a boy to go to college might be the very reason the father might wish to keep him from college. Adapt your speech to the audience.

II. OTHER SUGGESTED TOPICS

1. Wrong is Finally Punished.
2. Obey the Still Small Voice.
3. Health is Preferable to Wealth.
4. Know Thyself.
5. Knowledge is Power.
6. An Empty Sack Cannot Stand Upright.
7. Cultivate Roses but not on your Noses.
8. Opportunity.
9. Animals' Reason.
10. The Best Magazine.
11. Athletics.
12. Success; What is It?
13. Still Waters Run Deepest.
14. Why I am a Democrat.
15. The American Flag.
16. The Business Man.
17. The Militia.

18. Ghosts.
19. The "Four Hundred."
20. The Number Thirteen.
21. Mothers' Day.
22. "I Should Worry."
23. How to Read Books.
24. The City Slums.
25. Public Opinion.
26. Honesty is the Best Policy.
27. Culture vs. Riches.
28. Be on Time.
29. Heroism Means Immortality.
30. Success Means Hard Work.
31. Optimism Wins.
32. The Polite Clerk.
33. The Young Man in Love.
34. America's Greatest Orator.
35. America's Greatest Statesman.
36. America's Greatest Soldier.
37. America's Greatest Artist.
38. America's Greatest Woman.
39. The True Philanthropist.
40. The Fool-Killer Still Has a Job.
41. The Best Book I ever Read.
42. My Favorite Poem.
43. Why Some People Have no Friends.
44. The First Girl I Loved.
45. Handsome is as Handsome Does.
46. Who's Who and Why.
47. How I Spent my Vacation.
48. A Picture on Memory's Wall.
49. The Man Who Can Say *No*.
50. "I Thank You."

A good plan is to permit the student to speak for five minutes, and then for the next three minutes, while still on the floor, to answer questions presented by the class. This plan demands adequate preparation and is a good drill in thinking quickly and accurately while on one's feet.

IX

DEBATING

Introduction.—No form of public speaking can equal debating in importance. He who has the ability to arrange logically and adequately and to present clearly and forcefully truths that convince and persuade, is indeed a master among men.

Debating is selling *ideas,* and in comparison, selling articles, concrete in form and visible to the eye, is mere child's play.

The treatment of this subject in a single chapter will necessarily be confined to a statement of essential elements, with some brief suggestions as to methods. Some standard text on argumentation and debate should be used with a class, whenever time permits.

Definitions.—*Argumentation* is the kind of speech or writing which aims to establish the truth or the falsity of a proposition.

A debate is a formal arrangement agreed upon by two or more persons to discuss under set rules opposite sides of a proposition. These formal principles and rules will be tersely outlined in this chapter.

Facts are entities and relationships as they actually exist in the universe.

Opinions are merely man's conception of these facts. When our opinions agree with the facts they are called *truths.*

A proposition is the expression of relationship between two or more facts. It is a statement that something is or is not. You cannot debate a single fact. You must debate a proposition.

An *assertion* is an affirmation or denial without expressed or logical grounds.

Assumptions are truths accepted without proof.

Presumptions are statements considered true until proved otherwise.

Proof is sufficient reason for asserting a proposition as true. It includes *evidence* and *argument*.

Evidence.—Evidence is any matter from which an inference may be drawn. It is the *basis* of proof. There are three sources of evidence: 1. *Experience*, 2. *Testimonial*, and 3. *Circumstantial*.

1. Much of the evidence we use in arguing comes from our personal knowledge of facts. These facts we have learned 1. through *Observation*, and 2. through *Experiment*.

2. The second great source of material comes to us from what others have found out, or from witnesses, as they are, often called. Such testimonial evidence varies in value, as is pointed out below.

Expert Testimony is the opinion of a person of recognized standing in his profession upon matters relative to his special line of work which makes him competent to form an accurate judgment. A person whose expert testimony is generally accepted is said to be an *authority*.

Evidence from authority should stand the following tests:

1. Is the witness physically and mentally qualified?
2. Is he unprejudiced?
3. Has he had sufficient opportunity to know the facts?
4. Is he generally considered an authority in this particular field?

Testimony that is especially valuable:

1. That used by an opposing witness.
2. Concurrent testimony—or testimony substantiated by other authorities.
3. Unwilling testimony—or that which is given against one's own interest.
4. Negative testimony—or the omission of facts which would have been mentioned had they existed.
5. Undesigned testimony—an unintentional admission of circumstances which were meant to have been kept secret.
6. Consistent testimony—consistent (1) with itself, (2) with other facts, (3) with ordinary experience.

3. The third source of evidence is circumstantial. This is secured through a process of reasoning. The value of evidence secured in this way depends upon (1) the basic facts from which we draw inferences, and (2) the correctness of the reasoning process.

Argument.—Argument is the process of gaining the unknown from the known evidence. In debating, the methods used in convincing the minds of the audience of the validity of your conclusions are, 1. *Constructive proof,* and 2. *Refutation.*

1. *Constructive Proof.*—Constructive arguments may be either A. *Direct,* or argument from authority, or B. *Indirect,* or through a process of reasoning. There are two kinds of reasoning, a. *Inductive,* and b. *Deductive.*

a. When we reason *Inductively* we gather all the facts possible and then arrive at general truths or laws governing these particular facts. There are two general kinds of inductive reasoning. (1) *Casual relationship,* and (2) *Resemblance,* or *Example.*

(I) Casual Relationship. This is a very common method of reasoning. The two main divisions are: (1) From *cause to effect,* technically called *Antecedent Prob-*

ability; and (2) from *effect to cause,* often called *Argument from Sign.* The best way to make this clear is to give examples. We reason from cause to effect when we say that one result of the moving picture shows is that they lead boys to become bandits. We reason from effect to cause when we say that the cause of the great number of unemployed in the United States was our practically unrestricted European immigration.

(1) The tests to be applied to argument *from cause to effect* are:

1. Is the assumed cause adequate to produce the effect?
2. Are there other causes which might prevent the assumed cause from producing the effect in question?

(2) The tests for *effect to cause* are:

1. Is the cause adequate to produce the effect?
2. Could any other cause have produced the effect?
3. Was there no force to prevent the operation of the assumed cause?
4. Is the assumed cause not merely another effect of a common cause?

(II) Resemblance, or Example. There are two divisions of this mode of reasoning: (1) *Generalization,* and (2) *Analogy.*

(1) Generalization is a very common mode of reasoning. We observe a great many facts and, finding certain things true about some of them, we conclude they are also true of the others. For example: We observe that some high school boys are industrious, and conclude that all high school boys are industrious.

The tests for *generalization* are:

1. Have enough examples been observed to warrant the generalization?
2. Were these examples observed, typical?
3. Are we reasonably sure that there are no exceptions?

(2) Analogy. When two individual objects resemble each other in a certain number of points, we infer that they resemble each other in other points. Example: A student is known to loaf and fails to make a pass in his examination. We infer that if the second student loafs he, too, will fail to pass.

The tests for *analogy* are:

1. Are the details of comparison vital to the question at issue?
2. Do the points of resemblance outweigh the points of difference?
3. Is the fact known to be true of the analogous case more likely to be true of the case in question?
4. Are the assertions on which the resemblance is based true?

b. We reason *Deductively* when we take a general truth and apply it to particular cases. The usual form of deduction is the *syllogism*. This example was first used by Aristotle:

All men are mortal. (Major Premise.)
Socrates is a man. (Minor Premise.)
Therefore, Socrates is mortal. (Conclusion.)

Usually one of the premises is omitted; we then have what is called an *enthymeme*. As, Socrates is mortal because he is a man.

Another form sometimes used in debate is the *constructive dilemma*. Example: If a man acts in accordance with his own judgment, he will be criticized; and if he is guided by the opinions of others he will be criticized. But he must either act in accordance with his own judgment, or be guided by the opinions of others. Therefore, in any case he will be criticized. The logical dilemma is not so simple in construction as many debaters think. To construct a good dilemma is very difficult. As the word is used in everyday life, we are said to be in a dilemma when there are but two courses of action open to us, and when both of these lead to unpleasant results.

2. *Refutation.*—By refutation, or rebuttal, is meant weakening or destroying the contention of the opposition. We speak of *anticipatorial* rebuttal when the debater anticipates what the opponent may advance and answers it before it is made; a very effective rebuttal. We speak of *direct* rebuttal when the debater answers his opponent after the opponent has stated his argument. There are two methods of refutation: A. *General,* and B. *Special.*

A. General. The two means usually employed are: a. *Attacking the evidence,* and b. *Detecting the fallacies.*

a. Little need be said on the refutation of the evidence. If the evidence is not true, all there is to do is to show that the authority is untrustworthy since it fails to meet the tests suggested under *evidence,* or that the evidence is contrary to fact.

b. Fallacies. Any unsound mode of arguing is a fallacy. It will be impossible even to enumerate all possible fallacies; but a few of the principal ones are:

(I) Ambiguity of Language. This fallacy arises from (1) using ambiguous terms, and (2) ambiguous constructions. An example of the first is met frequently when (A) two words are given the same meaning; as, *socialists* and *sociologists;* (B) two meanings are given to the same word; as, *mob* (a destructive group of people and a large group of people); and (C) when meanings are implied which do not belong to the word; as, A man said he did not need to be a good speaker in going to Congress for he was told they elected a *speaker* of the House.

Secondly, in ambiguous construction we have an example in the telegram a large ranch owner wired to his friend, "If in need of mules don't forget me."

(II) Errors in Inductive Reasoning. These may be divided into:

(1) *Non Causa Pro Causa.* (Not the reason for the cause.) Two events may be closely associated but the one may not be the cause of the other. As hard times and the election of a certain man for president of the United States.

(2) *Post Hoc, Ergo Propter Hoc.* (After this, therefore because of it.) Example: A man is sick, takes quinine, gets well. The quinine made him well.

(3) *The Effect May, in Part, Be Due to Other Causes.* Example: High cost of living is due to the trusts.

(4) *Hasty Generalization.* This fallacy comes from the violation of the tests for generalization. Example: Radium cured a number of patients who had cancer. Therefore, Radium is a specific for cancer. Also, a certain man said he was always happy when April came, for he had noticed for forty years that if he survived April, he lived the rest of the year.

(5) *False Analogy.* Due to a violation of the tests for analogy. Example: Compulsory arbitration would be successful in the United States because it is successful in New Zealand.

(III) Errors in Deductive Reasoning.

(1) *Begging the Question.* (*Petitio principii.*) The most common method is to argue in a circle: assuming the truth of a premise, and from this premise deducing a conclusion, and then using this conclusion to establish the premise assumed in the beginning. Example: The reason the man did not die was due to his longevity.

Also, the soul is immortal because the rational element in mankind can never die.

(2) *Ignoring the Question.* (*Ignoratio elenchi.*) There are a great many methods of ignoring the main issue. The debater must ever be on his guard to detect this fallacy in his opponent and as far as possible to avoid it himself.

Some of the most common ways of ignoring the question are:

(A) Shifting Ground. Frequently an opponent no sooner is cornered on one proposition than he hedges to another issue; he will not meet the issue squarely. To illustrate: A lawyer who dwells upon the crime rather than upon the guilt of the prisoner is "shifting ground."

(B) Part Proof. Proving only one phase of the question, and maintaining that the entire question has been proved. Example: Concluding that Mexico should be annexed to the United States because such action would benefit the Mexicans.

(C) Argumentum ad Populum. Appealing to the passion and prejudice rather than to reason. Example: Antony's speech at Cæsar's funeral.

(D) Ad Ignorantiam. Assuming that a certain proposition is correct because the contradictory has not been proved. Example: The soul is immortal because it has never been proved to be mortal.

(E) Ad Hominem. Arguing against the character of the opponent rather than the principles he advocates. Example: Socialism is opposed to the church, because Karl Marx, one of the early advocates of socialism, was a materialist.

(F) Avoiding the Issue. To begin proving one thing

and finish by having proved something altogether different.

(G) Making Objections. Finding some fault with the issue. Every plan has some defects; hence merely pointing out a few objections does not prove that it should not be adopted.

(3) *Fallacy of Composition and Division.* Arguing that what is true of a part is true of the whole, and *vice versa.* Example: Hydrogen and oxygen are both gases, therefore water which is composed of these two elements must be a gas. The church is a good institution; Mr. Blank is a member of the church, therefore a good man.

(4) *Non Sequitur.* (Does not follow.) This fallacy is due to a violation of one or more of the rules of the syllogism.

B. Special Form of Refutation.

a. *Reductio ad Absurdum.* One of the most effective means of refutation is that of reducing an argument to an absurdity. The debater assumes for a moment that a given proposition is true, and then points out the absurd results to which it leads. By reason of its simplicity and directness, together with the humor that frequently accompanies it, this method is usually very effective.

b. *The Destructive Dilemma.* As it is ordinarily used, the dilemma is really a special form of *Reductio ad Absurdum.* It arises from the attempt to show that the opponent's proposition must lead to two and only two alternatives, and that both lead to absurd results. The opponent is thus placed as it is commonly said, "between the horns of a dilemma."

A dilemmatic argument may be attacked in three ways (1) "escape between the horns," i.e., present a third alternative; (2) "taken by the horns," i.e., denying the premises; and (3) offering a "rebuttal dilemma."

c. *Method of Residues.* This may be used as a constructive argument. All possible solutions to a problem are enumerated. At least one must be the proper solution. All but one are proved absurd or wrong. Therefor the remaining one is the proper solution. Burke used this method in his speech on *Conciliation with the American Colonies.*

d. *Exposing Inconsistencies* in your opponent's argument. This is not an uncommon fallacy in debating, and should be watched.

Structure—*Proposition.*—Secure a good question for debate, observing the following points. A good debating question requires these essentials:

I. It must have an affirmative statement.

II. It must be stated briefly and in clear, unambiguous language.

III. It should be debatable.

IV. It must not be too broad.

V. It must have only one central idea.

VI. It should be profitable to study.

VII. It should be interesting to the audience.

Analysis.—Study both sides of the proposition. Briefs are absolutely necessary. Never attempt to debate without making a comprehensive brief; merely an outline will not do. A brief should contain, first, three or four leading propositions, logically arranged, that cover the field of the argument, and each proposition reading as a reason for the question under discussion; then, each of these leading propositions should be followed by subheads giving reasons and evidence to support the major heading.

The first speaker on the affirmative will present in his introduction the following points, which include the steps in analysis:

I. Briefly, the origin and history of the question.

II. Definition of terms.

III. Exclusion of irrelevant matter.

IV. Statement of mutually admitted matter.

V. The special issues.

Special Issues.—It is not desirable that a definite scheme be followed in determining the special issues in a proposition for debate; but the following plan will aid as a check for beginners.

The affirmative may prove:

I. Cause for action, or evils in the present sytsem, or necessity for a change.

II. Method of action, or remedy for evils, or feasibility of plan.

III. Practicability of method, and best plan.

The negative may prove:

I. No adequate cause for action, or, that evils do not exist, or no need for proposed changes.

II. Method not adequate, or evils incurable, or plan not adequate.

III. Method impracticable, or better plan.

Main Discussion.—Confine your discussion to a few major issues. Avoid unimportant matter. Never read into a question a far-fetched, unusual, or technical meaning. Meet the proposition squarely. Convince the judges that you are willing to play fair and have no intention of quibbling over doubtful terms.

The chief speaker of the negative may accept or reject

the affirmative's interpretation. If he differs he should mention this in the beginning of his speech.

Every speech should have a beginning, a middle, and a conclusion; these should be joined together skillfully. Make each major issue stand out clearly. Make your speech show up logically, and climactically.

The affirmative has the initial burden of proof. The burden of proof may be shifted to the negative as the debate progresses. "He who affirms must prove." When the negative speakers advance a better plan, the burden of proof lies upon them to prove this plan superior. It is not incumbent on the affirmative to prove that the plan advanced by them is superior to every other plan, or even superior to any plan mentioned by the negative; but superior to the plan the negative uphold—this may be the present plan or a new plan.

Unsupported assertions by either side are worthless. The use of "We think—," "I believe—," "Authorities agree," etc., indicates poor debating. Guard against using assertions for evidence. Success in any argument is built on evidence. Arm yourself with authentic information. Get facts; then get more facts.

Have few issues. If possible reduce the argument to a single issue. Make a slogan of this. Repeat it over and over. Approach this slogan from many sides and angles but press it home, so that at the conclusion of the debate the judges and audience cannot help but remember this point.

Bring the issues direct to the people in the audience. Human beings are primarily interested in *themselves*. Each one is asking the question, "How does this affect me?" If your team supports the policy of canceling the allied war debts, bring home to each man in the audience the fact that such cancellation would stimulate European trade, with the result that more money would flow into the pockets of Jimmy Jones.

If arguing against the United States entering the League of Nations, prove that such participation would increase the taxes of Jimmy Jones. If debating against Government ownership of coal mines, stress the point that such ownership involves an annual interest charge to the government of about one billion dollars—again hitting Jimmy Jones square in the pocketbook.

The "money appeal" is not the only one to use. Some questions lend themselves readily to other "dominant motives" such as: (1) Profit, (2) Self-preservation, (3) Pleasure, (4) Leisure, (5) Reputation, (6) Power, (7) Entertainment, (8) Pride, (9) Affection, (10) Aesthetic.

Another point that the debater must remember is that clearness is one of the chief qualities of a successful debater. Speak so that you will be understood by everyone in the audience. Use simple language that is readily understood. Concrete, homely illustrations should be scattered abundantly throughout the debate. Humorous illustrations are best, as mankind enjoys being entertained; and we prefer an optimistic spirit in a speaker.

Do not expose your entire argument in the first speech. If you do, snap judgments may be formed—judges will jump at conclusions, before hearing your completed argument. Always make clear that some of your most important arguments are in reserve—that they will be advanced by the next speaker. Guard your grammar and diction. Have a clear, vigorous, unified, direct, unpretentious style.

Conclusion.—Summarize the points made by the opposition and also your own points. A good method is to make parallel comparisons. Emphasize your main points; hold them up clearly at the close. If your side has scored a good point during the debate, do not let the judges forget it.

Rebuttal.—It is a general rule in debating that no new argument can be introduced in the rebuttal speech. Additional proof, however, may be offered in answer to any attack upon any argument that was presented in the speaker's main speech.

The principal rule for good rebuttal is: *Answer only the strong arguments against you.* In debating any question there are various and sundry arguments more or less related to the question, but which are not vital enough to demand any particular attention, if, indeed, any attention at all. A debater should try to avoid a scattering effect in rebuttal work—hitting at various points without really delivering a solid shot at some vital point. The best form of rebuttal is the strengthening of your argument wherever it has been attacked; recalling the minds of the hearers to the main issues; showing that you have proved your case; showing that your proof is better than that of your opponent; that the lines of argument that you have offered are vital to the discussion, and that they have been established.

Refutation should be scattered throughout the debate. Whenever a debater is preparing his constructive case, he should anticipate the argument that may be advanced in reply, and provide against it. Anticipatory rebuttal is very effective. It is a good plan to allow a few minutes at the beginning of each man's speech for refutation of his opponent's arguments. Destroy first the argument of the opposition and the audience will be more easily convinced of the merits of your contention.

No one who intends to win a debate will think of entering the contest without a score of rebuttal cards. Each card should have a brief reply to *one* point that may be advanced by the opposition. Each card should be topically labeled and bear detailed reference.

Delivery—*Manner.*—The main speeches are usually memorized; especially when the contest is keen. Do not memorize the rebuttal speeches; but use the information you have on your rebuttal cards. Keep these cards in your hands.

The style of delivery should be that of a simple, fervent, and aggressive conversation. Do not "elocute," "orate," or talk as though you were "speaking a piece." There should be no marked difference between the style of your main and your rebuttal speeches.

Prepare speeches of sufficient length so that you are not compelled to stop before the one-minute warning bell is sounded. Stop promptly at the sound of the second bell—completing your sentence if you are in the midst of a short one. No one listens to you after the second bell, everybody is wondering if you do not know the purpose of the bell. To show surprise or disgust when the stopping signal is given is extremely bad form. It proves that you have not made careful preparation.

Speak to the audience, not to the judges. Stand erect, move only to show transitions. Do not pace the platform. Use only a few direct, emphatic, spontaneous gestures. Speakers should be free from all personal show in dress and manner. Show your argument, not yourself.

Judges.—If possible secure as many as five competent judges. Few things are so discouraging to a debater as to speak before incompetent, prejudiced judges.

Secure men who know a debate when they hear one. The mere fact that a man holds a professorship in a college or is a school superintendent does not qualify him to judge a debate. A man may be very intelligent in many respects and not know anything about music. Likewise he may know very little about debating.

The following plan of judging a debate overcomes some of the objections of the usual method of voting simply for the affirmative or the negative side: (1) Select three men who are especially qualified for their respective parts. (2) One judge will decide which side wins in Delivery. A second judge will decide which side wins in Argumentation. A third judge will decide which side wins in General Effectiveness. (3) The relative points awarded to each side by the respective judges are: For Delivery, 2 points; for Argumentation, 3 points; for General Effectiveness, 4 points. The side having the highest total number of points wins the debate. The decision when read would stand: 0—9, or 2—7, or 3—6, or 4—5, as the case might be.

The advantage of this plan over the old and inadequate method will readily be seen.

We trust the time will soon come when it will not be considered essential to have judges in a debate.

Ethics of Debating.—There are two cardinal principles of debating which should always be kept in mind and put into practice. These are: (1) Be honest, and (2) Be respectful to your opponent and to his arguments.

The necessity for honesty arises in two ways: in the presentation of your own argument, and in the handling of that of your opponent. The form of statement of your argument should be absolutely your own; that is, it should be in your own language, and not copied from some one else. Ideas may be borrowed; as a matter of fact, all of us borrow arguments by the wholesale; but the point is, the way of stating these arguments should be your own work. Of course, if the language of another is stated as quoted matter, that is admissible. Again, whenever you have occasion to restate an argument of your opponent, state it fairly. In this respect the amateur in debate needs especially to watch himself. In the first place, it is foolish to say that your opponent said so and so, when your hearers know better. Any appearance of unfairness in the handling of your opponent's argument only prejudices the hearers against your own argument.

(2) Good debating means a search for and presentation of the truth on each side of a given question. In a really debatable question all of the truth is never on one side. The very idea that a thing is debatable assumes that there *is* another side. Hence, your opponents and their arguments should always be treated with respect. Young debaters frequently make the mistake of opposing everything that is said on the other side, and attempt to annihilate an opponent instead of showing him his errors. One never gets far in any discussion by trying to force his opinions upon others. Instead of saying bluntly, "I am right—you are wrong," it is much more effective to say, "It seems to me that you (or the affirmative) are mistaken; but let us assume that you are right, and see where that leads us." You cannot bludgeon people into your way of thinking; but you can usually *win* them by going over to where they are and gently leading them to you.

It is said of Lincoln that he often surprised young

attorneys by the fair and strong statement of his opponent's case. Whenever a debater uses such expressions as "He gets up here and foolishly asserts so and so," "He harps about this point," etc., it shows that he has a wrong idea of what debating really is, and the wrong attitude toward those on the other side. Other exhibitions along the same lines are shown when a speaker dramatically challenges his opponents by turning from the audience and addresses them alone, accompanied, perhaps, by a quasi-withering look or gesture: or flaunts an authority in their faces; or otherwise conducts himself in an hysterical manner when there is no special cause for excitement, and when his argument would be far more effective if presented in a more respectful and dignified manner.

Finally, the debaters should remember that the judges are more competent to pass upon the total effect of the argument on each side than are the debaters themselves. The right principle to proceed on is to do the best you can in presenting your argument, and leave the decision absolutely to the judges. Here again reference is had more particularly to the debates of the interscholastic leagues. Wrangling over decisions is unsportsmanlike, and accomplishes nothing. The debater should take to heart the advice frequently given in other contests, "Be a good sport." And in debating, as in other things in life, it is fine training for one to learn how to lose as well as how to win.

EXERCISES

I. Make a brief outline of this chapter.

II. Name the arguments and fallacies in the following:

1. The cat upset the pitcher. I saw her tracks on the table.
2. There was a heavy rain last night, the roads will be too muddy for the automobile.
3. Blessed are the meek for they shall inherit the earth.
4. That boy is a rogue because his father is a rogue.
5. All dogs have brown eyes. I examined the eyes of twenty dogs, and each one had brown eyes.
6. Immigrants should be debarred from the United States because we would then be free from all labor troubles.
7. There must be a God, because I love Him.
8. That bad boy whispers because he is mean.
9. I don't believe what that man preaches because he is not honest.
10. Men are not happy. Those who are single have no wives to take care of them. Those who are married have wives to take care of. Since all men are either single or are married, men are not happy.
11. No cat has two tails. Every cat has one tail more than no cat. Hence every cat has three tails.
12. Hans is a great beer drinker, for the Germans are great beer drinkers.
13. Knowledge is power, for Bacon said so.
14. Are you the only rogue in your family?

III. Arguing from Resemblance, prove the truth or falsity of the following propositions:

1. Honesty is the best policy.
2. Irrigation greatly increases the value of the land.
3. Unclean milk is a menace to public health.
4. Animals reason.

IV. Cite a case of circumstantial evidence which caused you to change one of your plans during the past month.

V. Name five people who would be considered authority on farming.

VI. Give an example of unwilling testimony that you have heard; of undesigned testimony; of negative testimony.

VII. Discover in your newspaper or magazine an example of each form of argument mentioned in this chapter.

VIII. Discover in your newspaper or magazine an example of each form of fallacy outlined in this chapter.

IX. Test the following propositions for debate:

1. There should be no electives in the first two years of high school.

2. In criminal trials, three-fourths of the jury should be competent to render a verdict.

3. All mines should be under the control of the Government.

4. All Christian churches in the City of ———— should be united.

5. All high school interscholastic athletic games should be abolished.

6. Oral English should be one of the required studies in the high school.

7. The French Revolution was justifiable.

8. A lawyer should not defend a man whom he knows to be guilty.

9. The truth should always be spoken.

10. Church property should be taxed.

11. Pupils should be furnished free text books by the State.

12. The study of Latin and Greek is a waste of time.

13. The most successful business men are not strictly honest.

X. Bring to the class ten questions for debate that will stand the tests.

APPENDIX A

1. A three minute oral review of a magazine article.
2. Original speech.   Needed reform in the institution.
3. Announcement of some impending event.
4. Speech on assigned subject.   (Illustrating forms of support.)
5. Presentation and Acceptance speeches.
6. Sales-talk.
7. After-dinner speech.
8. Story.
9. Eulogy.
10. Denunciation.
11. Nominating speech.
12. Political speech.
13. Public lecture.
14. Anniversary address.
15. Argumentative address.
16. Sermonette.
17. Commemorative speech.
18. Dedication address.
19. Speech of welcome and reply.
20. Scientific address.
21. Commencement address.
22. Formal debate.
23. Unveiling a monument.
24. Speech of farewell and response.
25. Inaugural address.

APPENDIX B

STANDARDS FOR PUBLIC SPEAKING CONTESTS

Have you ever entered a candidate in a public-speaking contest, and after the verdict gone home so disgusted with the decision that you vowed you would never again have anything to do with a similar contest? Have you ever been a judge in a public speaking contest where there were six or more candidates and found a unanimous agreement as to the ranking of the several contestants? Now, frankly, do you know of any contest of any sort where there is such a manifest lack of unanimity as in a contest in public speaking?

There are at least two reasons: (1) Judges are seldom competent; and (2) when competent they fail to use like standards.

Because a man possesses sound judgment in business, art, science, etc., does this qualify him to know values in an oratorical or declamation contest? Are men ever selected to judge a musical contest just because they occupy a prominent position in the community? And the chances are that the average citizen knows as much about music as he does about public speaking or literary interpretation; that he can sing as well as he can read; and that he has studied harmony as much as he has the technique of speech. But is he ever mandamused to pass out medals at a sängerfest or an eisteddfod? Unfortunately, unqualified men and women must often be used to judge public speaking contests, because competent persons are not always available.

Even within the profession there is often a great disagreement as to what constitutes proper standards, and a still greater variation in the application of such standards. Lack of standardization is the one big cry in the whole field of speech education.

Space does not permit a discussion of the various attempts during the past twenty years to agree on a criteria for judging contests. Twenty years ago elaborate score cards were frequently presented to judges, but often so complex that the judges, either through ignorance or indifference, refused to use them. They preferred to just " lump it off."

Unless we can agree on the relative value of the more important points our contests will continue to be disappointments, and moreover, they will prove a deterrent, rather than an incentive, in promoting interest in the art of oral expression.

We would like to see the antiquated and obsolete " oratorical " replaced by a modern and practical " speech " contest, and the " Bobby Shaftoes-Curfew Must Not's " by a contest in *reading*. However, as long as we must have these " oratorical pyrotechnics " and the " yallercutin," would not the following score cards afford just criteria by which to judge them?

FOR ORIGINAL ORATORICAL CONTESTS

1. Composition (50).
   A. Material.
      (a) Originality................................. 5
      (b) Purposefulness............................. 5
      (c) Appropriateness........................... 5
      (d) Interest.................................... 10

B. Style.
    (*a*) Clearness.................................. 5
    (*b*) Power..................................... 5
    (*c*) Eloquence................................ 5
    (*d*) Unity.................................... 10
2. Delivery (50).
  A. Platform bearing.............................. 10
  B. Emphasis...................................... 10
  C. Force... 10
  D. Voice... 20
                                                   ———
                                                  100

FOR DECLAMATION CONTEST

1. Choice of selection (20).
  A. Length.. 5
  B. Appropriateness............................... 5
  C. Quality....................................... 10
2. Delivery (80).
  A. Spirit.. 15
  B. Platform bearing.............................. 15
  C. Emphasis...................................... 15
  D. Force 10
    (*a*) Loudness.
    (*b*) Volume.
    (*c*) Intensity.
    (*d*) Stress.

  E. Voice... 25
    (*a*) Enunciation.
    (*b*) Purity.
    (*c*) Melody.
    (*d*) Quality, etc.
                                                   ———
                                                  100

APPENDIX C

I. Structure.

A. THOUGHT.

(1) Subject not appropriate for occasion. (2) Treatment of subject inadequate. (3) Insufficient preparation—general—specific. (4) *Introduction*—poor, none; anecdote, illustration, general, personal, explanatory, philosophical, stating purpose; *Body*—too long, too short, uninteresting; means of support (restatement, general illustration, specific instance, quotation)—trite, too many, too long; illustration unfamiliar, inappropriate; quotation misquoted. No climax; anticlimax. *Conclusion*—poor, none; general, personal, anecdote, quotation, hortatory, prediction, summary.

B. COMPOSITION.

(1) *General*—lacks unity, coherence, clearness, force, beauty, climax; no humor, satirical. (2) *Sentences*—weak, redundant, ambiguous, false syntax, too long, too short, involved, not balanced, no subject, no predicate. *Words*—weak, slang, impure, technical, colloquial, not precise, repetition.

II. Delivery.

A. VOICE.

1. ARTICULATION.—Careless, indistinct, over precise, weak; lips too close together, too active, smacking; stammers; stutters; lisps; strained; sounds prolonged.

2. PRONUNCIATION.—Poor; wrong sound of vowels; omission of initial (final) consonants; omission of syllables; wrong accent.

3. CHARACTER OF TONES.—Impure, harsh, raspy, throaty, shrill, thin, flat, hollow, thick, nasal, breathy, metallic, little resonance.

4. PITCH.—Monotonous—*Key*—too high, too low.

5. INFLECTION.—Little, none, excessive, too great, suspended at close of sentences, too many falling inflections, semitone, singsong, oratorical.

6. MOVEMENT.—*Rate*—too fast, too slow, no variation. *Pause*—too long, too short, too often, choppy, wrong place. *Quantity*—too long, too short. *Transitions*—weak, inappropriate.

7. FORCE.—*Loudness*—too loud, too weak, lacks force at beginning—at end of sentences. *Intensity* —weak, none. *Volume*—too little, too much. Improper distribution of force. No climax; anti-climax.

8. EMPHASIS.—Missplaced, habitual, monotonous, wanting; uses one kind too often (loudness, time, pause, inflection, intensity).

9. QUALITY.—*Atmosphere* (intellectual, spiritual, vital).

B. PHYSICAL EXPRESSION.

1. *Approach to Audience.*—Too slow, too rapid, "cat-like," military, swaggering, stooped, spiritless.

2. *Position.*—Awkward, still, disrespectful, leaning, military, head bowed, too rigid, scrapes floor with feet, paces platform, rises on toes, begins speaking too soon—not soon enough; speaks while leaving platform. Improper position while seated on platform.

3. *Gesture.*—Too many, too few; movement of hands inappropriate, stiff, angular, ungraceful; hands in pockets, in front, behind back, akimbo.

4. *Facial Expression.*—Passive, sad, savage, scowling, smiling; looks at floor, at ceiling, at wall, out of doors, over audience; winks, stares.

C. GENERAL EFFECT.

Ineffective, indifference, arrogant, careless, flippant, heavy, satirical, antagonistic, nervous, flirts with audience, no enthusiasm, speech memorized.

APPENDIX D

I. Breathing (diaphragmatic).

Ah.   Halt!   Boot, saddle, to horse, and away.

II. Enunciation.

Thoughts black, hands apt, drugs fit, and time agreeing;
Confederate season, else no creature seeing;
Thou mixture rank, of midnight weeds collected,
With Hecate's ban thrice blasted, thrice inflected,
Thy natural magic and dire property
On wholesome life usurp immediately.

III. Pronunciation (or words of equal difficulty).

abdomen	combatant	data	inquiry	heroism
chasten	clematis	cello	exquisite	disputant

IV. Purity of Tone.

Let me go wher'er I will
I hear a sky-born music still;
It sounds from all things old,
It sounds from all things young,
From all that's fair, from all that's foul,
Peals out a cheerful song.

V. Melody.

1. KEY.   Read the second selection one octave lower than the first.

    (a) Now glory to the Lord of Hosts, from whom all glories are.

    (b) Holy! Holy! Lord God of Hosts.

2. AGILITY.

```
cheer-              em-
            pre-   i-                use-
      ful               nent-   a    ful
A          man is              ly        man.
```

3. INFLECTION.

    (*a*) Property, character, reputation, everything was sacrificed.

    (*b*) Is it possible a cur can lend three thousand ducats?

VI. Movement.

1. SLOW RATE (75 words per minute).

> Tears, idle tears, I know not what they mean,
> Tears from the depth of some divine despair
> Rise in the heart, and gather to the eyes,
> In looking on the happy Autumn-fields,
> And thinking of the days that are no more.

2. FAST RATE (250 words per minute).

> I sprang to the stirrup, and Joris, and he;
> I galloped, Dirck galloped, we galloped all three;
> "Good speed!" cried the watch, as the gate-bolts undrew;
> "Speed!" echoed the wall to us galloping through;
> Behind shut the postern, the lights sank to rest;
> And into the midnight we galloped abreast.

3. PAUSE (to be observed in other selections).

VII. Force.

1. LOUDNESS (soft tone).

> Softly! She is lying
>   With her lips apart.
> Softly! She is dying
>   Of a broken heart.

(Loud tone.)

> "Young man, ahoy!"
> "What is it?"
> "Beware! beware! The rapids are below you!"

2. INTENSITY (strong degree).

> I curse thee! and thou art cursed! May thy love be
> blasted—may thy name be blackened—may the
> infernals mark thee—may thy heart wither and
> scorch—may thy last hour recall to thee the prophet
> voice of the Sage of Vesuvius.

VIII. Emphasis.

(Emphasize words in italics (1) Loudness,
(2) Pause, (3) Time, (4) Intensity, (5)
Inflection.)

> Let us be *sacrificers*, not *butchers*.

IX. Quality.

(Read the following: (1) as intellectual, (2) as
emotional, (3) as volitional):

> Whoever you are, be noble;
>   Whatever you do, do well;
> Whenever you speak, speak kindly,—
>   Give joy wherever you dwell.

X. Stage Bearing.

BIBLIOGRAPHY

Compiled from the "Book List" of the American Library Association

BAUTAIN, L. E. M. The art of extempore speaking. New York, McDevitt–Wilson, 1915.

A general treatise on extempore speaking, the work of a French scholar of the last century. A book that will appeal to cultivated readers.

CLARK, S. H. Interpretation of the printed page. Chicago, Row, 1915.

A practical text for the English teacher with little or no special training in vocal interpretation in helping the pupil to interpret literature orally and silently.

CUMNOCK, R. McL., ed. Choice readings. Chicago, McClurg, 1913.

The selections occupy about four-fifths of the book, are well chosen and are grouped according to their characteristic sentiment.

ELSON, W. H., and KECK, C. M. Junior high-school literature. Books 1–2. Chicago, Scott–Foresman, 1919–20.

Represent literature of different types suitable for silent reading, memorizing, dramatization, etc.

FISK, M. I. The silent sex. New York, Harper, 1923.

Twelve amusing monologues.

FOERSTER, NORMAN, and PIERSON, W. W. JR. American ideals. Boston, Houghton, 1917.

Thirty-seven selections bringing together "certain essays, addresses and state papers that express from the point of view of American statesmen and men of letters, these ideals, past and present."

FULTON, R. I., and TRUEBLOOD, T. C. Standard selections. Ginn.

Practical text.

—— British and American eloquence. Boston, Ginn, 1912.

Selections from 101 speeches made by twenty-two noted English and American orators, with biographical sketches prefacing each group. Compiled to provide a convenient volume for a critical study by college students of the "message and methods of orators whose utterances have molded public opinion and guided the destinies of the two great Anglo-Saxon nations."

HOWARD, JOHN RAYMOND, *ed.* Poems of heroism in American life. New York, Crowell, 1922.

Contains two hundred poems grouped to correspond to historic periods. Introductory paragraphs give dates and essential facts that inspired the poems. Lists over seventy poems not included in Stevenson; *Poems of American History.* These for the most part deal with recent history.

JOHNSON, G. E. Dialects for oral interpretation, selections and discussions. New York, Century, 1922.

A convenient collection of readings and recitations in Scotch, Negro, French, Irish and Scandinavian dialects, four one-act plays and a discussion of dialect and the monologue.

—— Modern literature for oral interpretation. New York, Century, 1920.

Modern American authors are well represented in these selections of prose and poetry, chosen because of their power to awaken a responsive interest in students.

LONG, A. W., ed. American patriotic prose, with notes and biographies. New York, Heath, 1917.

A supplementary reader for upper grammar grades and junior high school.

MILLER, M. M. American debate. New York, Putnam, 1916. 2v.

Not a mere compilation, but the extracts from the more important debates are connected with the narrative of their historical background. Colonial, state and natural rights, 1761–1861. Land and slavery question, 1607–1860.

——, ed. Great debates in American history. New York, Current Literature Publishing Co., 1913.

From the debates in the British Parliament on the Colonial stamp act (1764–1765) to the debates in Congress at the close of the Taft administration (1912–1913). Speeches grouped by subjects, which range from Revolutionary politics to present-day economic and social questions.

O'NEILL, J. M., comp. Classified models of speech composition. New York, Century, 1921.

Most complete compilation of the best examples of the different types of English and American speeches, classified according to the occasion of their delivery.

O'NEILL, J. M. Modern short speeches. New York, Century, 1923.

Not a book of great oratory, but a collection of fine examples and excellent models of various kinds which illustrate plans, methods, means, of achieving such ends. An excellent text containing ninety-eight complete examples.

SHEFFIELD, A. D. Joining in public discussion. New York, Doran, 1922.

Intended particularly for the use of members of labor unions, public forums, and similar discussion groups.

SHURTER, E. DU B., ed. Winning declamations and how to speak them. New York, Noble, 1917.

Interesting as a collection both of the readings that have been familiar for years and of recent discussion of timely interest. Part one is for the middle and upper grades; part two for high schools and colleges.

SNOW, W. L., ed. The high school prize speaker. Boston, Houghton, 1916.

Some fifty prose and verse selections that have taken prizes or received honorable mention in the J. Murray Kay prize speaking contests held annually at Brookline, Mass., high school. Contains a number of old favorites.

THOMAS, C. S., and PAUL, H. G., ed. Atlantic prose and poetry. Boston, "Atlantic Monthly," 1919.

An attractive and diverse collection from the "Atlantic Monthly" files for junior high schools and upper grades. The war interest is apparent, but not obtrusive.

WOOLBERT, C. H. The fundamentals of speech. New York, Harper, 1920.

A practical and interesting college text, comprehensive in scope, including many well-chosen selections which would prove helpful in individual study.

University debaters' annuals. v. 1–8. New York, Wilson, 1914–1923. v. 1, 3, 4 out of print.

A series of yearbooks which include verbatim reports of debates held in the larger American colleges and universities grouped under subject and college. Full up-to-date bibliographies are provided for each subject and an index for the whole. Aims to provide a record of college work in debate and to supply specimen material for the use of students of debating.

Debaters' handbook series. 23v. New York, Wilson. Various
prices.

Each volume contains a well chosen collection of reprints of arguments
on both sides of the question with a brief and a carefully selected bibliography that invites one to further reading on that subject.

Handbook series. 18 v. New York, Wilson. Various prices.

This series includes a number of subjects on public questions on which
every man and woman should be well informed. The reprints are grouped
(for convenience) according to the stand taken by the speaker quoted on
the subject and an extensive bibliography guides one to further reading on
the subject.

INDEX

Just another Buckeye strayed
from the Buckeye state.
"Red" "Marg. Girtli."

The world is so full of a
    number of things,
I'm sure we should all be as
    happy as kings.
            Angeline Wojciak

While still young, tune your tongue.
            Mae Wojciak

The noblest mind the best
contentment has.
            Daisy Buczkowski
                (Santy Claus)

"If you, your lips
Would keep from slips.
Five things observe with care
Of whom you speak, To whom you speak
And How, and When and Where"
            Irene R. Manxing

M. Kerr:
I enjoyed your friendship through the Night school year.

Arthur C. Betz.

4/30/29

What is more beautiful than the memory of a sincere Friendship

Mary G. Carnana.

The one worth while.
Is the one who will smile.

H. J. Shar

Smile and the world smiles with you.
Cry and you cry alone. So it always pays to smile.

Rose V. Carnana

2/30/2

In remembrance of many enjoyable evenings at H. C. H. S.

2/20/29

Emma B. Gardo